Socialization as Cultural Communication

Socialization as Cultural Communication

DEVELOPMENT OF A THEME IN THE WORK OF MARGARET MEAD

THEODORE SCHWARTZ

Editor

UNIVERSITY OF CALIFORNIA PRESS

Berkeley, Los Angeles, London

Reprinted from *Ethos,* volume 3, number 2 (Summer, 1975)

University of California Press
Berkeley and Los Angeles, California
University of California Press, Ltd.
London, England
Copyright © 1976 by
The Regents of the University of California
First Paperback Printing 1980
Second Cloth Printing 1980
ISBN 0-520-03955-6 paper
      0-520-03061-3 cloth
Library of Congress Catalog Card Number: 75-17282
Printed in the United States of America

CONTENTS

Introduction

Within the field of anthropology, the subdiscipline of culture and personality studies has flourished in spite of the great conceptual and methodological challenges it has presented. Although this subdiscipline seemed to have declined relative to the growth of other anthropological pursuits, research and teaching in "C&P" continues to be a primary interest of many anthropologists. Course offerings attract large numbers of students, for the questions raised by culture and personality studies have an inescapable relevance and a perduring fascination. The cultural perspective these studies provide has been applied to the methods and theories of psychoanalytic, psychiatric, social, and cognitive psychology, with rewarding results. As a consequence of this wider-ranging application, the field of culture and personality is now perhaps more appropriately called psychological anthropology.

The success of psychological anthropology lies not so much in a set of well-demonstrated propositions as in its contribution to human consciousness. There has been a growth in our understanding of the cultural sources of human behavior—and of a human nature as dependent on its cultural as on its biological foundations. In this, the contribution of psychological anthropology has been complementary and, perhaps, comparable in magnitude to that of psychoanalysis. But this growth of consciousness is not easily measured in terms of the paradigms of the physical and life sciences. Neither (I think) is anthropology "pre-paradigmatic" in Thomas Kuhn's sense. Instead, anthropology and its psychological subdiscipline have evolved as a culture evolves. Its paradigm is the processual structure it finds in its object of study—culture itself. The "culture" of anthropology contains various islands of formal discourse and demonstration among a larger body of informal, often programmatic or polemic discourse. It leads not necessarily to a single consensual doctrine but, like a culture, to a complex structure of commonality and difference among the perceptions of imaginative individuals. A culture within a culture, anthropology serves as a self-reflexive part of the larger whole. Psychological anthropology in particular focuses on culture at its distributive locus—in populations of individuals.

The journal *Ethos* was created in 1972 in response to the rather puzzling lack during the past fifty years of a specialized journal to bring together the understandings or findings of psychological anthropologists. In creating a journal to represent the field, the editorial board agreed that it would be appropriate to dedicate some special issues to those individuals who pioneered the field and who have sustained its growth through all these years. This book originated as a special issue of *Ethos*. (A list of errata can be found at the end.)

There could be no more obvious pioneer than Margaret Mead. The year 1975 was the fiftieth anniversary of her first major field study, from which she wrote *Coming of Age in Samoa.* She was in the field again in Manus (Papua, New Guinea) where she has returned repeatedly over a span of forty-seven years. Anthropology's claim to having transformed human cultural consciousness rests to an extraordinary extent on her work. While most anthropologists have spoken to and read one another, she has spoken to and has been read by innumerable students and a vast public. As I observed her at work in the field, I mused on the need for a Manhattan Project to study the source of her energy, her creativity, and her appetite for and ability to encompass the complexity of very many lives within her own life and intellect. If, as I have suggested, culture may be seen as both the object of study and as the model or paradigm for anthropology itself, then Margaret Mead has been a master participant—intuitive, brilliant in her field work, vivid in her dramatizations of individuals and cultures. She could not describe a dead culture; it would come to life in her words.

Margaret Mead has had much recognition in the professional

community as past president of the American Anthropological Association and current president of the American Association for the Advancement of Science. A bibliography of her works alone will fill a volume.[1]

This book develops but one central theme from her work—the processes of cultural transmission. In keeping with the interdisciplinary focus of *Ethos* and with the interdisciplinary relevance of Margaret Mead's work, scholars of diverse fields—anthropology, sociology, psychology, psychiatry, and primatology—were invited to contribute articles on suggested topics related to the theme of *socialization as cultural communication.*

Socialization as used in this volume is to be conceived in its broadest sense as the way individuals become members of a society, embodying in their own experience, and acting out in their learned behavior, a part of the culture of that society. Although Margaret Mead prefers the term "enculturation" to characterize her own work, I chose the more widely used term. It is to be understood in a sense that encompasses both "socialization" and "enculturation," as they are sometimes usefully distinguished. It is characteristic of Margaret Mead that she sees socialization not as a set of discrete practices such as swaddling, early weaning, or training for independence but as context-sensitive interactions among parents and children, peers, youths, and adults. For her, manner (particularly affect, role modeling, and meaning) counts as much as the form of the behavior. For her, also, the channel of communication is open in both directions; socialization is not merely done *to* children by an "agent." Children elicit (or fail to elicit) needed or approved responses in older persons who respond in terms of their own needs —not as interchangeable units, but as distinctive personalities. Learning to elicit responses is a large part of learning a culture. At the same time, a culture's "messages" about life and behavior are communicated to the child in diverse and redundant ways in every contact with other individuals and with objects.

In Margaret Mead's earlier studies—in Samoa, Manus, New Guinea, and Bali—she dealt with these culture-transmitting interactions in still relatively traditional, not yet radically changing cultures. From Samoa to the present time, she related each study ex-

1. *Margaret Mead, A Complete Bibliography, 1925–1975*, edited by Joan Gordan, Mouton, The Hague, 1976.

plicitly to current, salient problems and trends in American culture. Although our attention is focused on the vivid outlines of an exotic culture, aspects of our own culture are constantly illuminated—the aspect of her work that accounts for her broad popular appeal. In her later work, particularly her restudy of the Manus in 1953 and thereafter, she turned her attention to understanding rapid and drastic culture change. In *Culture and Commitment* (1970), the two-way communication that is inherent in her model of socialization is translated into the dynamics of communication between generations. Here she examines change in the socialization process and in the very structure of culture itself.

The contributors to this volume have expressed their homage to Margaret Mead by developing aspects of this central theme of her work in reporting on their own research in diverse areas of behavior.

Psychoanalytic studies brought us to the child. For the most part, the focus was on the unfolding of endogenous processes in the child's interaction with the family—primarily with parents playing universal roles. L. L. Langness calls attention to Mead's preeminence among those anthropologists, following Malinowski, who explored the widely varying cultural contexts within which personality formation takes place, and who showed that personality formation is inseparable from the enculturation process. Psychological anthropology does not refute psychoanalysis; rather it corrects and completes it in one of its otherwise fatal deficiencies. Langness traces the widening circle of Mead's intellectual concerns, from cultural learning, to education, to the evaluation and reform of American culture and of the emerging world culture. Of greatest importance to our theme, Langness describes Mead's enormous contribution to the study of, to our very conception of, education. As in so many other things, Mead has been an antidote to the excessive emphasis on *formal* education in our culture. Mead related education to the broad process of cultural learning and teaching for which each culture had its methods and philosophy.

The chapters by Thelma E. Rowell and I. Charles Kaufman, which deal with primate socialization, do not return us to a precultural level of "pure" biology. Instead we find ourselves quite at home in a realm in which individual and group experience modulates primate behavior into transmissible patterns. In her studies of monkeys, Rowell stresses the continuity of socialization. Each partial departure from one relation (particularly mother-infant) is an entrance into new relations; it is not a simple transition to "independence." Rowell describes the bidirectionality of social learning in monkeys. She eschews the term "socialization" as it is sometimes narrowly employed and shows that the context of socialization is the troop or community of primates. The infant interacts with a mother of a particular social status even as the mother and the infant itself interact with others of the community. Rowell surveys the evolution, diversity, and common ground of primate caretaking behavior. She, like Kaufman, stresses the role of learning in primate behavior. Group traditions and innovations are transmitted through social learning—and in the case of innovation, transmission often flows from the young to their elders.

Kaufman radically extends our awareness of the centrality of learning in primate behavior beyond troop traditions to species-specific behavior. Such behavior was long considered to be genetic, an evolutionary precipitate of adaptive processes. In a longitudinal study of groups from two closely related macaque species, Kaufman demonstrated a causal nexus in which genetically derived maternal behaviors establish a species-invariant context. Within that context, a wider range of behaviors is reliably learned. This broad extension of the total behavioral phenotype through learning is "protocultural," for it depends on the physical presence of the behavioral act as specific model or on experience in direct interaction, that is, it does not operate through symbolic mediation.

The work reported by Rowell and Kaufman indicates a convergence of interests and conceptual frameworks between students of primate behavior and psychological anthropologists. In their increasing attention to longitudinal (or repeated cross-section) studies of specific individuals in groups, it is apparent that primatologists are on the verge of elucidating personality (or "protopersonality"?) formation in primates.

Four chapters are devoted to the socialization of affect. Our subject remains the same: cultural learning through social interaction. Here it is learning at the level of form, movement, feeling and sentiment.

Gregory Bateson takes us into the learning of trance in Bali as behavior and as state of consciousness. Like so much of human learning (as Bateson has long instructed us), indirection may be the most direct method. Bateson begins characteristically by exposing the epistemological difficulties of knowing what we seek to know about socialization. Particularly, he addresses the need to know the structure of the behavior in question as "seen" by the actor—whether that actor be rat, monkey, or human being. Fortunately the invisible becomes party visible in interaction: "evolution is always coevolution and learning is always co-learning." We are urged to take as our units of observation, both contexts and content (interactions). What follows is a suggestive analysis of kinaesthetic socialization in Balinese dance training which, in the experience of self-induced muscular clonus, provides one key to the trance state. This exemplary exercise proceeds from the multi-photograph plates of *Balinese Character,* an as-yet unrivaled work by Bateson and Mead.

Walter Goldschmidt explores once again this neglected pathway by examining his and his wife's beautiful photographs of the Sebei of Uganda. Photographs and films are of great value in the study of cultural communication. Although they are not immune to the selectivity of the observer, they capture far more than the photographer can control. And in such visual recordings, content and context are locked together. Their fullest value, however, depends on how well they are embedded—as Goldschmidt's are—in thorough ethnography. We know how to support our assertions in many more tangible areas of ethnography. But when it comes to the quality, intensity, distribution, and development of affect, which is so extensively nonverbal in expression, then visual documentation is essential to ethnography. Goldschmidt turns to his photographic materials for what they can contribute as a test of his observation that a low level of interpersonal affective involvement prevails among the Sebei; and he turns to them for indications of how this pattern of affect is transmitted. He finds them in the manner of socialization rather than in the mode (the gross form of the behavior). It would be premature, however, and I am sure not intended, to discount radically the effect of mode of interaction in socialization in spite of its variability within a society. Some, and not necessarily the most prevalent, modes of interaction may be prototypic, having greater causal force in the overall cultural-ideological system.

In George A. DeVos's chapter we come to a classic and perennial problem for anthropology and for psychoanalysis: that of the near-universal cultural prohibition of incest. For quite different reasons, Freud and Lévi-Strauss (among many others) would place the prohibition of incest at the very point of disjunction, figuratively speaking, of nature and culture. The diverse theories of the origin *or* function (by no means the same thing) of the "incest taboo" are fascinating, if unresolvable. DeVos makes an original contribution to this body of discourse and to psychology as well in his theory of affective dissonance (an extension and correction, in part, of Festinger's cognitive dissonance theory). Is there a repugnance, innate or born of familiarity, that leads to incest prohibition? If so, why is there the need for sanctions? Or is there an attraction, innate or acquired, that must be thwarted for the sake of society or the species itself? Affective dissonance subsumes the notion of ambivalence, positive and negative feelings about the same "object." But with respect to incest, affective dissonance refers to conflicting childhood and adult affectional ties.

John W. M. and Beatrice B. Whiting directly relate their cross-cultural study of the degree of intimacy between husbands and wives to Mead's work on the cultural patterning of sexual roles. The chapter illustrates the research paradigm which the Whitings have so productively developed. Rooming arrangement (in the same room, or apart) is taken as the cross-cultural index of aloofness or intimacy of husband and wife. Other aspects of aloofness of husband from wife as well as father from children correlate with separate rooming. The Whitings test a series of hypotheses linking aloofness, polygyny, mid-level agricultural societies, problematic sexual identity, and hypermasculine warrior males.

Mead does not generally separate affective and cognitive socialization, though the distinction serves well to group the chapters of this book into sections. It is doubtful that either cognition or affect is to be found free of the other's influence. It is also doubtful that either develop without the most profound cultural influence, even though they are the natural functions of the human body and brain. Some theories of the cognitive development of individuals see the process as one of maturation through a set of invariant, biologically and logically given stages. Any such formulation is fatally vulnerable to citation of a single exception—what Mead has called the "Yes,-but-the-Eskimo . . ." technique, which must lead from biology to biocultural compromise. Richard A. Shweder and Robert A. LeVine cite Mead's pioneering 1932 paper, where she contended that Piaget's theory of a universal animistic phase in the development of causal explanation in children did not apply to the Manus of Melanesia, whose children showed less animistic thought than adults. Shweder and LeVine apply this method to Kohlberg's formulation of the series of stages through which children change their understandings of the nature of their own dreams. Such changes do occur, they say, but there are alternative sequences—not a single logically given one. Such alternative sequences occur even among the children within a single culture—the Hausa of Nigeria. Their chapter, however, goes considerably beyond the invalidation of a developmental sequence based on structural-logical assumptions. They offer an alternative explanation to account for the sequence variability they observed. In their view, children are seen as changing their understandings, choosing from alternatives simultaneously available to them on the basis of the confirmatory-infirmatory evidence of their expanding experience. A synthesis of logical and experiential considerations seems to be a further step that must be taken in this discussion, and one must caution against the assumption of the child's autonomous development in relative isolation from the ambient ideology of its culture.

It is widely believed that the experiences of early childhood lay the foundation—well or poorly—not only for personality but for the individual's ultimate level of cognitive competence. Jerome Kagan questions not the influence of childhood experience but the permanence of that influence. He reports his research with Guatemalan village children, whose environment during the first year of life was poor with respect to cognitive, emotional, and social stimulation. In spite of the evident retardation of infants, Kagan found older children from the same community performing normally. He reviews other studies with animals as well as with human children that support his finding that early deprivation-retardation is reversible. (Are the effects of optimal conditions also reversible?) He urges us to a view of human resiliency and away from predestination set in early childhood. Kagan seems to predict surprise at and resistance to his position. Freud expected and encountered resistance to the opposite view in which the determinative effects of childhood were stressed. This area of research has major implications for educational and social policy.

Michael Cole and Sylvia Scribner go far toward meeting this challenge. Are there important variations in the structure and working of the intellect among different groups of people? Or do "apparent differences mask underlying universal equivalences"? What contribution does culture make to the implementation of

the human mind? Cole and Scribner feel it would be insufficient for
them simply to survey the facts, for psychologists and anthropologists disagree on their interpretation. They undertake to examine
the presuppositions and inferences that environ "the facts." They
argue that psychologists and anthropologists respectively tend to
differ in stressing processes versus content, contrived (or controlled)
versus "natural" situations, and experimental versus observational
methods. They hold that the members of these three seemingly op-
positional pairs are not as distinctive or separable as is usually supposed. The synthesis of these pairs should be accomplished in an
"ethnographic psychology" (psychological anthropology). In their
discussion, the authors include a valuable critical review of cross-
cultural studies of memory. The choice is opportune; so much of
culture is, in fact, memory—stored, potentially retrievable experience. Process itself may have cultural content, as the activity of remembering is implemented in the manner, to the extent, and in
the contexts that are requisite to each culture.

Robert I. Levy examines the teaching-learning patterns in the
schools serving American middle-class culture. He refers to an
article by Cole and Scribner, in which they pointed to a lack of
connection between formal schooling and the requirements of the
culture from which the students derive. In looking at predominant
philosophy and manner of teaching and learning in the schools,
and in following Bateson's principle of focusing on the context
rather than on the content, Levy finds consistency (a "conjunctive
pattern") between the schools and the ambient culture. The pattern
that he describes centers on the segmentation of learning into discrete units of achievement. Each task is calibrated for resolution
and reward, following moderate effort over relatively short time
spans. The pattern that he perceives concerns base-level features of
American (perhaps Western) culture. He describes alternative patterns from Polynesia and elsewhere, and alternatives already on
the scene in the West: "open education" and the "helping mode,"
which shift the emphasis in the teaching-learning process from the
teacher (as task master and reward dispenser) to the learner. To the
distinction between "content" and "process" elucidated by Cole
and Scribner, Levy adds an application of a third term: "context."
The discussion as a whole, throughout the book, evokes a fourth
term: "purpose," in the sense of "purposive socialization." This
phrase designates the increasingly self-conscious extent (probably

present to some degree in all cultures) to which we apply our uncertain knowledge of socialization, hoping for better results than we ourselves embody rather than traditional self-replication. It is a hazardous enterprise from which we are unable to refrain, short of the extirpation of our consciousness.

George Devereux takes us into the temporal logic of socialization as pre-experience and makes clear the uniquely human aspects of socialization as specifically cultural communication. The *referent* of cultural communication used in socialization may lie in the past, or in other places, or be nonexistent—but its *pertinence* is to future behavior. Devereux points out that until now, present learning has pertinence to a future conceived in the present or in the past—and may be disastrously inappropriate to a future arrived at through social change. Thus "a penny saved is a penny earned" may be a poor strategy, given a high inflation rate. Devereux takes issue with the position he attributes to Mead in *Culture and Commitment*—that under these circumstances, it is the young who must teach their elders. He points out that Mead, in her very assertion, continues as she always has to teach the young. What remains to be taught, he says, is the sense of time, of historical experience that continues to have future pertinence given the need for "continuous creative readjustment" regardless of what that future may be.

New Guinea and the Melanesian Islands surrounding it are well known for their richness of diverse traditional cultures and for the rapidity with which these cultures have undergone drastic change as a result of intense culture contact. Rhoda Metraux's chapter and my own, which follows, confront the same seeming paradox of the coexistence of both great change and fundamental continuity. Both chapters independently deal with the relations between younger and older generations spanning markedly different degrees of acculturation, particularly differentiated by the advent of formal, European-type schooling. Metraux uses a nonverbal technique—a test in which each individual is asked to create a design with colored plastic chips—in order to seek clues to "the cognitive processes that account for cultural continuity." She describes the changes that have taken place in Iatmul culture since it was described and analyzed by Bateson in *Naven* (1936). Then, Bateson developed the concept of eidos, which refers to the principles by which members of a culture structure relations of various kinds. Metraux succinctly describes the eidos of Iatmul culture in terms of the ways in which larger entities are composed of sequences of symmetric and complementary pairs. Given the mosaic test, the Iatmul produced quite beautiful and imaginative designs. Metraux found generational differences in the type of design made, but she found no difference between generations with respect to the process through which the pieces are combined or structured into the larger whole through sequential addition of symmetric and complementary pairs. However much the content of life has changed for the Iatmul, there thus seems to be an unbroken line of transmission in the manner of structuring that content—unbroken perhaps because it is invisible to consciousness, not subject to articulate choice.

My own chapter, taking off from the long-term documentation of change in Manus culture begun by Mead and Fortune in 1928, attempts a general formulation of the structure of generationally stratified cultures. An ethnographic analysis of mother's teeth exchange ceremonies and the father's sister's curse in Manus follows. The analysis centers on the conversion of these former intersegmental (clan, lineage) devices into intergenerational sanctions now operating between the stay-at-home older generation and their educated, salaried progeny dispersed throughout Papua New Guinea. I must admit to my surprise, after the iconoclasm I observed on my first trip in 1953, that on subsequent trips I found not only further drastic change but also more and more of what had seemed defunct traditional practices now adapted to new needs. There are both genuine and spurious revivals. Much that looks old, we know to be recent imports or improvisations. I often feel that to start from scratch now without the ethnographic base Mead and others established would be like studying embryology from scrambled eggs. The Manus case gives evidence of deep-lying continuity of cultural transmission that maintains the coexisting generations of Manus within a single community of belief, despite the great educational gap and spatial dispersion. And yet, the change and modernization is also real and tremendously impressive.

It is appropriate for the book to conclude with Alex Inkeles' chapter, "Becoming Modern." Inkeles reports on a vast study comparing large numbers of individuals, urban and rural, in industrial and nonindustrial employment, in six developing countries. He is concerned with "modernity" not as an attribute of nations to be measured in GNP and capital goods but as an attribute of individuals, a basic personality type measured by attitudes and capacities. We are offered a definition of modern man. Much effort went into devising a cross-national scale of individual modernity. The choice of traits will be controversial, subject to criticism as ethnocentric. What is ironic in this recurrent form of criticism, however, is that it claims certain valued traits as our own and sees their imputation elsewhere as ethnocentric. It amounts to a kind of reverse "negritude." But the traits describing modern man, wherever found, do seem rather one-sidedly positive. Has he no defects? If not, who are the multiply flawed people we see around us and in our mirrors? Inkeles reports that among the eight to ten factors revealed as having the greatest effect on individual modernity, those operating early in life (such as the father's education and own education) seem almost equally balanced with those coming into effect later in life (such as factory employment). Although education has the greatest single effect of all factors, it is evident from Inkeles' data, at least, that socialization of a modern personality is a lifelong process in which towns, factories, or rural cooperatives are also schools.

The chapters of this book are not random contributions. Each was "commissioned" to play a part in developing the theme derived from the work of Mead. Yet my expectations are exceeded. I am surprised and pleased at the extent to which they have woven themselves together into a coherent work. A picture emerges of socialization as cultural communication—complex, interactive, life-long; adaptive to change while providing for deep-level continuities; operating on affect, thought and behavior; and mediated through both intimate and formal relations ranging from mothering, to peer play, to schooling, to the arts, and to work in the adult world.

I wish to thank the contributors for papers worthy of the goal of the special issue of *Ethos*. I thank the editors of *Ethos*, particularly Walter Goldschmidt, who guided me and who made substantial editorial contributions of his own. I thank Lucy Kluckhohn, who did the final editing and who put it all together. I owe a great personal debt to Margaret Mead for the privilege and stimulation of having worked with her.

Theodore Schwartz
San Diego, 1976

Socialization as Cultural Communication

Margaret Mead in Samoa (Faleasao, Manu'a) with Talking Chief
Meauta Atufili Mageo of Pago Pago Village, 1971.

Biographical Sketch of Margaret Mead

Anthropologist, psychologist, teacher, lecturer, writer and observer of change in our time, Margaret Mead was born on December 16, 1901, in Philadelphia. She received her B.A. degree in 1923 from Barnard College, her M.A. degree a year later from Columbia University, and her Ph.D. in 1929, also from Columbia. Dr. Mead has been honored many times for her work and holds twenty honorary doctorates, including an honorary Doctor of Science awarded by Harvard in 1973, as well as many prizes and awards, among them The American Museum of Natural History Gold Medal, awarded in 1969. In 1975 alone, Dr. Mead was granted the Woman of Conscience Award from the National Council of Women; the Medal for Distinguished Service at Teacher's College, Columbia University; the Ceres Medal from the Food and Agriculture Organization (FAO) of the United Nations, and an honorary doctorate from The Philippine Women's University, Manila.

Dr. Mead began her career at The American Museum of Natural History in 1926 as assistant curator of ethnology in the Anthropology Department while completing her graduate work with the late Drs. Franz Boas and Ruth Benedict. In 1942 Dr. Mead was named associate curator; in 1964 she was appointed curator; and she is now curator emeritus of ethnology.

For several years, Dr. Mead was engrossed in the creation and installation of the Hall of Peoples of the Pacific at the Museum, which opened to the public in the spring of 1971. Dr. Mead's office and staff at the Museum served as the center for this project, as it does for most of Dr. Mead's work. The office complex consists of several rooms tucked away in a tower of the 106-year-old institution. From this office, her assistants coordinate a complicated calendar of appointments with scientists from around the world. Speaking engagements are kept in disciplined order and writing obligations and classes are scheduled. The rooms are literally a mine of information because of the complete files Dr. Mead keeps of all her past research and all her writings, plus the thousands of books on all the subjects with which Dr. Mead concerns herself.

Dr. Mead began her field work in the Pacific in 1925 when, as a fellow of the National Research Council, she made a study of adolescent girls in Samoa. This research led to her first book, *Coming of Age in Samoa* (1928). In 1928–29, as a fellow of the Social Science Research Council, Dr. Mead studied the children of Manus, one of the Admiralty Islands, and in 1930 she did research with an American Indian group. During 1931–33, Dr. Mead studied the relationship between sex and temperament among the Arapesh, Mundugumor, and Tchambuli peoples of New Guinea, which resulted in her book, *Sex and Temperament in Three Primitive Societies* (1935). This was followed by field work in Bali and New Guinea (1936–39).

After twenty-five years' absence, Dr. Mead revisited the Admiralty Islands in 1953 to study changes occuring there as the Manus people were in the process of becoming part of the mid-twentieth-century world. Dr. Mead went back to the Admiralty Islands to continue her work in 1964, 1965, 1971, 1975 and in 1967 to make a film. During one of her recent field trips in the spring of 1973, she returned to New Guinea, to revisit a mountain Arapesh group. During her lifelong study of the peoples of the Pacific, Dr. Mead has had to learn to use seven languages of the area.

Dr. Mead's field work and research into both Western and non-Western societies have resulted in an enormous amount of writing, including 24 books she has authored and another 18 she either co-authored or co-edited. She has also written a large number of scientific papers, monographs, journal articles and popular articles, including a regular column in *Redbook* magazine.

Dr. Mead has also written and narrated various films, including the series "Films on Character Formation in Different Cultures," produced with Gregory Bateson and distributed by the New York University Film Library. Other films have been "Four Families" (1959, National Film Board of Canada), "Margaret Mead's New Guinea Journal" (1968, National Educational Television), and "New Lives for Old" (1960, The Horizon for Science Series of the Educational Testing Service of Princeton, New Jersey).

In recent years, Dr. Mead has studied contemporary Western culture in the light of knowledge gained during field work in small, homogeneous and stable societies. She has focused her work on problems of education and culture; the relationship between character and social forms; personality and culture; culture change; the cultural aspects of nutrition, mental hygiene and family life; cross-national relationships; national character; and problems of the environment, food, population and human settlements in a global context.

Dr. Mead's comments on social change and the difference between generations have stimulated wide interest on both sides of the "generation gap," and her defense of change in *Culture and Commitment* (1970) has gotten people on both sides of the "gap" to look at social change with more understanding. (This may have influenced *Time* Magazine's choice of Dr. Mead as "Mother of the World" in 1969). In 1971 Dr. Mead published *A Rap on Race: A Dialogue with James Baldwin.* Two recent books are *Twentienth Century Faith: Hope and Survival* and her autobiography called *Blackberry Winter: My Earlier Years*, both published in 1972. A biography of Ruth Benedict by Dr. Mead was published in 1974 by Columbia University Press. Dr. Mead has recently completed her new book with photographer Ken Heyman, entitled *World Enough: Rethinking the Future*, which was published in 1975 by Little, Brown & Co.

Among Dr. Mead's many interests are the study of culture building, cultural change, and ekistics—the study of human settlements. Dr. Mead was a founder of the World Society for Ekistics, of which she was president from 1969 to 1971. Dr. Mead has held offices with many organizations: in the past, she has been president of the World Federation for Mental Health, the Society for Applied Anthropology, the American Anthropological Association, the Scientists' Institute for Public Information and the Society for General Systems Research; vice-president of the New York Academy of Sciences, and a member of the Board of Trustees of Hampton Institute and the Menninger Foundation. She is currently Chairman of the Board of the American Association for the Advancement of Science and secretary of the Institute for Intercultural Studies.

Among her academic affiliations, Dr. Mead is adjunct professor of anthropology at Columbia University, and visiting professor of anthropology in the Department of Psychiatry, College of Medicine, University of Cincinnati. She was Fogarty Scholar-in-Residence at the National Institutes of Health in 1973. From September, 1969, to June, 1971, Dr. Mead was chairwoman of the Social Science Division and professor of anthropology at Fordham University in New York City.

Margaret Mead and the Study of Socialization

L. L. LANGNESS

The scientific study of socialization began little more than fifty years ago. Margaret Mead's professional career began at approximately the same time. This is not merely coincidental, although the direct relationship between the two events might be seen more clearly if *cross-cultural* studies of socialization are emphasized (Williams 1972). Is there by now any informed person who is unaware of the impact made on such studies by Mead's first book, *Coming of Age in Samoa?* And if we have so incorporated the early lessons Mead gave us into our scientific tradition that we have lost sight of their significance, perhaps we should pause for review:

It was a simple—a very simple—point to which our materials were organized in the 1920's, merely the documentation over and over of the fact that human nature is not rigid and unyielding, not an unadaptable plant which insists on flowering or becoming stunted after its own fashion, responding only quantitatively to the social environment, but that it is extraordinarily adaptable, that cultural rhythms are stronger

L. L. LANGNESS is an associate professor-in-residence, Departments of Anthropology and Psychiatry, University of California, Los Angeles. He wishes to thank Walter Goldschmidt, Robert B. Edgerton, Theodore Schwartz, Thomas Weisner, Harold G. Levine, Cecile R. Edgerton, and Jill Korbin for various suggestions and advice.

and more compelling than the physiological rhythms which they overlay and distort, that the failure to satisfy an artificial, culturally stimulated need—for outdistancing one's neighbors in our society, for instance, or for wearing the requisite number of dog's teeth among the Manus—may produce more unhappiness and frustration in the human breast than the most rigorous cultural curtailments of the physiological demands of sex or hunger. We had to present evidence that human character is built upon a biological base which is capable of enormous diversification in terms of social standards (Mead, 1939a:x).

It is easy to confuse simplicity with unimportance. The importance of this shift in our view of human nature, as well as Margaret Mead's contribution to it, a shift that broke the stranglehold biology and genetics held on studies of child development, simply cannot be overemphasized (Hallowell 1955, Langness 1974, Simpson 1958). *Coming of Age in Samoa,* subtitled "A Psychological Study of Primitive Youth for Western Civilization," was the first intensive study of what was to become the subdiscipline known as Culture and Personality (Honigman 1972:125). We have by now become so accustomed to prefacing our statements, "in this culture," we tend to forget that it was not always so.

Although Mead made her second field trip to Manus specifically to study animistic thinking, she ultimately included mention of this only as an appendix to the more general book that resulted from it, *Growing Up in New Guinea.* Perhaps she did this because the results were negative, perhaps because, as she said at the time, she wanted to wait until she had replicated the study in an additional society. In any case, the result seems to have been to minimize the importance of an early, convincing, and still unsurpassed challenge to what still hangs on in some circles as part of a general theory of intelligence:

The results of these various lines of investigation show that Manus children not only show no tendency towards spontaneous animistic thought, but that they also show what may perhaps legitimately be termed as negativism towards explanations couched in animistic rather than practical cause and effect terms. The Manus child is less spontaneously animistic and less traditionally animistic than is the Manus adult. This result is a direct contradiction of findings in our own society, in which the child has been found to be more animistic, in both traditional and spontaneous fashions, than are his elders. When such a reversal is found in two contrasting societies, the explanation must obviously be sought in terms of the culture; a purely psychological explanation is inadequate (Mead 1932b:186).

Only now, 40 years later, is serious attention once again being directed to comparative studies of basic cognitive processes (Cole and Scribner 1973, Price-Williams 1975). "The Comparative Study of Primitive Education," the subtitle of *Growing Up in New Guinea,* was not only a broader field of inquiry which included her study of thinking, but also developed, of course, into what we now conceive of as the cross-cultural study of socialization.

Mead's field work on the Omaha reservation in 1930, although terribly unpleasant for her (Mead 1972), resulted in *The Changing Culture of an Indian Tribe* (1932a). This was one of the earliest full-length treatments of culture change, an interest that was to become formalized in anthropology in the 1930s and 1940s (Keesing 1953); and it was certainly one of the earliest "acculturation" studies (Siegal 1955). Mead has herself commented upon this:

The first real evidence of the emergence of a new viewpoint that gave weight to both sides of a culture contact situation came only in 1935 with the publication of a first report by the Social Science Research Council's Subcommittee on Acculturation and with the appearance of a paper by Gregory Bateson, in which, using techniques that anticipated cybernetic methods, he included both groups within an analyzable system. For my own awareness of the problem I owe a special debt to my mother's study, "The Italian on the Land," which I watched her make when I was four. In her research, she treated Italians as future members of the society into which they had migrated and regarded the nature of that society as relevant to their lives. I also knew and appreciated the work of Christie MacLeod who, in writing *The American Indian Frontier,* had taken into account the interrelationships that shaped Euro-American culture contacts (Mead 1966a:xiv-xv).

Thus it is fair to say, I believe, that by 1932 Margaret Mead had settled on the three major and closely related interests she would thenceforth pursue: Culture and Personality studies, Education, and Culture Change. Virtually all of her subsequent work has dealt with one or the other of these general topics. Over the years she has continually narrowed, refocused, or expanded her views as her experience has required. In addition, and running through all of her work, from *Coming of Age in Samoa* to the present, has been a serious and explicit concern with methodology. It is ironic that although Mead has been subjected to endless criticism about her presumed lack of methodological rigor, she has been far more open and honest about her methods than have most other anthropologists (Harris 1968). She has been methodologically innovative as, for example, in her work on animistic thought where she employed children's drawings, psychological tests, and experimental observations (Mead 1931, 1932*b*), on Bali where she introduced new photographic and recording techniques (Bateson and Mead 1942, Mead and MacGregor 1951), and on national character where she had to develop techniques for studying culture at a distance and cope with a difficult problem of sampling (Mead 1951*c*, 1953*b*, Mead and Metraux 1953). She has also often clarified anthropological methods for others (Mead 1933, 1939*b*, 1946, 1954, 1956*c*, 1969, 1970*a*).

Margaret Mead's interest in education, and particularly in American education, led her to recognize very early in her career that if a social scientist wished to be heard and to make an impact it would be necessary to appeal directly to the public rather than to peers. Thus she addressed her first books, and, indeed, most of her subsequent work, to the public. Even so, she did not, strictly speaking, "popularize" in the derogatory sense that has often been charged. There is no doubt that Mead was entirely aware of what she was doing:

I can emphasize that this was the first piece of anthropological fieldwork which was written without the paraphernalia of scholarship designed to mystify the lay reader and confound one's colleagues. It seemed to me then—and it still does—that if our studies of the way of life of other peoples are to be meaningful to the peoples of the industrialized world, they must be written for them and not wrapped up in technical jargon for specialists. As this book was about adolescents, I tried to couch it in language that would be communicative to those who had most to do with adolescents—teachers, parents, and soon-to-be parents. I did not write it as a popular book, but only with the hope that it would be intelligible to those who might make the best use of its theme, that adolescence need not be the time of stress and strain which Western society made it; that growing up could be freer and easier and less complicated (Mead 1973).

In this way, as we all know, Mead has long been the foremost spokesman for the profession and she has done more for the public awareness of anthropology than any other anthropologist.

It is in the area of education that Mead's particular concern with socialization is most directly apparent. But it is important to recognize that education, as Mead employs the term in her early work, implies not only the institutionalized and formal methods of schooling employed in the Western world, but also the completely informal and unstructured means employed in the small-scale, preliterate world. The term education is employed by her synonymously with socialization. Neither term, however, describes precisely what she was attempting to study. The term that best describes it—enculturation—did not appear until 1948 when it was introduced by Melville J. Herskovits (Titiev 1964:239).

The aspects of the learning experience which mark off man from other creatures, and by means of which, initially, and in later life, he achieves competence in his culture, may be called *enculturation*. This is in essence a process of conscious or unconscious conditioning, exercised within the limits sanctioned by a given body of custom. From this process not only is all adjustment to social living achieved, but also all those satisfactions that, though they are of course a part of social experience, derive from individual expression rather than association with others in the group (Herskovits 1948:39).

In the introduction to *Coming of Age in Samoa* Mead had defined her task as follows:

because of the particular problem which we set out to answer, this tale of another way of life is mainly concerned with education, with the process by which the baby, arrived cultureless upon the human scene, becomes a full-fledged adult member of his or her society (1928:13).

Her opening sentence in *Growing Up in New Guinea*:

The way in which each human infant is transformed into the finished adult, into the complicated individual version of his city and his century is one of the most fascinating studies open to the curious minded (1930:1).

And then later:

We have followed the Manus baby through its formative years to adulthood, seen its indifference towards adult life turn into attentive participation, its idle scoffing at the supernatural change into an anxious sounding of the wishes of the spirits, its easy-going generous communism turn into grasping individualistic acquisitiveness. The process of education is complete. The Manus baby, born into the world without motor habits, without speech, without any definite forms of behavior, with neither beliefs nor enthusiasms, has become the Manus adult in every particular. No cultural item has slipped out of the stream of tradition which the elders transmit in this irregular unorganised fashion to their children, transmit by a method which seems to us so haphazard, so unpremeditated, so often definitely hostile to its ultimate ends (1930:259–260).

Many other examples can be found. Mead appears to have never been particularly interested in how an infant becomes *social,* or even in how it becomes *human.* She was interested from first to last in how it becomes *cultural*—and she seems to have meant cultural in a remarkably sophisticated, meaningful, and modern sense. The contemporary concept of culture that would come the closest to what she had in mind would perhaps be that of Clifford Geertz:

We are, in sum, incomplete or unfinished animals who complete or finish ourselves through culture—and not through culture in general but through highly particular forms of it: Dobuan and Javanese, Hopi and Italian, upper-class and lower-class, academic and commercial. Man's great capacity for learning, his plasticity, has often been remarked, but what is even more critical is his extreme dependency upon a certain sort of learning: the attainment of concepts, the apprehension and application of specific systems of symbolic meaning. Beavers build dams, birds build nests, bees locate food, baboons organize social groups, and mice mate on the basis of forms of learning that rest predominantly on the instructions encoded in their genes and evoked by appropriate patterns of external stimuli: physical keys inserted into organic locks. But men build dams or shelters, locate food, organize their social groups, or find sexual partners under the guidance of instructions encoded in flow charts and blueprints, hunting lore, moral systems, and aesthetic judgments: conceptual structures molding formless talents (Geertz 1965:113).

The distinction involved here between enculturation and socialization is by no means trivial:

So it is important to reaffirm the difference between the study of enculturation—the process of learning a culture in all its uniqueness and par-
ticularity—and the study of socialization—the set of specieswide requirements and exactions made on human beings by human societies. Unless,
in each case, the full details of enculturation are recorded and, later, are
examined as meticulously as are techniques of drumming or singing,
and are analyzed, in context, in many systematically chosen cultures, the
probability of our developing a cross-culturally viable theory of socialization is negligible.

Each time a member of some other discipline arrives at a generalization about socialization based on an indiscriminate use of anthropological materials, each time an anthropologist applies to his own work the
treatment of socialization currently in vogue in the behavioral sciences,
which has not passed through the refining crucible of comparative study
of enculturation, the confusion is further compounded. Controversies
arise in which the anthropologist, or someone with a genuine knowledge
of enculturation, objects that the particular generalization made by a
behavioral scientist does not take culture (by which he means *cultures*)
into account; in reply, the behavioral scientist insists that he has taken
as a basic premise the idea that man is a cultural animal, that all culture
is learned, and so forth. But to the extent that they are talking past each
other, the controversy remains unresolved (Mead 1963:187).

It is probably true to say that although she rarely bothered to define it, Mead employed the concept of culture throughout her entire career far more consistently, insightfully, and successfully than
most other scholars. This is at least partly responsible for her success and durability as an anthropologist. Although she was influenced by A. R. Radcliffe-Brown, as her monograph, *Kinship in the
Admiralty Islands* (1934) shows, she was not led astray as were many
of her peers by the simplicities of Radcliffe-Brown's version of
structuralism. She retained and used the concept of culture in spite
of Radcliffe-Brown's insistence (1957) that there could be no science of culture. Likewise, she was not plunged into relative inertia
because of the difficulties of operationalizing or defining culture as
were still others of her colleagues. Mead continued to demonstrate
in her articles, books, and lectures just what completely cultural
animals we really are. If her early work, *Sex and Temperament in
Three Primitive Societies* (1935) is a dubious but plausible over-
statement of this, *Male and Female* (1949) is a more mature and
convincing one. Even more convincing is the work on Balinese

character (Bateson and Mead 1942, Mead and MacGregor 1951) and the work on culture and national character she conducted during and just after World War II. *And Keep Your Powder Dry* (1942), Mead's penetrating analysis of American character, is perhaps the best single example here, with *Soviet Attitudes Toward Authority* (1951*b*) being another very good one.

While it may be true that theory is more often implicit than explicit in Mead's work, it has always been informed by a clearly formulated, consistent, and strongly held view of the nature of man and culture (Webb 1968). Furthermore, she has never been uncomfortable when grappling with explicit theoretical issues in the study of culture. Her theoretical position is probably best seen in such works as "The Concept of Culture and the Psychosomatic Approach" (1947), *The Study of Culture at a Distance* (Mead and Metraux 1953), "The Cross-Cultural Approach to the Study of Personality" (1956*a*), "Cultural Determinants of Behavior" (1958) and *Continuities in Cultural Evolution* (1964). That the culture concept has become recognized as the "most central problem of all social science" (Malinowski 1939:588), "the foundation stone of the social sciences" (Chase 1948:59), "the key concept of anthropology" (Devereux 1956:23), and so on, is in important measure due to the persistence and talent Margaret Mead brought to her work.

Although Mead worked in cultures that can easily be thought of as exotic, and although she wrote books that often became popular, she never indulged in sensationalism, nor did she concentrate on the esoteric. Her work has always been serious and comparative; it has most frequently contrasted other ways of life with those of her countrymen. In *Coming of Age in Samoa* she discussed American educational problems as they related to her findings about Samoa. In *Growing Up in New Guinea* she did likewise. This early interest grew and developed in literally hundreds of conferences, articles, and lectures and led eventually to *The School in American Culture* (1951*a*). While Webb's claim that, "with the exception of the technical monographs (for example her work on the Mountain Arapesh) she never really has written about anything other than Western society," (1968:158) cannot be taken seriously, it is quite apparent, as he also suggests, that two of her major interests have always been the reformation of American culture and the creation of a better world. Her attitude towards this can be seen clearly in the following passage from *Balinese Character,* written just as America was entering the Second World War:

we are faced with the problem of building a new world; we have to re-orient the old values of many contrasting and contradictory cultural systems into a new form which will use but transcend them all, draw on their respective strengths and allow for their respective weaknesses. We have to build a culture richer and more rewarding than any that the world has ever seen. This can only be done through a disciplined science of human relations and such a science is built by drawing out from very detailed, concrete materials, such as these, the relevant abstractions—the vocabulary which will help us to plan an integrated world (Bateson and Mead 1942:xvi).

Insofar as anthropology and the other social sciences had as their original purpose the idea of social reform (Becker 1971), and as the current trend in the social sciences is quite clearly back towards this original and only meaningful purpose (Hymes 1969), Mead's attitude and consistency on this point, which has often been denigrated in the recent past, must surely be seen as a virtue.

Mead's continuing interest in culture change, which originated with *The Changing Culture of an Indian Tribe,* eventually resulted in the practical manual *Cultural Patterns and Technical Change* (1953a). Her revisit to Manus, twenty-five years after her initial field work there, rather drastically revised her views of the process of culture change:

The transformation I witnessed in 1953 taught me a great deal about social change—change within one generation—and about the way a people who were well led could take their future in their own hands. It helped correct the widely held belief that slow change, however uneven, was preferable to rapid change. The Manus children I studied earlier, in 1928, had taught me about the consequences of the kind of education advocated by contemporary educators. For Manus children, given great freedom, grew up to accept—even though grudgingly—the standards of the adult world. I learned that it is not enough to depend on the next generation; adults themselves must take part in change (Mead 1966b).

New Lives for Old: Cultural Transformation—Manus, 1928–1953 (1956b), although not the first restudy of a culture done by anthropologists, was an unusually dramatic example, and it quickly became one of the best-known and most influential studies of its kind. As above, it questioned for the first time the assumption that culture change must go slowly if it were not to be disruptive. More important, it helped to shape and clarify Mead's theoretical position with respect to the evolution and microevolution of culture as recorded in *Continuities in Cultural Evolution,* and it also helped her to formulate her recent and insightful *Culture and Commitment: A Study of the Generation Gap.* The contrast Mead develops in *Culture and Commitment,* between *postfigurative, cofigurative,* and *prefigurative cultures,*[1] although perhaps not as completely developed as we might wish, is one that deserves our most serious attention. It is one of only a few formulations dealing with the immensity of the changes confronting us that does not confuse the contemporary situation *subjectively* viewed (the young have always rebelled against authority, etc.) with the same situation *objectively* viewed (the position of young people in the world today is, in fact, totally without precedent). Only an anthropologist with Margaret Mead's interests and vast experience—with socialization and enculturation, cognition, with culture change and communication, and with evolution—could convincingly write as follows:

Today, as we are coming to understand better the circular processes through which culture is developed and transmitted, we recognize that man's most human characteristic is not his ability to learn, which he shares with many other species, but his ability to teach and store what others have developed and taught him. Learning, which is based on human dependency, is relatively simple. But human capacities for creating elaborate teachable systems, for understanding and utilizing the resources of the natural world, and for governing society and creating imaginary worlds, all these are very complex. In the past, men relied on the least elaborate part of the circular system, the dependent learning by children, for continuity of transmission and for the embodiment of the new. Now, with our greater understanding of the process, we must cultivate the most flexible and complex part of the system—the behavior of adults. We must, in fact, teach ourselves how to alter adult behavior so that we can give up postfigurative upbringing, with its tolerated con-

1. Postfigurative cultures are those in which children learn primarily from their forebears. Cofigurative cultures are those in which both children and adults learn from their peers. A prefigurative culture is one in which adults learn from their children as well as from their forebears and peers (see Mead 1970*b*).

figurative components, and discover prefigurative ways of teaching and learning that will keep the future open. We must create new models for adults who can teach their children not what to learn, but how to learn and not what they should be committed to, but the value of commitment (1970b:72).

In spite of her emphasis on children, Mead never restricted her work merely to child-rearing practices, emphasizing instead the wider cultural context and the roles of siblings, parents, and grandparents in the enculturative process. She recognized very early that much of the study of enculturation—the process of transmitting particular cultural forms and symbols to particular individuals and groups—revolved around the problem of communication; and she also realized early that the communicative process was not entirely verbal. Whereas all of this might be said to be merely implicit in her early work, it was the early work (with the added stimulus of Gregory Bateson's similarly emerging ideas on culture and communication) that guided her to undertake the remarkable study of Balinese character. *Balinese Character* was an attempt to demonstrate, on the one hand, how culture is organized and communicated in all its nuances from generation to generation, and, on the other, how anthropologists could communicate their knowledge of this process to others without relying so exclusively on the printed word. It was a most rewarding experiment which has, unfortunately, never been replicated. The best statement of what they were attempting is found in their own introduction to the book:

In this monograph we are attempting a new method of stating the intangible relationships among different types of culturally standardized behavior by placing side by side mutually relevant photographs. Pieces of behavior, spatially and contextually separated—a trance dancer being carried in procession, a man looking up at an aeroplane, a servant greeting his master in a play, the painting of a dream—may all be relevant to a single discussion; the same emotional thread may run through them. To present them together in words, it is necessary either to resort to devices which are inevitably literary, or to dissect the living scenes so that only desiccated items remain.

By the use of photographs, the wholeness of each piece of behavior can be preserved, while the special cross-referencing desired can be obtained by placing the series of photographs on the same page. It is possible to avoid the artificial construction of a scene at which a man, watching a dance, also looks up at an aeroplane and has a dream; it is also possible to avoid diagramming the single element in these scenes which we wish to stress—the importance of levels in Balinese interpersonal relationships—in such a way that the reality of the scenes themselves is destroyed.

This is not a book about Balinese custom, but about the Balinese—about the way in which they, as living persons, moving, standing, eating, sleeping, dancing, and going into trance, embody that abstraction which (after we have abstracted it) we technically call culture (Bateson and Mead 1942:xii).

This was an ambitious attempt to avoid the earlier, more literary style of Mead, without resorting to the analytic extremes of Bateson's early work, *Naven* (1936). Had World War II not intervened, the impact of this fruitful innovation would doubtless have been much greater than it was. *Balinese Character* might well be seen as the first formal study of "socialization as cultural communication," and therefore as the original inspiration for this particular volume, a slightly belated testimonial to an exceedingly valuable idea.

Mead has always been in the forefront of anthropological research. As we have noted, she helped to break the monopoly biology and genetics held for a time on ideas of human development. She produced the first work in Culture and Personality. She was the first seriously to challenge Piaget on cognitive processes. She was one of the earliest anthropologists formally to study culture change and, more particularly, acculturation. She was also the first cultural anthropologist to appeal successfully to the public. She studied the process of enculturation before the term existed. Her view of the culture concept was considerably more advanced than that of most of her colleagues. She pioneered in the area of national character studies and the study of culture at a distance, and she consistently maintained, at times in the face of outright derision, that anthropology was a reformer's science. She innovated methodologically and, with Bateson, she introduced the idea of culture as communication. Open to suggestion, she took selectively and critically, and for her own purposes, from psychoanalytic theory and from Radcliffe-Brown. Finally, she has given real meaning to the study of rapid change and the concept of the generation gap.

It has often been noted that there exists no "school" of Mead, no tightly knit band of disciples, no clique or loyalists, no true believers, no central theme or discovery to be institutionalized in Mead's name. So be it—all behavioral and social scientists have been influenced by the work of Margaret Mead, an influence that has gone far beyond the sciences themselves to permeate virtually every literate household. Whatever her critics say, and granted that like all such gifted and productive people she is open to criticism, her positive contributions are monumental. Her influence on the profession, on related disciplines, and on the public, as well as on the theme of this volume, are simply without precedent.

REFERENCES

BATESON, GREGORY. 1936. *Naven*. Cambridge University Press.

BATESON, GREGORY, and M. MEAD. 1942. *Balinese Character: A Photographic Analysis* (Special Publications of the New York Academy of Sciences, 2). New York Academy of Sciences.

BECKER, ERNEST. 1971. *The Lost Science of Man*. George Braziller.

CHASE, STUART. 1948. *The Proper Study of Mankind*. Harper.

COLE, MICHAEL, and SYLVIA SCRIBNER. 1973. *Culture and Thought*. John Wiley and Sons, Inc.

DEVEREUX, GEORGE. 1956. Normal and Abnormal: The Key Problem of Psychiatric Anthropology, *Some Uses of Anthropology: Theoretical and Applied* (J. B. Casagrande and T. Gladwin, eds.), pp. 23–48. Anthropological Society of Washington.

GEERTZ, CLIFFORD. 1965. The Impact of the Concept of Culture on the Concept of Man, *New Views of the Nature of Man* (John R. Platt, ed.), pp. 93–118. University of Chicago Press.

HALLOWELL, A. IRVING. 1955. *Culture and Experience*. University of Pennsylvania Press.

HARRIS, M. 1968. *The Rise of Anthropological Theory*. Thomas Y. Crowell Co.

HERSKOVITS, MELVILLE J. 1948. *Man and His Works*. Alfred A. Knopf.

HONIGMANN, JOHN J. 1972. North America, *Psychological Anthropology* (F. L. K. Hsu, ed.). Schenkman Publishing Co.

HYMES, DELL (ed.), 1969. Reinventing Anthropology. Pantheon Books.

KEESING, FELIX. 1953. *Culture Change: An Analysis and Bibliography of Anthropological Sources to 1952*. Stanford University Press.

LANGNESS, L. L. 1974. *The Study of Culture*. Chandler and Sharp Publishers, Inc.

MALINOWSKI, B. 1939. Review of Six Essays on Culture by Albert Blumenthal. *American Sociological Review* 4:588–592.

MEAD, M. 1928. *Coming of Age in Samoa*. Wm. Morrow and Co.

———. 1930. *Growing Up in New Guinea*. Wm. Morrow and Co.

———. 1931. The Primitive Child, *A Handbook of Child Psychology*, (Carl Murchison, ed.). Clark University Press.

———. 1932b. An Investigation of the Thought of Primitive Children with Special Reference to Animism. *Journal of the Royal Anthropological Institute* 62:173–190.

———. 1932a. *The Changing Culture of an Indian Tribe*. Columbia University Press.

———. 1933. More Comprehensive Field Methods. *American Anthropologist* 35:1–15.

———. 1934. *Kinship in the Admiralty Islands*. American Museum of Natural History *Anthropological Papers* 34, II.

———. 1935. *Sex and Temperament in Three Primitive Societies*. Wm. Morrow and Co.

———. 1939a. *From the South Seas*. Wm. Morrow and Co.

———. 1939b. Native Languages as Field Work Tools. *American Anthropologist* 41:189–205.

———. 1942. *And Keep Your Powder Dry*. Wm. Morrow and Co.

———. 1946. Research on Primitive Children, *Manual of Child Psychology* (Leonard Carmichael, ed.), pp. 735–780. Wiley.

———. 1947. The Concept of Culture and the Psychosomatic Approach. *Psychiatry* 10:57–76.

———. 1949. *Male and Female*. Wm. Morrow and Co.

———. 1951a. *The School in American Culture*. Harvard University Press.

———. 1951b. *Soviet Attitudes Toward Authority*. McGraw Hill.

———. 1951c. The Study of National Character, *The Policy Sciences*, (D. Lerner and H. D. Haswell, eds.). Stanford University Press.

———. 1953a. *Cultural Patterns and Technical Change*. UNESCO.

———. 1953b. National Character, *Anthropology Today* (A. L. Kroeber, ed.), p. 642–667. University of Chicago Press.

———. 1954. The Swaddling Hypothesis: Its Reception. *American Anthropologist* 56:395–409.

———. 1956a. The Cross-Cultural Approach to the Study of Personality, *Psychology of Personality: Six Modern Approaches* (J. L. McCary, ed.), pp. 203–252. Logos Press.

————. 1956*b*. *New Lives for Old: Cultural Transformation—Manus, 1928–1953*. Wm. Morrow and Co.

————. 1956*c*. Some Uses of Still Photography in Culture and Personality Studies, *Personal Character and Cultural Milieu* (Douglas G. Haring, ed.). Syracuse University Press.

————. 1958. Cultural Determinants of Behavior, *Behavior and Evolution* (Anne Roe and George G. Simpson, eds.), pp. 480–504. Yale University Press.

————. 1963. Socialization and Enculturation. *Current Anthropology* 4 (2):184–188.

————. 1964. *Continuities in Cultural Evolution*. Yale University Press.

————. 1966*a*. Consequences of Racial Guilt: Introduction 1965. Capricorn Books Edition, *The Changing Culture of an Indian Tribe*, pp. ix–xxiii. Capricorn Books.

————. 1966*b*. Manus Revisited—Preface 1965. *New Lives for Old*, pp. xi–xvi. Wm. Morrow and Co.

————. 1969. Research with Human Beings: A Model Derived from Anthropological Field Practice. *Daedalus* (Spring 1969), pp. 361–386.

————. 1970*a*. The Art and Technology of Field Work, *A Handbook of Method in Cultural Anthropology* (R. Naroll and R. Cohen, eds.), pp. 246–265. The Natural History Press.

————. 1970*b*. *Culture and Commitment: A Study of the Generation Gap*. The Natural History Press.

————. 1972. *Blackberry Winter*. Wm. Morrow and Co.

————. 1973. Preface to the 1973 edition of *Coming of Age in Samoa*. Wm. Morrow and Co.

MEAD, M., and FRANCES COOK MACGREGOR. 1951. *Growth and Culture: A Photographic Study of Balinese Childhood*. G. P. Putnam's Sons.

MEAD, M., and R. METRAUX. 1953. *The Study of Culture at a Distance*. University of Chicago Press.

PRICE WILLIAMS, DOUGLASS R. 1975. *Explorations in Cross-Cultural Psychology*. Chandler and Sharp Publishers, Inc.

RADCLIFFE-BROWN, A. R. 1957. *A Natural Science of Society*. Free Press.

SIEGEL, BERNARD J. (ed.). 1955. *Acculturation: Critical Abstracts, North America*. Stanford University Press.

SIMPSON, GEORGE G. 1958. The Study of Evolution: Methods and Present Status of Theory, *Behavior and Evolution* (Anne Roe and George Gaylord Simpson, eds.), pp. 7–26. Yale University Press.

TITIEV, MISCHA. 1964. Enculturation, *A Dictionary of the Social Sciences* (Julius Gould and William L. Kolb, eds.), p. 239. The Free Press.

WEBB, MALCOLM C. 1968. The Culture Concept and Cultural Change in the Work of Margaret Mead. *The Proceedings of the Louisiana Academy of Sciences* 31:148–165.

WILLIAMS, THOMAS RHYS. 1972. *Introduction to Socialization.* The C. V. Mosby Co.

Growing Up in a Monkey Group

THELMA E. ROWELL

METHODOLOGICAL PROBLEMS

Primates as an order have an exceptionally long generation interval. Compared with other mammals of equivalent weights, gestation is long, lactation is long, and the juvenile period is long. Thus the minimal generation time is about 20 months for a marmoset smaller than a laboratory rat, 4 years for a typical Old World monkey the size of a dog, perhaps 10 or 12 years for a great ape. Nor does maturation cease with sexual maturity: increasingly, it is becoming clear that interaction patterns, the "social role," of adult primates of either sex continues to change for many years (e.g. Sackett and Ruppenthal 1973). This is not necessarily a peculiarity of primates, however; social maturation probably continues beyond sexual maturity in other social mammals.

We can, of course, make cross-sectional descriptions of social development, obtaining means and ranges of such measures as time spent in contact with mother, or frequency of maternal intervention in interactions between infants and others at particular ages. This method can be extended relatively easily to infants develop-

THELMA E. ROWELL is assistant professor in the Department of Zoology at the University of California, Berkeley.

ing in widely different situations, including highly controlled and modified laboratory situations, with the effect of extending the range of the readings at a particular age. Development, however, is a process whose interest largely derives from the resultant end product, so that longitudinal studies are more satisfying. Yet even with enormous resources the answer to a simple question like "is there an effect of mothering received on maternal behavior towards first offspring" is nearly a lifetime research commitment on apes, and involves a time span far longer than the average project funding even for monkeys.

We have then two distinct types of information: first, descriptions of social behavior at successive ages, with a measure of variation to be encountered between individuals in the same general environment, and the extension of variation to be expected if environmental conditions are changed. Second, there are, or should be studies of what amount to causal processes, correlation of early variation in social experience with later variation in adult behavior at maturity. Because of the time needed to obtain the latter type, discussion of social development in monkeys must be augmented with the inspired reading of cross-sectional data as a series in time (cf. Kummer 1968), the extrapolation of laboratory data to natural situations with quite different social environment, and other forms of inspired guesswork. In this article I aim towards a consideration of social development in undisturbed groups of monkeys in their natural habitat, about which little data are available, because wild monkeys are shy and most live rather invisibly in dense vegetation. Data from provisioned wild troops in Japan provide some information, but social behavior has undoubtedly been altered by feeding if only because it allowed the numbers of animals in a troop to increase enormously (up to 700 in a troop). Individuals have, however, been followed through their whole lives, and genealogies are known. A step further removed are the rhesus macaques free ranging on islands off Puerto Rico. These also have a very dense population, are dependent on localized provided food, and are in an alien habitat; but known genealogies have been followed for long periods. Other sites are being developed which should provide valuable longitudinal information, such as wild populations of baboons at Gilgil in Kenya and Gombe Stream in Tanzania.

KINSHIP

Except for these studies, field students have guessed about the kinship of their animals, in fact very often individual identification was not possible. Captive groups typically start with strangers and studies are rarely long enough to see lineages develop from scratch (Kaufman's studies, below, are a notable exception). In both these circumstances there is a tendency to describe social interactions as between age/sex classes. This is better than nothing as a first approximation, but there is a danger of extrapolating from this an expedient to handle incomplete data to the assumption that monkeys actually interact with examples of an age/sex class, whereas in reality they interact with individuals.

Where kinship groups exist in a captive group, or are known in a wild group, it is clear that a major part of an individual's identity depends on its relations. In a captive vervet group that has been followed into the third generation, Bramblett (1970) found that both sexes were ranked according to their maternal lineage. Subadult males defended their mothers and only their own mothers if the senior, adult male who normally defended the group was absent; if all adults were removed, each infant was defended by its oldest male sibling only. Grooming, spacing, and other behavior could also be best described in terms of kinship links. Loss of kinship information can result in gross oversimplification. For example, a catalogue of the types of interaction seen between, say, adult males and infants under six months, which might perhaps be published under a title like "the role of adult males in the socialization of infant monkeys" would in fact be the sum of several different relationships with varying degrees of overlap in the type of interactions they include. Ransom and Ransom (1971) avoided this type of oversimplification in an illuminating way. In their study of interactions between male baboons and infants in a troop at Gombe Stream, four very different types of relationship were analyzed.

Most studies of infant development in captivity have explored the relationship of mother and infant in the first months, and the way in which the infant's dependence on the mother lessens. This interest stems in large part from the current stress on maternal care and the development of independence in Western society, but it also is a simple-seeming system that lends itself to experimental manipulation and is reliably duplicated. In contrast, in wild or large, long-standing captive groups of monkeys, a mother and her new infant appear not so much as interacting individuals but as a single unit, with very different social properties from the pregnant female that preceded it. Social development becomes not so much a matter of leaving the mother but of entering new relationships, a gradually growing, but never complete separation of the interaction patterns of mother and infant.

SPECIAL STATUS OF YOUNG INFANTS

The infant monkey is not usually threatened or attacked, nor does it threaten or attack others. As a badge of this immunity it has distinctive markings: its fur is a different texture, and usually a different color from that of adults or juveniles. Thus dark brown stumptail macaques have blond infants, while light grey hanuman langurs have dark brown infants. Distinctive adult patterns are lacking—the brilliantly colored de Brazza's monkey (*Cercopithecus neglectus*) with orange browband and long white beard has an all-over brown infant, the talapoin infant has a pale pink face, lacking the dark cheek-lines and yellow side-whiskers of the juvenile and adult.

Infant monkeys all look much more alike than do adults of different species, and their infancy is recognized and responded to by other species. I have seen a captive baboon female lipsmack and grunt appreciatively at a newborn vervet infant in the next cage, to the alarm of its mother who probably knew that baboons are predators of vervets. Occasionally we find monkeys in the wild living with troops of the wrong species—an adult male vervet lived in one of the baboon troops I studied in Uganda, and Aldrich-Blake (1968) reported a female coppertail monkey that lived with a blue monkey troop (*Cercopithecus ascanius* with *C. mitis*) and even had a hybrid infant. It is probable that these were the result of infant theft and adoption at an interspecies encounter. The infants were reared successfully because not only do infants look alike, but behavior towards an infant appropriate to ensuring its survival is much the same for all monkeys, and the behavior of the infants which helps to elicit such responses is also very similar.

There are differences in rates of increase of locomotor independence—Chalmers (1972) has found a correlation between habitat and developmental rates, with infants growing up high in trees being slower to go out of mother's arm's reach, reasonably enough, than infants of terrestrial species, which first run safely along the ground. In other respects the arboreal infants developed as fast as closely related terrestrial species, and the arboreal mothers were not more restrictive.

SOCIAL EXPERIENCE OF YOUNG INFANTS

All infants in the first three months or so need suckling, carrying, grooming, protecting. During this time they are learning about their companions. Sackett (1970) presents evidence that there is an inborn recognition of, and preference for adults of own species. Yet the evidence of animals living with the wrong species in the wild, even though their own species uses the same range and the troops must on occasion meet, and the evidence of numerous hand-reared pet monkeys that continue to prefer human company even after being placed with groups of their own species suggests that this innate tendency may be to a greater or lesser extent overruled by early experience. Presumably it is normally reinforced by the early experience. The young monkey also learns to recognize the members of his troop, and the social interaction patterns to be expected between them and his mother and himself. An infant patas monkey, for example (personal observations) develops decided preferences among the would-be caretakers in the group which seem to be the result of experience of the type of handling it may receive from them. It tries to avoid caretakers that are rough or restrictive. The type of care given depends partly on the relationship of the caretaker to the mother and partly on the maturity of the caretaker. Juvenile females gradually come to treat infants less as playthings and more maternally, possibly as a result of learning which types of caretaking allow her to keep the infant for longer periods of time (Lancaster 1971). Thus the infant may aid in the social development of the older animal as well as vice versa. The infant's preference among alternative caretakers does not always coincide with that of its mother. In a cage situation mothers are reluctant to allow females ranking higher than themselves to take the infant because they have trouble in taking it back; yet the high-ranking female is often the most relaxed and permissive caretaker, and so is favored by the infant. This is the first point at which the mother's and infant's interaction patterns begin to diverge.

Besides the infant's special and generally recognized status as an infant, it is also responded to from the moment it leaves its mother as an individual with known kinship. A juvenile female will glance at its mother before picking it up, even though she is not the closest other monkey. An adult female in a captive group will unerringly interfere in an infant play group if her friend's child is, in her opinion, being treated roughly, and cuff away the others (Rowell, Hinde, and Spencer-Booth 1964). Occasionally one sees a juvenile female retrieve an infant and carry it back to its own mother, perhaps to the other side of the group (e.g. Breuggeman 1973). An infant that is known to have influential protectors will be treated with great respect at least if any of its protectors are in sight. An adult male vervet will carefully avoid walking directly up to an infant because if one happens to scream at his approach a pack of females will instantly attack him, assuming him to have harmed it (Lancaster 1970). In this way an infant learns its own status including its rank, which is basically that of its mother. Differences between infants in the way they behave gradually become apparent, and are probably in large part the result of their different social experience.

INTERSPECIFIC VARIATION IN SOCIAL EXPERIENCE

Although the caretaking needs of the infant and the social stimuli it provides are similar in different species of monkey, there is great variation between species as to who provides the care, and hence great variation in the social experience of the infant. At one extreme, the young infant is at first almost exclusively the concern of its mother, who fends off interested adults and juveniles by threats or by continually avoiding or turning away so they must look over her shoulder at the infant, according to her rank. As the infant gets older it is permitted to interact first with siblings and maternally related females, later with peers. But the pattern established very early, of interacting mainly with maternal relations, continues throughout life or until a male leaves his natal troop. Although all ages and both sexes do some caretaking, females of all ages do much more than males. Something like this pattern is typical of most of the species of monkey where infant development has been extensively studied—the rhesus and the pigtail macaques and the baboon and the vervet. It is by no means, however, the only social environment that the infant monkey may experience. In the

Barbary ape (*Macaca sylvana*), studies of two separate populations (Deag and Crook 1971, Burton 1972) have emphasized the frequent interaction of males of all ages with infants. Burton gives the impression that the majority of the infant's social interactions other than with its mother are with males. In a mangabey (*Cercocebus albigena*) Chalmers (1968) found that yearlings were cared for mainly by adult males, and similar behavior is reported from some Japanese macaque troops (*M. fuscata*), though in both these species adult males interact only cursorily with small infants. All the species mentioned live in groups containing several adults of both sexes. Other species live in groups of one male and several females, obviously offering a different social environment for infants. The patas (*Erythrocebus patas*) male is so peripheral to his group of females that infants must scarcely be aware of his existence until they are several months old. At the other extreme, marmosets and tamarins live in pairs, and the infant (usually one of twins) is cared for by father, mother, and juvenile siblings almost equally, though after the first three weeks the infant is returned by father and juveniles to the mother only for nursing (Nicoll, personal communication).

Multiparous female baboons are interested in a new infant, in that they investigate and groom it and occasionally pick it up if the mother permits, but their behavior towards the infant may also be ambivalent. They may behave as if they were jealous of the infant taking the mother's attention, and tweak at it maliciously behind her back (Ransom and Rowell 1972). Care is given more by nulliparous females. In contrast, once a patas infant is about three weeks old and starts to leave its mother other adult females frequently take it so that in the field it is very difficult to tell which infant belongs to which female (Gartlan, personal communication). In a caged group of patas, we have seen a female regularly take and suckle an infant younger than her own. In langurs the infant is taken and shared among all females in the group from birth, so that it is even more difficult to discover which infant belongs to which mother.

This catalogue of diversity could be continued, but the point has, I hope, been made that the environment for social development varies a great deal from one monkey species to another. The only generalization that can be made is that never is the mother the infant's only caretaker. We would expect such different experiences to produce different "personalities" among the adults. Monkey species do have very different and characteristic temperaments, as any zoo keeper would agree, but we have no study yet which relates child-rearing practices to later adult behavior in different monkey species.

A ZOOLOGIST'S VIEW OF CARETAKING

A zoologist must always ask "what is the selection pressure that has caused this behavior to evolve?" Monkeys other than mothers spend time and energy caring for infants, and such expenditure must be selected against unless it is advantageous, in the strictly limited sense that the animal that does it must thereby be enabled to leave more offspring than one that does not.

For the first part of the answer we should return to our opening statement. It takes a lot of time to produce a primate infant, and a lot of energy goes into it, so that each individual already at birth represents considerable parental investment. It will probably be more efficient to rear this one successfully than to give up and start again. (Compare for example a newborn mouse, one of a litter of ten needing only three weeks gestation, thus a much more expendable individual in terms of maternal energy output.)

Monkeys live in relatively closed groups, so there is some chance that a male protecting an infant is protecting one of his, or his father's or his son's offspring. It may be since paternity is not known in multimale groups at least, that a blanket approach is the most economical—giving care to all infants ensures that own progeny receive it; providing the proportion of own progeny is sufficiently high, such behavior has selective value.

Hamilton (1964) pointed out that strictly speaking the problem is not one of leaving as many progeny as possible, but of causing the birth and survival to maturity of as many individuals of the most similar possible gene combinations. A full sibling has more similar genetic constitution than do offspring, and the offspring of a full sibling are likely to have a genetic constitution very nearly as close as that of own offspring. Thus there may be as much selective advantage in ensuring the survival of siblings or the offspring of siblings as there is in reproducing oneself. This is particularly true where the infant is expensive to produce, as are infant monkeys. "Altruism" is closely akin to enlightened self-interest.

I have suggested elsewhere (Rowell 1972) that it may be advantageous for protection to be extended from younger to older members of a monkey group as well as vice versa. Old monkeys have long memories that may enable the group as a whole (including their own offspring) to circumnavigate some infrequent environmental crises—to find the remaining water in a drought of a severity that only occurs once every twenty years, for example. In exchange for such rarely used information it may well be selectively advantageous for a group to include aged individuals even if they must occasionally wait for them in progressions or defend them against predators they no longer have the agility to avoid.

If the evolution of caretaking behavior towards infants by animals other then the mother can be explained in general by the selective advantage of ensuring the survival of closely related young carrying a high proportion of the protector's genes, we must then ask the significance of variation, within the order, of the extent and intensity of nonmaternal parental care. One possibility is that the variation simply represents "play" in the system—the differences between species in who gives care, and how much, are by-products of other selection pressures, and are not large enough to affect infant survival. Alternatively, different habitats may give selective advantage to different patterns of child care, so that the variations we see may represent adaptations to specific environmental pressures. We are now entering the field of pure speculation, but one general point can still be made: it is unlikely that the answer will be found by considering a single set of behavior patterns out of the context of other interspecific behavioral differences. For example Deag and Crook (1971) point out that infant barbary apes are unusual in that they wander a long way from their mothers as soon as they become mobile. If infants were retrieved by their own mothers when the troop is alarmed, as is usual for vervets or rhesus monkeys, such errant infants would surely fall easy prey to dogs or jackals. At least we can say that the combination of behavioral characteristics of wandering infants and strongly parental males is fortunate for the species, though whether one trait had a causal relationship to the other in evolution, we cannot of course know.

There remains the problem of the freeloader. A monkey that did not waste energy looking after infants might live in a troop of normal caretakers and actually be at a slight advantage—his offspring would be protected by others and he could put his saved energy towards leaving more offspring, some of which would carry his genetic tendency towards nonaltruism. Presumably a group that came to carry too high a proportion of freeloaders would be unable to protect its infants successfully, and a balance between these conflicting selection pressures would be achieved. It ought to be to the advantage of altruistic monkeys to develop behavior to exclude or coerce nonaltruistic animals in the group, since such animals ultimately pose a threat to the survival of their own offspring. Bramblett (1970) suggests that female vervets expected protective behavior of the adult male in his captive group, and that some of their punitive behavior directed toward the adult male occurred when he was not adequately fulfilling this role. Rhesus males will attack a female whose infant is screaming, usually because she is preventing it from suckling or otherwise rejecting it; and when a mother baboon finally accepts her weanling on the nipple and his tantrum ceases there is typically a chorus of greeting grunts from nearby animals, apparently indicating approval, which perhaps might also be taken as an attempt to influence the behavior of a troopmate towards a more parental attitude.

ENCULTURATION?
LEARNING HOW TO MAKE A LIVING

Infant monkeys learn about their surroundings as well as their society from group companions. Some of their earliest coordinated movements are attempts to intercept food the mother's hand is conveying past the infant to her mouth. For several weeks the infant talapoin only attempts to eat food that older animals are already eating, picking up scraps and taking fragments from mouth or hand, long after he has the coordination to get food for himself. In the cage such behavior may persist for several months, the infant waiting on a shelf while others go to the tray to fetch food, but in the wild infants forage for themselves earlier, by about three months (personal observation). Juvenile monkeys often smell the mouth of an animal that is eating and then go and fetch the same sort of food for themselves (Gartlan 1969, on vervets). This behavior has been especially noticed in the genus *Cercopithecus*, which are mostly forest living; far more plant and animal species are available as food in tropical forest than in any other environment, and many of them are relatively rare. Thus a young forest monkey has a formidable learning task to acquaint itself with the whole range of foods used and how they are gathered and eaten.

Monkey troops do not always utilize all available foods in their home range, and adjacent troops with similar resources may use different items. Thus Harding (1972), observing predatory behavior of baboons in Kenya, had one troop that frequently killed antelope kids but showed no interest in guinea fowl, flocks of which could feed through the troop unmolested. A neighboring troop included guinea fowl in its diet. Such differences in behavior must be the result of troop traditions, juveniles learning specific food habits from their parents.

ESTABLISHING NEW TRADITIONS

It is of great interest to consider how these traditional differences between troops might arise, and a unique opportunity to study this phenomenon has been most elegantly exploited by workers of the Japan Monkey Centre. It is to be expected that new techniques for obtaining food will develop most frequently in a period of major habitat change. Such a change was produced for the monkeys of Koshima islet: food began to be left for them regularly so they would come and spend more time on the open beach where their behavior could be studied. They quickly accepted the offerings of sweet potato and wheat, but had some problems with sand adhering to them, which they attempted to rub off with their hands in the usual Old World monkey fashion. One juvenile female discovered that sand could be removed better by washing sweet potato in water, and, a year or so later, that sand could be separated from wheat by floating the wheat on water. Kawai and his co-workers were able to follow the spread of these new behavior patterns through the group. Mothers learned from offspring, juveniles learned from juvenile peers. Adult males were much slower to learn than females probably because they had little contact with the innovative juvenile subgroups, and the older an animal the less likely he was to learn a new habit (Kawai 1965). The new environment generated other new habits, such as swimming for sport, which later included fetching possible food items from under water, walking on hind legs, and using a begging movement of the hand towards the observers. All these behavior patterns were first developed by juveniles and spread slowly up the age scale through the population. Itani (1958) observed the acquisition of new diet items in another troop (Takasakiyama). He suggests five probable routes of acquisition of such new habits (in this particular case, eating candy), which depend on the particular social organization of *Macaca fuscata*:

1. Mothers learn from their infants.
2. Subadult and adult males learn from infants in their care.
3. Adult males learn from females during consort pairing in the mating season, or from females with whom they have strong grooming relationships.
4. Mothers learn from their adult offspring.
5. Elder brothers and sisters learn from younger siblings.

Again, these transmission routes (except perhaps number 3) are from younger to older members of the group.

Learning about the environment from group companions is thus a two-way process. The young learn the established traditions of their troop concerning food, and also the paths and limits of the home range and possible sources of danger from the older members of the troop, which also maintain a memory store of appropriate responses to infrequent but recurring environmental changes. The young, in their exploratory behavior develop new techniques, especially during periods of environmental change, which older animals then learn and which are incorporated in the tradition of the troop.

Although in the Koshima group it was possible to identify a single author of the innovations, when watching young monkeys playing and exploring new objects I have been struck with how several heads are better than one. In a group of juvenile talapoins investigating a sink stopper, for example, one animal handled the object while one or more looked over his shoulder. To begin with, that others were waiting made him retain interest and work harder on the problem. Eventually he left it for a while and the next monkey took it and tried some of the same manipulations he had just been watching, but added a few variants of his own; this process continued until collectively they dismantled the sink stopper, posted one part through the wire of the ceiling, and hung the other on a nail in the wall, after using it as a hat. One juvenile playing alone would not have had the persistence, and is unlikely to have had all the required insights to make so much of such unpromising material.

CULTURAL DIFFERENCES IN
SOCIAL INTERACTION PATTERNS

Monkey troops differ not only in their ways of interacting with their environment, but in their pattern of social interactions. Again the best known example comes from Japan. Itani (1959) described care of yearlings and two-year-olds by adult males especially during the birth periods when the mothers were turning their attention from the yearlings to the newborn infants. Males of three troops showed this behavior extensively. In eight other troops it has never been seen, while in seven more occasional isolated incidents have been observed. One may speculate whether males learn the behavior by imitation of other males, or whether infants, being cared for by males, are conditioned to care for infants in their turn. Presumably the paternal behavior of the barbary ape, now a species characteristic, arose as such a cultural variant.

Social behavior of rhesus monkeys from an urban environment is different from that of forest-reared monkeys, and the difference continues when both are maintained in the laboratory (Singh 1966). Urban monkeys are more aggressive, and also more active and manipulative, which characteristics are appropriate for the highly competitive urban environment. While the environment must have some direct effect on the individual's behavior, we are probably dealing here with another cultural difference as well.

The hamadryas baboon has an entirely different social organization from the common baboon, troops consisting of several separate one-male harem units. This difference is based on a single interaction pattern, the herding of females by males: a male goes to a female who is not following him closely enough and bites the back of her neck. She responds to this by following him more closely. By studying animals in a natural zone of interbreeding, Nagel (1973) was able to show that this herding behavior is genetically determined in the males, but is learned by females as juveniles. Hybrid males show partial, and rather ineffective herding and so are at a disadvantage in breeding. Females, whether pure hamadryas, pure common, or hybrids can successfully adapt to the prevalent social organization of a troop. The behavior is innate for males, culturally determined for females.

CONCLUSIONS

Social development of primates is a process that continues throughout life, in which younger animals can alter the behavior of older ones as well as vice versa. For this reason I have avoided using the term "socialization," which to me implies a process applied "from above" by older animals to originally asocial infants until they conform to some standard known as "adulthood." Not only is the infant monkey the least asocial creature in existence, but its social development does not resemble "socialization" as I arbitrarily describe it. Infants bring highly specific infantile stimuli to an interaction, and while they are learning about older animals, they may themselves be contributing to the social development of their partners. Juveniles learn the traditional customs of their troop concerning diet, routes, and dangers. In return they contribute to the tradition as during their characteristic exploratory play they discover new properties of the environment which may be learned from them by older kin. Young adults behave deferentially towards older ones although they may have become stronger than their seniors, and in return they gain from the older animal's store of experience. It is in terms of such reciprocal relationships that the selective advantage of living in close-knit permanent troops may be understood.

REFERENCES

ALDRICH-BLAKE, F. P. G. 1968. A Fertile Hybrid Between Two *Cercopithecus* species in the Budongo Forest, Uganda. *Folia Primatologica* 9:15–21.

BRAMBLETT, C. A. 1970. Maternal Determinants of Behavior in Vervet Monkeys (*Cercopithecus aethiops*). MS. Abstract: Vervet monkeys and their mothers. *Bulletin of the American Anthropological Association* 3:29.

BREUGGEMAN, J. A. 1973. Parental Care in a Group of Free-ranging Rhesus Monkeys (*Macaca mulatta*). *Folia primatologica* 20:178–210.

BURTON, F. D. 1972. The Integration of Biology and Behavior in the Socialization of *Macaca sylvana* of Gibraltar. *Primate Socialization* (F. Poirier, ed.), pp. 29–62. Random House.

CHALMERS, N. R. 1968. The Social Behavior of Free-living Mangabeys in Uganda. *Folia Primatologica* 8:263–281.

————. 1972. Comparative Aspects of Early Infant Development in Some Captive Cercopithecines, *Primate Socialization* (F. Poirer, ed.), pp. 63–82. Random House.

DEAG, J. M., and J. H. CROOK. 1971. Social Behavior and "Agonistic Buffering in the Wild Barbary Macaque (*Macaca sylvana*, L.). *Folia Primatologica* 15:183–200.

GARTLAN, J. S. 1969. Sexual and Maternal Behavior of the Vervet Monkey, *Cercopithecus aethiops*. *Journal of Reproduction and Fertility*, supplement 6:137–150.

HAMILTON, W. D. 1964. The Genetic Evolution of Social Behavior 1 and 2. *Journal of Theoretical Biology* 7:1–52.

HARDING, R. S. O. 1972. Predation by a Troop of Olive Baboons (*Papio anubis*). *American Journal of Physical Anthropology* 38:587–592.

ITANI, J. 1958. On the Acquisition and Propagation of a New Food Habit in the Natural Group of the Japanese Monkey in Takasaki Yamo. *Primates* 1:84–98.

————. 1959. Paternal Care in the Wild Japanese Monkey *Macaca fuscata fuscata*. *Primates* 2:61–93.

KAWAI, M. 1965. Newly Acquired Precultural Behavior of the Natural Troop of Japanese Monkeys on Koshima Islet. *Primates* 6:1–30.

KUMMER, H. 1968. Social Organization of Hamadyas Baboons. S. Karger Basel.

LANCASTER, J. B. 1970. Female Bonding; Social Relations Between Free-ranging Adult Female Vervet Monkeys. American Anthropological Association (preliminary report).

————. 1971. Play-Mothering: The Relations Between Juvenile Females and Young Infants Among Free-ranging Vervet Monkeys. *Folia Primatologica* 15:161–183.

NAGEL, U. 1973. A Comparison of Anubis Baboons, Hamadryas Baboons, and Their Hybrids at a Species Border in Ethiopia. *Folia Primatologica* 19:104–165.

RANSOM, T. W., and B. S. RANSOM. 1971. Adult Male-Infant Relations among Baboons (*Papio anubis*). *Folia Primatologica* 16:179–195.

RANSOM, T. W., and T. E. ROWELL. 1972. Early Social Development of Feral Baboons. *Primate Socialization* (F. Poirier, ed.), pp. 105–144. Random House.

ROWELL, T. E. 1972. *Social Behaviour of Monkeys*. Penguin.

ROWELL, T. E., HINDE, R. A., and Y. SPENCER-BOOTH. 1964. "Aunt"-infant Interactions in Captive Rhesus Monkeys. *Animal Behaviour* 12:219–266.

SACKETT, G. P. 1970. Unlearned Responses, Differential Rearing Experiences, and the Development of Social Attachments by Rhesus Monkeys, *Primate Behavior* (L. A. Rosenblum, ed.). Academic Press.

SACKETT, G. P., and G. C. RUPPENTHAL. 1973. Induction of Social Behavior Changes in Macaques by Monkeys, Machines, and Maturity, *Fourth Western Symposium on Learning: Social Learning* (P. J. Elich, ed.), pp. 99–119.

SINGH, S. D. 1966. The Effects of Human Environment on the Social Behavior of Rhesus Monkeys. *Primates* 7:33–40.

Learning What Comes Naturally:

The Role of Life Experience in the Establishment of Species Typical Behavior

I. CHARLES KAUFMAN

Culture has generally been considered to be a human phenomenon, by custom if not by definition. The perpetuation or transformation of human social structure has been viewed as a cultural process. In fact this whole volume is addressed to this process.

Among nonhuman species the question of existence of culture has had no definitive answer.[1] Social structure in nonhuman populations is generally thought to have evolved, primarily through processes of natural selection, and to be maintained on a genetic basis. The evolutionary process may be seen to have provided *through group living* several adaptive advantages—sufficient territory to supply food for all the members, a mutual defense system, and an internal stability derived from the social structure which facilitates reproduction as well as the education and social devel-

I. CHARLES KAUFMAN, M.D. is professor of psychiatry and director of the Primate Laboratory for Bio-Behavioral Studies, at the University of Colorado Medical Center, Denver.

The research reported was supported by project grants MH-4670 and MH-18144 from the U.S. Public Health Service. I thank my colleagues A. J. Stynes and L. A. Rosenblum for their contributions to the research projects.

1. For further discussion of this question see Kummer (1971:117–130) and Rowell (above).

opment of the young in ways appropriate to their environment. Among group-living species, however, different selective pressures have led to a diversity of social structures.

Among primates there is considerable variation in the nature of social adaptations. For example, when monkeys in primeval forests came down from the trees to the ground, the male adult baboons became physically powerful, with huge canines, so that they could protect by battle the rest of the troop. In contrast, the male adult patas monkeys became excellent runners, able to decoy predators while mothers and infants hid. The same problem, predation, led to different adaptations in these two species.

Futhermore, in more recent studies it has become clear that even within a species, social structure may vary from one troop to another, often in relation to differences in ecological variables. Also, troops may differ in certain behavioral patterns, as a result of the innovative behaviors of individuals which become troop traditions (see Rowell, above). In such cases, where there are patterns of troop-specific behavior transmitted through learning, one may speak seriously of culture, or at least of "protocultures," a qualification reflecting the nonsymbolic mode of transmission. But further, it is the thesis of this chapter that highly stable forms of species-specific behavior are based on a causal nexus in which there are important experiential links as well as genetic links.

BACKGROUND TO THE PRESENT STUDIES

When I started my first Primate Laboratory (in 1961 at the Downstate Medical Center in New York) I decided that we would study the animals *living in groups* because monkeys in nature are very social creatures. I hoped that by studying groups we would be able to observe the full repertoire of behavior that occurs in natural troops containing animals of all ages and both sexes. I also decided that we would study *two closely related species* rather than only one, in the belief that a more comprehensive base of comparative data might augment the possibility of making evolutionary generalizations and extrapolations. Thus we have been studying since that time both the bonnet macaque (*M. radiata*) and the pigtail macaque (*M. nemestrina*), Old World monkeys.

Over the years we have formed many groups of both species, generally starting with wild-born animals. Each group has initially consisted of 1 adult male and from 4 to 12 adult females. The animals have bred very well so that by now close to 200 infants have been born, and many of these have been studied into their maturity. As both of these species belong to the same genus, we anticipated that they would show many common traits, among them structural aspects of the central nervous system and the potentialities for social development and learning. We also expected that they would differ in significant ways, and that these differences would be markers of their different evolutionary adaptations. Concerning this, we may question: once selection pressure has promoted a genotypic alteration whose behavioral manifestations favor survival, what are the processes that in succeeding generations reproduce this behavioral phenotype? Simply put, just how do characteristic differences in behavior arise from differences in genes? It is easy to picture in a primitive organism a simple transition from genetic substance to a behavior like a tropism. For example, a tendency to move toward or away from light or darkness would require only a simple biochemical system. A very different transitional process is required, however, to explain how baboons and patas monkeys arrive in adulthood at their particular behavioral modes for dealing with predators. Evolutionary theory obliges us to assume that these different adaptational solutions to the problem of predation are based on different genotypes. We must keep in mind, however, that the behavioral differences we have described characterize adult animals, take years to develop, and only emerge through the typical life experiences of patas monkeys and baboons respectively. In the course of evolution an important adaptation was the increase in time between birth and maturity, a major consequence of which is a much greater opportunity to learn. There are many kinds of learning, however, and species differ in their learning abilities. Washburn, Jay, and Lancaster have pointed out that learning "is not a generalized ability; animals are able to learn some things with great ease and other things only with the greatest difficulty" (1965:1546).

Among the kinds of learning, Mead pointed out "there is one kind of transmitted experience in which—if we ignore for a moment the presence of language—there is no break between the kind of learning described for red deer or prairie dogs and that which occurs in human society, that is, learning which can occur only when the behaving, individual model is present, because the learning is unverbalized, inarticulate, recorded in no artifact, and repre-

sented in no symbolic form. Posture and gesture systems and the un-
symbolized parts of a language—stress, cadence, and accent—all
belong to this category. As the senior female red deer or the old
ewes lead the herd or flock so older members of human groups guide
the behavior of the younger members through the experience of a
mass of patterned behaviors, specific to a given ecological setting,
and characteristic of a given society, with much of this never becoming conscious teaching or conscious learning" (1958:487–488).

The mother in primate society has a special role in this kind of
social learning. Despite the very considerable variation in the social
structure of higher primates, one feature is constant, the close tie
of the mother-infant pair and the mother's caretaking responsibility for her offspring. Young infants in every species invariably are
found near or with their mothers who nurse them, look after them,
and teach them what their species needs to know to thrive in their
environment. It has become clear that the tie between the mother
and her offspring endures for many years in many species, often
with considerable intensity. Goodall (1965) reported that chimpan-
zess continue to return to their mothers into their maturity. I have
noted the same thing concerning pigtail monkeys (1970), and Sade
(1965) has reported similar findings for the rhesus macaque. Darwin
in 1871 said, "the feeling of pleasure from society is probably an extension of the parental or filial affections, since the social instinct
seems to be developed by the young remaining for a long time with
their parents; and this extension may be attributed in part to habit,
but chiefly to natural selection" (1898:106–107). With regard to
nonhuman primates I would have to modify Darwin's statement to
stress the greater role of the mother, since the functional role of
males can hardly be called paternal.

With respect to learning it seems clear that primate mothers provide the basic education in affective behavior and in techniques of
communicating, relating, and living with others in social groups.
Young monkeys and apes learn a great deal by observation and imitation. Hall pointed out that "early learning goes on in intimate relationship with positive emotional attitudes" (1963:204) in the affectional context provided by the mother and others" (1963:222).
Many emotional reactions seem to be learned from observation, or
kinesthetically derived from the mother's reaction. Learning what
is dangerous seems to be in this category. All in all, the mother's
role in primate society is very considerable; in the education, social

development, and general rearing of the young it is probably the greatest single force. We can safely say that maternal behavior and the mother-infant relationship are very literally the matrix of primate society.

We may apply some of these considerations to the development of macaques. From field and laboratory studies (Hansen 1966, Harlow, Harlow, and Hansen 1963, Hinde and Spencer-Booth 1967, Imanishi 1963, Kaufmann 1966) we know that early development follows a somewhat typical sequence in all the macaques studied. Maternal behavior is strongly motivated at birth and for some time thereafter, so that the mother and infant are very close, physically and otherwise. A stage follows in which the infant makes efforts to disengage from the mother, but these efforts are frequently thwarted as the mother attempts to keep the infant close. Following this, however, there is a progressively greater apartness of the pair, which the mother either encourages or allows. The infant spends more and more time away from the mother, involved in play, increasingly with peers, as it develops autonomy and acquires the skills of its species and gender. As Washburn has said, "We see the power of play, social learning and identification creating adults whose biology and learning have both fitted them for their adult roles. The patas male is built to flee and he has learned when this behavior is appropriate. The baboon male is built to fight, and he has learned the behavior of his troop. Biology and experience make possible the appropriate behaviors of the species" (1968:204). Put more directly in terms of the thesis of this paper, in higher primates, species-typical experience is generally required for species-typical behavior to develop.

MY STUDIES OF PIGTAIL AND BONNET MACAQUES

I would like to consider the details of this developmental sequence in the two species we have studied, living under identical conditions in the laboratory. But first let me make some general comments about our studies of pigtail and bonnet macaques.

As we observed many groups during the past 13 years, we made an inventory of their behavioral repertoire (Kaufman and Rosenblum 1966) and compared the two species. As we expected, we found that they do indeed have many of the same behaviors and social characteristics. We also found three major differences. The *first* difference concerns their tendencies to physical closeness and thus their spatial configurations. Bonnets characteristically tend to remain physically close to each other, often in huddles (fig. 1). Pigtails in contrast do not often make physical contact with neighbors (fig. 2), unless they are involved in an active social interaction such as mating or grooming or fighting. Even sleeping arrangements maintain this difference. We have seen this difference consistently with every group we have formed over the years, and the difference has endured even in the face of marked changes in ambient temperature, available space, and available food and water.

We discovered a *second* significant difference between the two species when we began our experimental mother-infant separations; the mother was removed from the pen in which the group lived, leaving the four- to six-month old infant in the group with all the familiar animals. After removal of a pigtail mother, her infant is agitated and distressed and seeks comfort and attention from the other female adults, but usually the other females do not comfort the motherless infant and may even be physically abusive (fig. 3). Within a day or so the infant then shows a reaction (fig. 4) remarkably like the "anaclitic depression" shown by bereaved human infants, described by Spitz (1946). (The adaptive significance of this response and its possible relationship to human depression have been discussed at length elsewhere [Kaufman and Rosenblum 1967, Kaufman 1973].) The sequence of behavior following the removal of a bonnet mother is quite different. When the bonnet infant initially gets agitated, it almost immediately gets attention from the remaining adult females. The infant may actually be adopted by one of the females even if she is caring for an infant of her own (fig. 5). A bereft bonnet infant may even be held and comforted by its father (fig. 6). Such behavior by a pigtail father we have never seen. At the conclusion of the experimental separation when the mother is returned, in the pigtails there is usually a very intense reunion with increased closeness between mother and infant lasting for as many as three months after reunion. The reunion behavior is much less intense when a bonnet mother is returned. We have even seen bonnet infants remain with the female who adopted them rather than return to the mother, such behavior occurring more often with younger infants.

The *third* and final major distinction between the species only became obvious when we followed several groups into third and fourth generations (Kaufman 1970). We have now observed such groups for 13 years. In the pigtail group, now containing more than thirty animals, all but two having been laboratory born, we find that social behavior occurs primarily among animals sharing maternal lineage, that is to say, among a mother and all her descendants (fig. 7). In the bonnet group this is not so. When we sum such positive social behaviors as *physical contact* and *proximity, grooming*, and *play*, we find that pigtails demonstrate considerably more of such interactions with their clanmates than do bonnets. In fact, pigtails socially interact *primarily* with their clanmates, which is not true of the bonnets.

These major differences between the two species have been consistently maintained in our two laboratories (Downstate Medical Center, 1961–1968, and University of Colorado Medical Center, 1969 to present) with many groups of animals formed at different times with different wild-born monkeys, leading us to consider them to be characteristic traits of the two species, as characteristic as the difference in the length of their tails. Further, we must assume that these differences arose as adaptations to selective pressure.[2] Although we assume that these differences are genetically encoded, however, our data suggest that they may all be accounted for by differences in ontogenetic experience, centered primarily around differences in maternal behavior and the resulting differences in infant development and attachment.

I mentioned earlier the tendency of bonnets to maintain physical contact, to the extent that they frequently huddle. This closeness is not affected by pregnancy or delivery. After a baby is born its mother returns to close contact with her neighbors. In contrast, pigtail females with infants tend to remain apart from other females. Whereas mothers in both species provide their infants with the intensive care characteristic of higher primates, the pigtail mother does it pretty much by herself while the bonnet mother does it in the company of her peers (Kaufman and Rosenblum 1969a). The pigtail mother guards her infant from the attention of others (fig. 8), while the bonnet mother permits considerable attention to her infant and even lets other females interact with it (fig. 9). Conse-

2. The field data available so far do not yield an explanation for these adaptations. I have speculated that some aspect of basic ecology favored a limitation of pigtail groups to clan size, living either as a single group or as part of a colonial arrangement. In this regard pigtails appear to be more arboreal (Bernstein 1967) than bonnets (Simonds 1965). Other speculations are perhaps just as likely, but in any event the explanation awaits further study.

quently, as soon as the first month of life bonnet infants interact socially with animals other than mother significantly more than do pigtail infants.

Over the next several months in both species, infants begin to initiate departures from their mothers. Our data (Kaufman and Rosenblum 1969*b*) indicate clearly that most of the early breaks in contact are initiated by the infant. These early breaks are brief in duration and do not take the infant very far from the mother who is all the while closely watching and guarding it. Gradually there is an increase in the amount of time the infant spends away from the mother, but it tends to remain on the same level of the pen. Meanwhile, the mother rarely fails to watch her infant constantly when it is away from her, and if she perceives any threat to the infant she quickly retrieves him. There are a number of other protective behaviors shown by mothers in both species. When we compare the amount of protective behavior (fig. 10), however, we find that it is considerably greater on the part of pigtail mothers than bonnet mothers.

Soon the infants leave their mothers behind by moving to other levels of the pen. Both the frequency and duration of these *vertical departures* dramatically increase after the first month, reaching a high asymptotic level in the eighth month. As with the early breaks from mother, our data make it clear that the infants, not the mothers, are responsible for the departures to other levels. When we compare the two species on both the frequency and total duration of these maximal distance departures, however, we find clear evidence of a distinction between pigtail and bonnet infants. Starting in the third month bonnet infants quite consistently spend more time than pigtails away from their mothers and at different levels of the pen. This would appear to signify a greater relative security of bonnet infants in both their physical and social environment, as well as a real difference in the nature of their attachment to the mother. Consistent with this, from the mother's side, our data show that *retrieval*, which reflects maternal apprehension about the separated infant, appears considerably less often, peaks earlier, and then wanes more rapidly in bonnet as compared to pigtail mothers. We could say that bonnet mothers *let* their infants go, and that bonnet infants *go*.

As the infants grow into the middle of the first year of life, maternal solicitude wanes. In both species the mothers become less restrictive. They encourage their infants to leave them and they even deter the infants from returning. They deprive the infants of the nipple, and when the infant persists too much the mothers punish them by gentle biting. When we compare the total amount of these various maternal abdyadic behaviors, however, we find that pigtail mothers show considerably more (fig. 11).

To summarize briefly the comparison between maternal behavior in the two species we can say that the pigtail mother is at first more protective and later more punitive, a combination that fosters a closer attachment to or dependence upon the mother, whereas the bonnet mother, by being both less protective and less punitive, facilitates the developing independence of her young.

Meanwhile, as the first year of life progresses, in both species the infant displays a growing interest in the inanimate environment and in its peers, at the same time as its physical capacities, dexterity, and coordination are continually improving. The early uncoordinated departures from mother are soon transformed into repeated playful practice of its physical prowess, which we term *exercise play*. Then increasingly play becomes interactional so that towards the end of the first year of life *social play* is the most common infant behavior that does not involve the mother. It should be noted that the total time involved in play is the same in both species. Whereas pigtail infants engage in more *exercise play* (fig. 12), however, bonnet infants engage in more *social play* (fig. 13).

HYPOTHESIS

I think we are ready to consider now answers to the questions raised earlier about the processes whereby the behavioral manifestations of genotypic adaptations are perpetuated from one generation to the next. My most general thesis (in line with Washburn and Mead) is that in each species there are predispositions to learn more easily certain things from species-typical life experiences. With respect to the two species of macaques I have studied, the thesis is more specific and states that the differences in social relations and particularly maternal behavior are *the* particular species-typical life experiences that are crucial to the social development of infants in each species as they grow to maturity.

The data presented make it clear that a developmental distinction between pigtail and bonnet dyads exists from birth. The preference for physical contact among bonnet adults is associated, generally, with a more relaxed maternal disposition. While providing good care to their infants, bonnet mothers are less restrictive and more tolerant, that is, they allow infants to go and to return. As a consequence bonnet infants have different experiences than do pigtail infants. Their social interactions begin earlier, and they are freer to approach other members of their group whether peers or adults. They are less attached to their mothers, leaving them more often and going further away. They engage in more social play than the pigtails who engage in more solitary play. It is my thesis that it is the mother's behavior, within the context of the characteristic social structure, which provides the experience for the developing infant that perpetuates (through ontogenetic realization) the species-characteristic difference in spatial patterning and temperament, the *first* difference we found between the species.

The same thesis would apply to the *second* difference cited between the species, namely the reaction to separation. The protected and restricted pigtail infant is more closely attached to, or dependent upon, his mother than is the bonnet, so that her loss is a greater catastrophe for the pigtail, especially since he is not likely to be comforted and cared for by other mothers whose own attachments are primarily to their own offspring and descendants. The bonnet infant has a wider experience of both the inanimate and social environment, is less dependent upon his own mother, and when bereft of his mother is met by a more receptive attitude on the part of the other adult females. For all these reasons he is better able to cope with the loss of mother.

With respect to the *third* main difference between these two species, namely the maternal clan structure of the pigtail but not the bonnet group, the explanation appears to lie also in the effect of the characteristic maternal behavior on the development of the young. The protective, restrictive behavior of the pigtail mother combined with her intermittent rejection create in the infant an intense attachment to the mother and a strong tendency to remain close to her (Hinde 1974, Kaufman 1974). The attachment is intensified when siblings are born (Kaufman and Rosenblum 1969a) and then spreads to include the siblings, who are similarly closely attached to the mother. The same process applies to the next generation. Thus we find that the maternal clan is the primary social structure of the pigtails. The social structure of the bonnets is different. The maternal clan is not the primary unit. Peer relations appear

FIG. 1. A typical huddle of bonnet macaques, including 3 pregnant females.

FIG. 2. A group of pigtail macaques showing the typical spacing out and lack of physical contact except between mother and infant.

FIG. 3. An agitated pigtail infant, grimacing and screaming while fleeing from an abusive rebuff by an adult female he had approached (from Kaufman and Rosenblum 1967).

FIG. 4. A depressed pigtail infant uttering the distress call, "coo."

FIG. 5. A bonnet female with 2 separated infants she adopted and her own infant. She cared for and nursed all 3.

FIG. 6. A bonnet male holding a motherless infant whom he protected and cared for.

FIG. 7. A pigtail maternal clan of 3 generations, mother on the right with her youngest infant who is falling asleep, another offspring in the center, and the oldest offspring on the left, holding her own infant.

FIG. 8. A pigtail mother cradling her newborn infant (with cord and placenta still attached) and giving an open-mouth threat to another mother who is approaching too close.

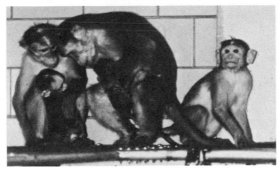

FIG. 9. A bonnet mother cradling her newborn infant while approaching with interest another mother-infant pair.

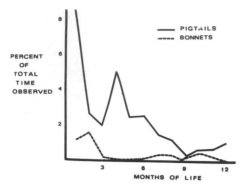

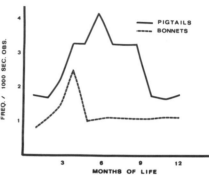

FIG. 10. Mean duration in the two species of maternal protectiveness over the first year of life. This index represents the combined scores for *departure restraint*, *guard*, *retrieval*, and *watch* (from Kaufman and Rosenblum 1969a).

FIG. 11. Frequency of maternal abdyadic behaviors in the two species over the first year of life. This index represents the combined occurrence of weaning, *punitive deterrence, infant removal*, and *contact-deterrence* (from Kaufman and Rosenblum 1969a).

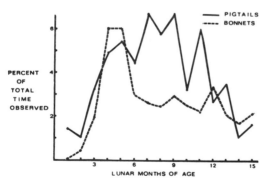

FIG. 12. Mean duration of *exercise play* in pigtail and bonnet infants during the first 15 months of life (from Kaufman and Rosenblum 1969b).

FIG. 13. Mean duration of social play in pigtail and bonnet infants during the first 15 months of life (from Kaufman and Rosenblum 1969 b).

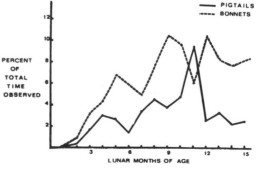

to be as important as clan relations. The whole group itself appears to be the primary unit, exhibiting close physical contact among all the members of the group. (At night a bonnet group sleeps in one huge huddle.) Since the physical closeness persists through the birth process, infants experience interactions with all the other members of the group both early and frequently. Conviviality with all the members of the group is an early and enduring characteristic (except during dominance encounters). Special closeness to the mother does not appear to last long beyond infancy. Bonnets seem to form equivalent bonds with all *familiar* animals.

In discussions with colleagues, but especially with students, repeatedly the question has been asked, "which is the better mother, the bonnet or the pigtail?" Some answer that the bonnet is, since her infant is more independent and secure, less fearful, and better able to cope with the loss of mother. Others answer that actually the pigtail is the better mother, since her infant forms much closer and more meaningful affective attachments. I generally point out that each of these answers are actually judgments derived from *human* value systems which do not apply to monkeys, whose maternal behaviors evolved millions of years ago as adaptations to selective pressure.

Another question that has been asked often is whether we can apply what we have learned of these differences in monkey maternal behavior and their effects on social development to the rearing of human children. I have pointed out that the goals in raising children derive from consideration of specifically human values. In that regard, Mead (1954) has suggested, based on her cross-cultural studies, that our children should be reared, as in Samoa, by many relatives and without intense bonds to parents. She believes that when a child is raised by one close inseparable mother the result is intense attachments, but these are few in number. She thinks that there is less proneness to trauma when a child is cared for by numerous warm, friendly people. She says that we have not devised a technique that makes it easy for our children to leave a familiar environment and be able to tolerate "without fear strangers who look, speak, move and smell very different. In a situation where the mother must take the child day by day to market, to the clinic, on the bus, on the underground, among strangers, the present tendency to advise very close ties between mother and child is doubtfully the best. Wider experience in the arms of many individuals known in different degrees of intimacy, if possible of different races, may be a much better preparation" (1957). Personally, I believe that the essence of human existence *is* the intensity of the intimate tie and the capacity to love. Whether we agree with Mead, or do not, about what kind of children we should have, or as to the accuracy of her psychodynamic formulations about development, however, we certainly agree with the appropriateness of her effort to extrapolate *from one human culture to another,* even if we question whether a rearing system could be successfully transposed from a primitive culture to an urban one. It would not appear to be appropriate, however, to seek in monkey mothers literal models for human behavior. Rather, by studying monkeys too we may learn about processes of adaptation, and about the relation between evolutionary and ontogenetic processes.

CONCLUSION

We know from the diversity of social structure throughout the animal order that the formation of bonds, affiliations, and social structure does not follow simply from the contiguity of creatures and the opportunity to interact. Although interactions form the basis of relationship, factors of both biological and experiential nature influence the frequency and kinds of interaction, the responses to them, and their effect on the subsequent relationships. From the data presented we have seen that two closely related species show differences, in individual behavior and in social structure, which appear to perpetuate themselves from one generation to the next ontogenetically, by providing species-typical life experience for the young, especially mediated through maternal behavior.

With respect to my hypothesis we need more data of a different kind for further substantiation. For example, we need to study the behavioral characteristics of hybrids, and we need to study the social development of infants who are reared by mothers of the opposite species. From such studies we would be better able to understand the interaction among biological predisposition, maternal behavior, social development, and social structure. Meanwhile, I hope that the data I have presented make tenable the hypothesis that species-typical, genetically determined behavior develops as a consequence of species-typical life experience.

As a final note I would like to suggest, in line with Lidz (1963), a modification of Heinz Hartmann's famous dictum that the infant is born adapted to survive in an average expectable environment. Hartmann's statement is undoubtedly correct as far as it goes, but we need to add that *in* the average expectable environment of all societal species, institutions or regulatory systems have arisen that take into account the essential needs of the young, including the need to grow up to be a typical and functional member of the group. These regulatory systems provide an experiential educational process which is calculated to realize, in the young growing up, the biological predispositions evolved through natural selection. In this way one learns what comes naturally.

REFERENCES

BERNSTEIN, I. S. 1967. A Field Study of the Pigtail Monkey (*Macaca nemestrina*). *Primates* 8:217–228.

DARWIN, C. 1898. *The Descent of Man.* Second Edition. Appleton.

GOODALL, J. Chimpanzees of the Gombe Stream Reserve, *Primate Behavior* (Irven DeVore, ed.), pp. 425–473. Holt, Rinehart and Winston.

HALL, K. R. L. 1963. Observational Learning in Monkeys and Apes. *British Journal of Psychology* 54:201–226.

HANSEN, E. W. 1966. The Development of Maternal and Infant Behavior in the Rhesus Monkey. *Behaviour* 27:107–149.

HARLOW, H. F., M. K. HARLOW, and E. W. HANSEN. 1963. The Maternal Affectional System of Rhesus Monkeys, *Maternal Behavior in Mammals* (H. L. Rheingold, ed.). Wiley.

HINDE, R. A. 1974. Mother-Infant Relations in Rhesus Monkeys, *Ethology and Psychiatry* (N. F. White, ed.), pp. 29–46. University of Toronto Press.

HINDE, R. A., and Y. SPENCER-BOOTH. 1967. The Behavior of Socially Living Rhesus Monkeys in their First Two and a Half Years. *Animal Behavior* 15:169–196.

KAUFMAN, I. CHARLES. 1970. Some Biological Considerations of Parenthood, *Parenthood: Its Psychology and Psychopathology* (E. James Anthony and Therese Benedek, eds.), pp. 3–55. Little, Brown, and Co.

———. 1973. Mother-Infant Separation in Monkeys: An Experimental Model, *Separation and Depression* (J. P. Scott and E. C. Senay, eds.), American Association for the Advancement of Science. 194:33–52.

————. 1974. Mother-Infant Relations in Monkeys and Humans: A Reply to Professor Hinde, *Ethology and Psychiatry* (N. F. White, ed.), pp. 47–68. University of Toronto Press.

KAUFMAN, I. CHARLES, and L. A. ROSENBLUM. 1966. A Behavioral Taxonomy for *Macaca nemestrina* and *Macaca radiata*: Based on Longitudinal Observation of Family Groups in the Laboratory. *Primates* 7:205–258.

————. 1967. The Reaction to Separation in Infant Monkeys: Anaclitic Depression and Conservation-Withdrawal. *Psychosomatic Medicine* 29:648–675.

————. 1969a. Effects of Separation from Mother on the Emotional Behavior of Infant Monkeys. *Annals of the New York Academy of Sciences* 159:681–695.

————. 1969b. The Waning of the Mother-Infant Bond in Two Species of Macaque, *Determinants of Infant Behaviour*, IV (B. Foss, ed.), pp. 41–59. Methuen.

KAUFMANN, JOHN H. 1966. Behavior of Infant Rhesus Monkeys and their Mothers in a Free-ranging Band. *Zoologica* 51:17–28.

KUMMER, H. 1971. *Primate Societies*. Aldine-Atherton.

LIDZ, T. 1963. *The Family and Human Adaptation*. International Universities Press.

MEAD, M. 1954. Some Theoretical Considerations on the Problem of Mother-Child Separation. *American Journal of Orthopsychiatry* 24:471–483.

————. 1957. Changing Patterns of Parent-Child Relations in an Urban Culture. *International Journal of Psychoanalysis* 38:1–10.

————. 1958. Cultural Determinants of Behavior, *Behavior and Evolution* (Ann Roe and George Gaylord Simpson, eds.). Yale University Press.

SADE, D. S. 1965. Some Aspects of Parent-Offspring and Sibling Relations in a Group of Rhesus Monkeys, with a Discussion of Grooming. *American Journal of Physical Anthropology* 23:1–18.

SIMONDS, P. E. 1965. The Bonnet Macaque in South India, *Primate Behavior* (Irven DeVore, ed.), pp. 175–196. Holt, Rinehart and Winston.

SPITZ, R. A. 1946. Anaclitic Depression. *Psychoanalytic Study of the Child* 2:313.

WASHBURN, S. L. 1968. Speculations on the Problem of Man coming to the Ground, *Changing Perspectives on Man* (B. Rothblatt, ed.). University of Chicago Press.

WASHBURN, S. L., P. C. JAY, and J. F. LANCASTER. 1965. Field Studies of Old World Monkeys and Apes. *Science* 150:1541–1547.

Some Components of Socialization for Trance

GREGORY BATESON

Let me be clear from the beginning that by "components" I do not mean events or pieces of events that can be counted to become members of a statistical sample. I am doubtful whether in human behavior there are any such. In certain games, such as baseball and cricket, the named actions of the players appear to be repeated many times over and upon the samples so created a sort of statistic can be computed, assigning "batting averages" and the like to the various players; and such "averages" are indeed a rough indication of "better" and "worse." But it is clear that every play of the game is unique and that every ball pitched or bowled is conceptually inseparable from others, forming with them a larger strategy. The most elementary requirement of statistics—uniformity of sample —is therefore not met.

"Into the same river no man can step twice," not because the universe is in flux, but because it is organized and integrated.

The behavioral stream of events, like baseball or cricket, is segmented in time; and this segmentation is not to be violated by treating its numbers as quantities. As in the segmentation of an earthworm, each segment can have an ordinal name from "first" to

GREGORY BATESON is a Fellow of Kresge College, at the University of California, Santa Cruz.

"last," but no cardinal number can be applied. The total number of segments, whether in the worm or the game, is the name of a pattern. Segmentation is itself not a quantity; it is a component or premise of the morphology of the worm.

But still there is an economy, a parsimony of description to be gained by recognizing the repetitive character of the segments, whether these be of life or of game or of worm. We shall require fewer words and phrases, fewer linguistic bits, in our description if we take advantage of the repetitive and rhythmic nature of what is to be described.[1] In seeking for components of socialization, it is such a parsimony that I would hope to achieve. My ultimate goal is simple and not very ambitious. It is merely to discover a few notions, a few categories, which can be used over and over again.

But in the whole realm of behavioral science, our ignorance is perhaps most conspicuously medieval when we pose questions about the classification of sequences of behavior. We have a whole host of words which name *classes* of action without identifying the members of the class. For some unknown reason, we cannot spell out the characteristics of any of these classes: What is "play"? What is "aggression"?

"He picked up his pen," "the cat scratched him," "he was hurrying," "she ate the steak," "he sneezed," "they quarreled," etc., etc. Not one of these descriptive statements can be classified without more information.

Here is an exercise: consider for each of the above statements what you would need to know in order to say "that was play" or "that was exploration" or "practice" or "hystrionics" or "humor" or "somnambulism" or "aggression" or "art" or "courtship" or "love" or "mourning" or "exploration" or "manipulation" or even "accident." "Ritual" or "magic"? Or was it mere "spinal reflex"?

And are any of these categories mutually exclusive?

It is not too much to say that a science of psychology might begin here. If we only knew what that rat or that graduate student was doing while he was "acting" as "subject" of our "experiment"! And what are those men with masks in New Guinea doing? Is it "dancing"? Is that actor "pretending" to be Hamlet?

The exercise is nontrivial.

---

1. In the wide biological field, where description must be passed on from one generation to another, a similar parsimony is de rigeur. This necessity explains (for me) the phenomena of *homology*, both phylogenetic and metameric.

Note first of all that such exercises concern how we, the observers, shall classify the items of behavior. How shall *we* structure our description? And what, if you please, is an "item" of behavior?

But these primary questions turn on another more difficult. What we are watching are not the impacts of billiard balls but of organisms, and they in turn have their own classification and structuring of the events in which they participate. The rat has surely a much more complex structure than the earthworm, and the structure is, surely, more complex again for the graduate student, though he, at least, will try to help the observer by trying (and seeming) to do what is asked of him. Our first task is to learn how the subject structures his living. Only after that is done can we build a "psychology," a science of biological categories.

This indeed is the trap of the laboratory in which the experimenter is caught: that the units of behavior are defined by the *structure of the experiment,* which structure is unilaterally determined by only one of the participants . . . and that the wrong one. Under such circumstances, the only units that can be investigated must always be simpler, smaller, and of lower logical type than the structure of the experiment. It is all very well to perform an experiment with a "naive" rat. When he becomes "test wise," the sophistication of the experiment will have to transcend that test wisdom.

This need to transcend, that is, to use in the explanations, propositions of higher logical type than the descriptive proposition used in the explanandum, has a logical corollary in the familiar rule that no scientific hypothesis can ever be verified by inductive procedure. The proposition of lower type can contradict but never verify that of high type. This rule is especially cogent when the explanandum contains propositions such as ideas in the heads of rats and people.

Finally, what about cultural contrast? How, if at all, can the anthropologist recognize "play," "manipulation," and so on, among people of another culture? And what about dolphins and octopuses?

All of these questions are embarrassing and all must be faced to make sure that we do not claim insight to which we are not entitled by our experience, but I, personally, do not believe that the gross difficulty of these questions makes invalid all attempts to understand what goes on in other cultures and among nonhuman organisms.

As it seems to me, there are several components of our problem which suggest that it may be not insoluble and which, conversely, suggest that research which ignores all these advantageous components is likely to be a tilting at epistemologically monstrous windmills. First, "socialization" (by definition) requires *interaction*, usually of two or more organisms. From this it follows that, whatever goes on below the surface, inside the organisms where we cannot see it, there must be a large part of that "iceberg" showing above surface. We, biologists, are lucky in that evolution is always a co-evolution and learning is always a co-learning. Moreover, this visible part of the process is no mere by-product. It is precisely that production, that set of appearances, to produce which is supposedly the "goal" of all that learning which we call "socialization." Moreover, this aggregate of externally observable phenomena, always involving two or more "persons,"[2] contains not only what has been learned but also all the imperfect attempts of both persons to fit together in an ongoing process of interchange.

Above all, out there and imaginable for the scientist, are the *contexts* of all those failures and successes that mark the process of "socialization."

In other words, the scientist who would investigate "socialization" is lucky in that nature displays before him phenomena that are already *ordered* in two ways that should be of interest to him. He can observe "out there" both the *actions* of the interacting persons and, by a sort of inductive perception, the *contexts* of these actions.

Clearly a first step in defining units or parts of the process of socialization will be the explication of these two levels of order: the "actions" and the "contexts."

Before illustrating this program, however, a word must be said about those phenomena that are only *subjectively* observable.

I can know something of the inner determinants of my own actions, and something of what the *contexts* of my actions look like to me. But how much egomorphism should I allow myself in interpreting the actions and contexts of others? No final answer can be given, since both internal and external sources of information are certainly valuable—especially as corrective of each other. The excesses of "behaviorism" can only be corrected by empathy, but the

2. The "person," after all, is the *mask*. It is what is perceivable of a human organism. It is a unilateral view of the interface between one organism and another.

hypotheses that empathy proposes must always be tested in the external world.

Without identification of context, nothing can be understood. The observed action is utterly meaningless until it is classified as "play," "manipulation," or what not. But contexts are but categories of the mind. If I receive a threat from him, I can never get empirical validation of my interpretation of his action as "threat." If his threat is successful and deters me from some action, I shall never be sure that he was really threatening. Only by calling his bluff (and was it "bluff"?) can I get an indication of how he *now*, at this later moment and in this new context of my "calling his bluff," classifies his potential threat. *Only* by use of introspection, empathy, and shared cultural premises—the products of socialization—can anybody identify how context appears to another.

One form of habitual error can, however, be pilloried. This is the trick of drawing a generalization from the world of external observation, giving it a fancy name, and then asserting that this named abstraction exists *inside* the organism as an explanatory principle. Instinct theory commonly takes this monstrous form. To say that opium contains a dormitive principle is no explanation of how it puts people to sleep. Or do the people contain a dormitive instinct that is "released" by the opium?

What is important is that the conscious use of introspection and empathy is always to be preferred to their unconscious use. When all is said and done, we are still human and still organisms, and it is silly not to compare what we personally know about being human with what we can see of how other people live, and silly not to use what we humans know of living as a background for thinking about the being of other species. The *difference* between man and planarian must be enlightening because these two creatures resemble each other more than either resembles a stone.

What is disastrous is to claim an objectivity for which we are untrained and then project upon an external world premises that are either idiosyncratic or culturally limited. Biology, alas, is still riddled with hypotheses that are unconscious projections upon the biosphere of social philosophies generated by the Industrial Revolution. It was right—and inevitable—for Darwin and the others to create hypotheses out of the climate of their own culture and epoch, but disastrous to not see what they were doing.

The danger inherent in the use of subjective insights is not that these are necessarily wrong. The subjective view is, in 1974, still the richest and most rewarding source of understanding in biology. (So little do we know of the nature of life!) The danger arises from what seems to be a fact of natural history: that the insights given by introspection and empathy seem irresistibly true. Like the axioms of Euclid, the premises of subjective insight seem "self-evident."

With this caveat regarding the subjective, I now return to the two species of order—the actions and the contexts of action—which characterize the observable part of socialization, and I ask what clues to the understanding of this external order can be derived from my own internal experience of living. As I see it, the fundamental idea that there are separate "things" in the universe is a creation of and projection from our own psychology. From this creation, we go on to ascribe this same separateness to ideas, sequences of events, systems, and even persons.[3] I therefore ask whether this particular psychological habit can be trusted as a clue to understanding the order or sorts of order that are (expectably)[4] immanent in the socialization process; and the answer is not what naive positivism might lead us to suspect. The more complex entities—ideas, sequences, persons, and so on—seem to be suspiciously intangible and suspiciously devoid of limiting outlines, and we might therefore be led to suppose them illusory, creations only of the mind and, therefore, to be distrusted in scientific analysis.

But, precisely at this point, there is a paradoxical reversal: the socialization that we try to study is a *mental* process and therefore only the productions and processes of mind are relevant. The dissection of experience into ideas, sequences, and events may be "really" invalid but certainly the occidental mind really thinks in terms of such separations. If, therefore, we are to analyze processes of socialization we must examine and map these separations and, by this act of separating a group of phenomena, I commit myself to natural history. My aim is to study those separations (valid or not) that

---

3. Opinions differ as to which separating line was primary. Some suppose that the first distinction is that between self and notself.

4. Note that already the psychological habit of isolating and naming processes as if they were things creeps in with this word "expectably" and with my reference to *the* socialization process. But are there any total divisions between things? Is there a place or time where one thing begins and another ends? If so, then clearly there could be no causal or logical interaction between them!

characterize the thought of those whom I study, of whom "I" am one.

This leaves conspicuously unanswered the analogous question about the organization of mind in the Orient and elsewhere. From an external view of what is reported, it seems that there are several arduous pathways by which experience of other ways of knowing can be achieved. Some of these other epistemologies are also accessible to Westerners by pathways not less arduous. What is reported by East and West alike is that, in these special states of mind, the way of knowing is precisely *not* organized in separate or separable *gestalten*.

In the jargon of this essay, it seems that for these states there are no separable components of socialization and possibly no meaning attachable to "socialization." Or perhaps such words could refer only to some buzzing of irrelevant memory, recalling other more prosaic states.

For the mystic shares with the pragmatist that fact of natural history—whereby the premises of mind, in whatever state it be, seem self-evident. His thoughts may be more abstract and perhaps more beautiful. From where the mystic sits, the premises of the pragmatic and the egocentered will appear parochial and arbitrary, but his own premises are, for him, completely self-evident.

In sum, what can be said about the mystics defines our upper limit, an upper level of abstraction into which we need not pursue the search for data, since socialization is not there, but *from* which we can look out at the data generated in other levels. The epistemology onto which we map the facts of socialization must be more abstract than the facts to be mapped.

Gradually the outlines of how to think about components of socialization or about any sort of mental change begin to appear. We are to concern ourselves with the psychologically "self-evident" and with a premise that the psychologically self-evident is divisible into components. This latter premise, is, itself, self-evident at the psychological level where the components appear to be (and therefore *are*) separable. But at a higher level of abstraction, where the mystics live, it is claimed that such separation is not only not self-evident, it is almost inconceivable. It is some traveler's tale from the world of illusion or *maya*. The mystic may laugh at us but still the task of the anthropologist is to explore the world of illusion, perhaps with the eyes and ears of the mystic.

To be "self-evident," a proposition or premise must be out of reach and unexaminable: it must have defenses or roots at unconscious levels. Similarly, to be "self-evident," a proposition or premise must be either self-validating or so general as to be but rarely contradicted by experience.

Enough has now been said to be background for considering a cluster of cultural phenomena in an attempt to recognize components that shall compose the socialization "behind" those cultural phenomena.

The most direct approach is that of looking at sequences of interchange between parents or other teachers and children in which the former are "socializing" the latter. Margaret Mead and I have provided data for such a study on a rather large scale in *Balinese Character*, where data in actual socialization are set side by side with other Balinese material. In this book, the plates, each with from five to nine pictures, were built according to what we thought or felt were cultural and characterological themes. These themes do not appear, however, in the naming of the plates, which is done in terms that appear to be episodic or concrete: "Cremation," "Cock Fighting," "Eating Snacks," "A Bird on a String," "Fingers in Mouth," and so on. But, in fact, every plate is a complex statement, illustrating either different facets of some quite abstract theme or the interlocking of several themes.

Each picture is raw data except for the fact of selection—the aiming of the camera and the choice of the particular print for reproduction. Beyond that, of course, the juxtaposition of the various pictures on the plate is, necessarily, ours. It is our first step towards computing some sort of theory from the data. The method is comparative but not statistical, reticulate rather than lineal.

Faced with these data, I ask again whether there is a useful species of component of culture? Are the themes useful in the formal sense that by recognition of them we can describe the Balinese culture and socialization in a more economical manner?

Consider plate 17, which is entitled "Balance." The two preceeding plates (15 and 16) are called "Visual and Kinaesthetic Learning I" and "Visual and Kinaesthetic Learning II." The three plates following "Balance" are called "Trance and *Beroek* I," "Trance and

Beroek II," and "Trance and *Beroek* III." The whole series of six plates from plate 15 to plate 20 are interrelated. (In addition, plate 17 in my copy has on it a penciled note in my handwriting: "This plate should more appropriately follow the series on 'Elevation and Respect' and point up the balance problems of the elevated. Cf. also 'Fear of Space' (plate 67) and 'Fear of Loss of Support' and 'Child as (elevated) God' (plate 45)."

In a word, the book is built in such a way that the interlocking nature of the themes is stressed and their separateness as "components" is made most difficult to disentagle. I have chosen the "Balance" plate for this essay because it illustrates a point of meeting of many different themes.

The context of plate 17 is described in the book as follows:

Plates 14, 15, and 16 taken together give us indications about the Balinese body image. We have, on the one hand, the fantasy of the inverted body with its head on the pubes; and on the other, the Balinese method of learning through their muscles, the discrepant muscular tensions which are characteristic of their dancing, and the independent movement and posturing of the separate fingers in dance. We have, in fact, a double series of motifs—indications that the body is a single unit as perfectly integrated as any single organ, and contrasting indications that the body is made up of separate parts, each of which is as perfectly integrated as the whole.

This plate illustrates the motif of the perfectly integrated body image, while Plates 18, 19, and 20 illustrate the fantasy that the body is made up of separate parts and may fall to pieces (*beroek*).

The nine pictures which make up "Plate 17, Balance," are as follows:

Two frames of a small boy learning to stand and walk while holding on to a horizontal bamboo. In the second picture he holds onto his penis in addition to the bar. (Other records not reproduced in this book support the proposition that male toddlers hold onto their penes when balance is precarious.)

One frame of a small girl, with hands holding each other in front of her belly.

One frame of a child nurse stooping to pick up a baby and one of an adolescent girl stooping to pick up an offering.

One frame shows a small boy scratching his knee. He simply stands on the other leg and lifts the knee to within reach of his hand. (Again there is massive support in the data for saying that Balinese movement is extremely economical. They contract just those muscles needed for each action.)

The three remaining frames are of works of art representing witches in different stages of transformation. It seems that to embark upon a horrendous "trip" in the realms of altered consciousness a woman should go out in the night with a small altar, a live chicken, and small offerings (*segehan*) for the chthonic demons. All alone she will then dance with her left foot on the chicken and her right hand on the altar. As she dances she will gradually assume the shape and appearance of the witch (*Rangda*).

In other words, whether or not the Balinese "know" what they are doing and intend this outcome, they somehow sense and recognize in art that their kinesthetic socialization prepares the individual for altered consciousness—for a temporary escape from the ego-organized world.

The use of dance as an entry into ecstasy and an ego-alien world is ancient and perhaps worldwide, but the Balinese (and perhaps every people) have their particular version of this pathway. Plates 15 and 16 together with 18, 19, and 20 illustrate the matter.

Balance is a partly involuntary and unconscious business, dependent on "spinal reflexes." When provided with appropriate context, these reflexes go into oscillation that is called "clonus," a phenomenon that is familiar to everybody and which is easily produced. (While sitting, place the leg with thigh horizontal and foot supported on the floor. Move the foot inwards towards you so that the heel is off the floor and the ball of the foot supports the weight of the leg. When the weights and angles are correctly adjusted, an oscillation will start in the muscle of the calf with a frequency of about six to eight per second and an amplitude of about half an inch at the knee. This oscillation is called *clonus* in neurophysiology and is a recurrent series of patellar reflexes, generated in a feedback circuit. The effect of each contraction is fed back as a modification of tension to the calf muscle. This change of tension triggers the next patellar reflex.)

The process of clonus involves three propositional or injunctional components: two of these are the usual paired components of any cybernetic oscillation which generate the sequential paradox in, for example, a buzzer circuit. In words: "If the circuit is 'on';

then it shall become 'off.' " And "if it is 'off'; then it shall become 'on.' " But, in addition to these two contradictory components, there is a process that sets values for the parameters of the whole system. The thresholds or other components of the oscillation can be changed by "meta" injunctions that presumably come from the brain. The two contradictory components are immanent in spinal cord and muscle.

The potentially ego-alien nature of such action is basic. Anybody, by ignoring (repressing the perception of) the meta-injunctions that control the parameters, can have the reflexive experience of seeing his or her leg engage in involuntary movement; and this oscillatory trembling can serve the same function as that of involuntary hand movements in the induction of hypnotic trance. The involuntary movement is first a detached object of perception: "I" see my leg move but "I" did not move it.

This detachment of the object proposes then two lines of development: (1) the possibility of "out of body experience," and (2) the possibility of integrating to perceive the body as an autonomous, ego-alien entity. Either the detached "I" or the detached "body" can become the focus of elaboration. Of these paths, it is the second that Balinese follow so that, by a curious inversion, the word *"raga,"* which seems to have the primary meaning of "body," comes to mean "self."

By extension from the experience of clonus, the various perceivable parts of the body become, in fantasy or mystic experience, each separately animated. If the arm or the leg can act of its own accord – (and, indeed, clonus is a completed self-corrective circuit; it is a true aliveness)—then a similar separate aliveness can be expected and can be found in any limb.

The Balinese cemetery is haunted not by whole ghosts but by the ghosts of separate limbs. Headless bodies, separate legs, and unattached arms that jump around and sometimes a scrotum that crawls slowly over the ground—these are the boggles of Balinese fantasy.

From this it is a small step to perceiving the body as a puppet or to imagining such supernaturals as *Bala Serijoet* (plate 20, fig. 4), the "Multiple Soldier" whose every joint—shoulders, elbows, knees, ankles, and so on—is separately animated and provided with an eye.

These fantasies generate or are generated by a paradox, a dialectic between integration and disintegration. Is there a whole? Or is it only parts? Or are the parts combined into a whole? And this paradox of disintegration-integration proposes a whole spectrum of entities, ranging from separated animated limbs to such supernaturals as *Sangiang Tjintjia* or *Betara Tunggal* (plate 20, fig. 6). This is the totally detached, totally integrated, "God of god," (*Dewaning Dewa*). He is completely integrated, sexless, enclosed within his own effulgence and totally withdrawn.

It is my impression, though I do not recall any Balinese telling me this, that as the woman by occult practices can cause her own transformation into the form of the Witch of witches (*Rangdaning Durga*), so also by occult practices the adept becomes transformed into a supernatural of the *Sangiang Tjintjia* genus.

Plates 16 and 18 illustrate another aspect of the character formation that centers in balance. In both of these plates the kinesthetic integration of the individual is invaded. His or her individuation is violently destroyed to achieve a new integration.

In plate 16, the famous dancer, Mario, teaches a preadolescent boy to dance, forcibly guiding the pupil's hands and body into the correct postures and almost throwing him across the dancing space.

In plate 18, two little girls are put into the trance state in which they will dance. The procedure is a little complicated: two dolls, weighted with bells, are threaded on a string about fifteen feet long which is strung between two vertical bamboo sticks. The sticks are held by two men in such a way that clonus in their biceps will change the tension in the string causing the dolls or *dedari* (angels) to dance up and down, while the weighted dolls provide a feedback promoting the clonus in the men's arms. When the *dedari* are dancing fast, the girl who is to go into trance takes hold of the shaking stick so that she is violently shaken by the man's clonus.

Meanwhile the crowd around is singing songs about *dedari*. The girl's action in holding the stick breaks the rhythm of the clonus and she takes control of the stick beating with its end upon the wooden stand that supports it. She beats out a few bars of the song that the crowd is singing and then falls backward into trance. She is then dressed up by the crowd and will dance as *dedari*.

Curiously enough, a conspicuous element of the dance is the balancing feat of dancing while standing on a man's shoulders (plate 10, fig. 3).

In sum, the business of explanation and the business of socializa-

Plate 16. Visual and Kinaesthetic Learning II (Bateson and Mead 1942)

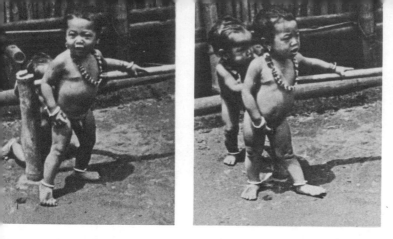

Plate 17. Balance (Bateson and Mead 1942)

Plate 18. Trance and *Beroek I* (Bateson and Mead 1942)

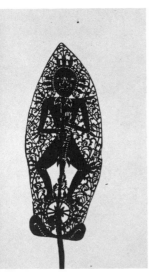

Plate 20. Trance and *Beroek III* (Bateson and Mead 1942)

tion turn out to be the same. To make a premise "self-evident" is the simplest way to make action based upon that premise seem "natural." To illustrate this, data from Bali have been adduced.

A large part of Balinese behavior is based upon paradigms of experience which are, for the Balinese, unquestionable. These are the paradigms of balance and of the interaction between the moving human body and the gravitational field in which it must move. This interaction is rooted in the unquestionable on both sides. On the one side are the reflexes of balance of which surely many components are genetically determined and, on the other side, are the universal characteristics of bodily mass and earth's gravity. These are combined to make it "self-evident" that the cemeteries would be haunted by autonomous parts of bodies.

And yet there is no universal cross-cultural imperative that would insist that everywhere in the world these generalities of balance and gravity shall become major cultural premises; or even that the synthesis of gravity and spinal reflex shall take the particular shape that is characteristic for Balinese culture.

REFERENCE

BATESON, GREGORY, and MARGARET MEAD. 1942. *Balinese Character: A Photographic Analysis* (Special Publications of the New York Academy of Sciences, 2). New York Academy of Sciences.

Absent Eyes and Idle Hands:

Socialization for Low Affect among the Sebei

WALTER GOLDSCHMIDT

Diverse aspects of institutionalized behavior among the Sebei[1] suggest a generally low level of affect in their interpersonal relationships. Among such evidences are the essentially remote relationships between husbands and wives, the tendency of the Sebei to use one another instrumentally, the regular demand for pay or other forms of compensation for acts performed, including ritual acts even when performed by relatives, and the low concern for the deceased (either in body or in spirit) in their funerary rituals (Goldschmidt 1973), as well as the general lack of empathy toward those who are suffering, or toward domestic animals. LeVine (1973:140ff.) has remarked on the weak affectivities as a widespread aspect of the African personality and the Sebei support his contention and represent an extreme instance.[2] I should make it clear that I am talking about low affect level, not hostility, anxiety, or anger. It is psycho-

---

WALTER GOLDSCHMIDT is professor of anthropology and psychiatry at the University of California, Los Angeles.

1. The Sebei are a Southern Nilotic (Kalenjin) people living on the north slope of Mount Elgon in Uganda. Data presented here, when not otherwise referenced, are from my detailed ethnography (Goldschmidt, in press).

2. Super and Harkness (1974) have argued that this is not so among the closely related Kipsigis, based upon a very different kind of evidence. I cannot resolve the differences between myself and Super and Harkness; LeVine's response (1974) is of no help, since the Sebei are similar to the Kipsigis in both economy and cultural derivation.

logical disengagement that is the characteristic mood, a lack of involvement of individuals with one another in all relationships, a
lack that finds expression in such other things as inconsistent values
(Edgerton 1971:122) and little commitment to tradition. Children
play together quietly rather than boisterously and they phantasize
adult roles rather than engage either in team sports or intensive
competition.

Ecological circumstances may make a low level of affect functionally meaningful for these originally pastoral peoples, at least for
the men. Under these earlier conditions Sebei men had to be prepared to engage in military operations, had to be stoic in the face
of both hardships and dangers, and had to delay marriage and/or
remain separate from their spouses. It may also be that this social
callousness is the obverse of the pattern of independence that characterizes pastoral societies in general (Goldschmidt 1971). Without
appropriate comparative data from other societies operating under
similar conditions, more cannot be said than to recognize this as a
possible reason why the pattern exists. But in this essay, I am not
concerned with why this interpersonal quality should exist, but
how it is transmitted; how the child first acquires these sentiments,
this outlook.

The matter is not self-evident, for most of the standard practices
do not suggest such an outcome. Sebei women, as in most of Africa,
regularly carry their children on their backs as they go about their
duties so that there is a good deal of body contact; infants sleep by
their mothers; there is little or no display of tension involved in
toilet training during the first (or often even second) year of the
child's life, and children are generally given the breast at the slight-
est demand. Though they are given supplemental milk at an early
age, weaning is variable; some children take the breast until their
playmates tease them while other children are weaned abruptly at
an early age. The difference in treatment occurs because babies are
not weaned until they give up the breast voluntarily unless the
mother becomes pregnant, in which case the continued suckling is
felt to be harmful to the mother, so that often (but not universally)
they wean the child forcibly and harshly by putting pepper or to-
bacco juice on their nipples or by pinching the child when he tries
to suckle. I have no detailed statistics on the proportions of children
treated in these alternate ways, but I would judge that at least half

of the population was self-weaned without traumatogenic action on the part of the mother.

None of these aspects of child care, which were credited with such salience by Freudian-oriented anthropologists a generation ago, can account for the transmission of the low level of interpersonal affect that I have found characteristic of the Sebei. Yet as Margaret Mead has herself said, it is not either weaning or toilet training or any particular element in the handling of the child's needs that is crucial to the transmission of these qualities, but it is the emotional tone that she brings to the relationship.

Before I turn to the interaction between mothers and infants, a word should be said about the role of Sebei fathers. I never saw a father dandle or hold a baby, so far as I can remember, and the one exception pointed out to me by my wife was a man who was exceptional in other ways, including the fact that he was the only adult male Sebei I know or heard of who had refused to be circumcised. In one of our picture tests for values there was a scene in which a man is bouncing a baby (Edgerton 1971:307). About half the respondents (N = 128; divided equally between men and women) saw the scene as playful and/or happy (as clearly intended) and a few commented that this was right, and that they themselves play with their children. One man added "more people should play with their children instead of neglecting them." But significantly, about half find it necessary to explain this unusual behavior: the child is sick, it is crying, the mother is away. Ten of them saw the man as a woman, an ayah, the member of another tribe; others had what appear outlandish or irrelevant responses, and five saw the man as harming the child. Thus, fully half of the respondents found this picture so unfamiliar that they had to redefine it to make it comprehensible. Later in the child's life, the father's role is that of chief (and harsh) disciplinarian, but in the early years he typically has no role; he is emotionally an absent father.

Mothers, of course, do hold their children. Yet the only ones I remember seeing fondling their infants were unmarried or childless ones holding babies belonging to another woman. But what impressed me even more was the quality of interaction between the mother and her infant; the apparent remoteness and disengagement of the mother when carrying or nursing her child. This quality is depicted in figures 1 and 2, the mother gazing abstractly in the middle distance, supporting the child with the minimum of body contact. These haunting pictures of disengaged mothers led me back to my photographic files, and it is the data derived from these that I wish now to present.[3]

I found 28 instances in which a mother was either holding her child while standing or was seated on the ground with her child on her lap, not including those posed photographs taken at the mother's request. Most of the instances are in scenes where the mother and child were incidental and in only a few did she seem to be particularly aware of the camera. Thus, the pictures were not taken for the purposes of the analysis I am here engaged in; indeed, I had not conceptualized the idea of low affect in Sebei culture nor concentrated, in my ethnographic analysis, on child-rearing practices. I did early perceive the absence of the fathers (there are no unposed pictures showing a father holding a child). I think, therefore, that these photographs can be taken as a representative sample of the manner in which mothers handle their infants when outside the house, whether alone or in a group. While it is conceivable that they behave differently indoors, I have every reason to believe that this is not so; certainly I saw no evidence suggesting this nor did either my wife or I receive any indication, verbal or otherwise, of such a differential. I should add that the pictures were taken in widely separate sectors of Sebei territory at two time periods (1954; 1961–1962). Some were taken by me, some by my wife, for we both habitually carried cameras with us and photographed events or scenes whenever so inclined.[4]

In only one of these pictures was noninstrumental interaction evident between the mother and the child (fig. 3); it is the single incident in these 28 pictures of eye contact. It is also the only instance of a hand placed on the child in a noninstrumental and apparently playful interaction.

In table 1, I have summarized my analysis of these ictures, giving the data on two modes of expressing affect: use of eyes and use

3. In this I am obviously inspired by the pioneer work of Bateson and Mead in Bali (Bateson and Mead 1942, Mead and Macgregor 1951, Mead 1956, 1970). It is a singular fact that over 30 years after their seminal use of photographic analysis of interpersonal behavior, there is still no corpus of literature based upon their pioneering techniques.

4. The Sebei were un-self-conscious photographic subjects (except when posing), and never objected to the presence of the camera.

TABLE 1
MATERNAL EYES AND HANDS

	Nursing	Not nursing	Total
Eyes on child	0	2	2
Eyes not on child			
on work	1	1	2
at camera	0	2	2
elsewhere	10	11	21
Total	11	14	25
Total	11	16	27
One hand on child*	1	5	6
No hand on child			
on work	1	1	2
clasped	5	5	10
free	4	5	9
Total	10	11	21
Totals	11	16	27

* In no instance did the mother have both hands on her child.
Note: in one nursing picture the direction of gaze is uncertain (but there is no eye contact); in another the positioning of the hands is uncertain.

of hands. I have listed separately those instances in which the infant was nursing from those in which it was not.

The nursing mother is not observing her child; her attention is elsewhere. Aside from the instance noted above, the mother is looking at the face of the child in one other photograph; she is feeding it milk in her cupped hand (fig. 4). In one instance she is tying a coin in the child's hair, which I have scored as looking at her work (fig. 5). But in most instances her attention is with some external event, or rather, it seems to me, some internal concern, remote both from the child and the events that surround her.

In no photograph, whether standing or seated, whether nursing or not, does the mother hold the child with *both* hands; indeed, in more than three out of four instances, neither hand is on the child. The most characteristic manner for the mother to hold her infant is to support its back with the forearm letting the child straddle her hip, as seen in figure 1. This frees the mother's hands for work or gesturing (fig. 5). When the hands are not in use, the mother characteristically clasps the hand of the arm supporting the child over the wrist of the other arm (10 of the 28 instances; see fig. 7). This suggests that this manner of holding the child is not functionally relevant to other activities, but is a gesture expressive of her attitude. Like her eyes, her hands are disengaged. Mead (1956:88), showing pictures of Balinese women and their children not unlike these of the Sebei, speaks of "inattentive hands." The hands of Sebei women are, in comparison to the sample of Balinese mothers and infants Mead has given us in her pictures, even less attentive than the hands of the Bali mothers.

I eliminated some six or eight posed pictures for obvious reasons, but I must include a single exception. When a Sebei mother asked that her child's picture be taken, she characteristically sat on a chair, turned the child to face the camera, holding it in place, and stared into the lens—a result devoid both of interest and esthetic value. There is a single exception (fig. 6), the only madonna pose in my small gallery. It is of interest because this mother, as it happens, is not really a Sebei woman, but a member of an ethnic enclave the Sebei call Bumachek, a Bagwere (Bantu) people who moved into Sebei territory about a century ago, adopted many Sebei customs, but retained many distinctive features of attitudes and sentiment. Among these is an apparently greater emotional lability than occurs among the Sebei.

Hands and eyes are (along with the voice, not amenable to photographic recording) the major means of expressing affect to a baby. One cannot look at these pictures or examine these statistics without an awareness that these modes of communication are rare. (Indeed, these photographs indicate the low level of interpersonal communication. No two persons, with the exception already noted, appear to be in mutual interaction in the scenes in figures 2 and 3.) But I am not arguing that it is these acts per se that are the significant element in transmitting affectlessness to the child, though they may very well be, but that they are indicative of the mother's sentiments, of her emotional stance vis-à-vis her infant. What I see in these photographs is an absent mother—an emotionally absent mother (fig. 7).

From the perspective of the child, the mother is available as a source of sustenance; she feeds him and cleans him, and is thus responsive to his biological needs. She doesn't tease him, provoke him, or behave seductively toward him (we never observed mothers manipulating the genitalia); she is emotionally blank and the infant gets no ego gratification from her. That he should therefore see other persons in later life as serving chiefly his instrumental needs rather than his ego satisfactions seems entirely understand-

FIG. 1. Mother standing with suckling child, Binyiny, 1954

FIG. 2. Mother seated with suckling child, Sasur, 1962

FIG. 3. Mothers and children, Benet, 1954. The single instance of communicative interaction in the photographs.   Note suckling child at right.

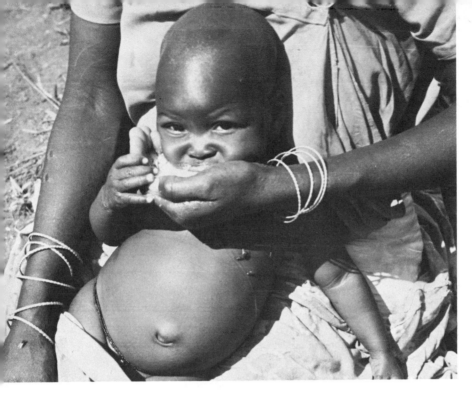

FIG. 4. Supplemental feeding of child. Note idle position of right hand

FIG. 5. Mother working while child suckles

FIG. 6. Posed photograph. The woman is Bagwere (Bantu), not Sebei.

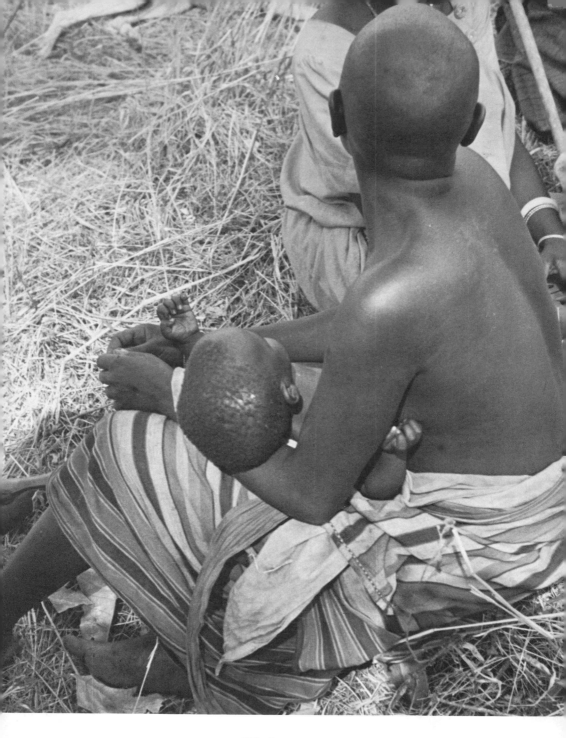

FIG. 7. Absent mother

able. Thus is the low level of affect transmitted to the next generation at infancy, reinforced in subsequent institutionalized behavior.

REFERENCES

BATESON, GREGORY, and MARGARET MEAD. 1942. *Balinese Character.*
Academy of Sciences, Special Publications, vol. 2.

EDGERTON, ROBERT B. 1971. *The Individual in Cultural Adaptation: A
Study of Four East African People.* University of California Press.

GOLDSCHMIDT, WALTER. 1971. Independence as an Element in Pastoral
Social Systems. *Anthropological Quarterly* 44 (3):132–142.

———. 1973. Guilt and Pollution in Sebei Mortuary Rituals. *Ethos*
1 (1):75–105.

———. (in press) *Culture and Behavior of the Sebei.* University of California Press.

LeVINE, ROBERT A. 1973. Patterns of Personality in Africa. *Ethos*
1 (2):123–152.

———. 1974. Comment on the Note by Super and Harkness, *Ethos*
2 (4):382–386.

MEAD, MARGARET. 1956. Some Uses of Still Photography in Culture and
Personality Studies, *Personal Character and Cultural Milieu* (3d rev.
ed.; D. Haring, ed.), pp. 79–105. Syracuse University Press.

———. 1970. The Art and Technology of Field Work, *A Handbook of
Method in Cultural Anthoropology* (Raoul Narrol and Ronald Cohen, eds.), pp. 246–265. The Natural History Press.

MEAD, MARGARET, and FRANCES COOK MACGREGOR. 1951. *Growth and
Culture: A Photographic Study of Balinese Childhood.* Putnam

SUPER, CHARLES M. and SARA HARKNESS. 1974. Patterns of Personality
in Africa: A Note from the Field, *Ethos* 2 (4):377–381.

A ffective Dissonance and Primary Socialization:

Implications for a Theory of Incest Avoidance

GEORGE A. DE VOS

THE UNIVERSAL APPEARANCE OF INCEST PROHIBITIONS

One of the yet unresolved mysteries of human nature is the universal appearance of some form of incest taboo in every society regulating sexual expression within the primary family. Often these prohibitions are socially extended in systems of exogamy in one form or another, depending upon the kinship structure of the society, to include individuals classified through kinship as "too close" for legitimate marriage, if not sexual congress. Most theorists who give time to a detailed analysis of this subject have come to the conclusion that the enforcement of social sanctions is not sufficient, however, to explain the cultural universality of incest prohibitions. Although differing widely in proposed etiology, some recognized the presence of self-limiting, deeply felt repugnance that makes the act unconscionable to most individuals (Westermarck 1921, Freud 1950). Nevertheless, most anthropologists have been loath to find recourse in some instinctual or psychological theory of

GEORGE A. DE VOS is professor of anthropology at the University of California, Berkeley.

aversion to explain this universal abhorrence of sexuality exercised between close-blood relatives. Instead, most of their attempts at explanation have in desperation turned back to some form of social structural theory.

For example, although the brother-sister taboo is universal, it is quite evident that there are, depending upon social structure, highly differential strains toward such incest, and conversely, a greater prohibition and exercise of avoidance behavior in some societies than in others. But to counter social structural analyses are the situations cited by Spiro and Wolf. In the absence of kinship prohibition, individuals brought up together at childhood exhibit some form of aversion to marriage in adulthood.

Limitations of space do not permit me to present a critique of the various attempts by social scientists to account for incest prohibitions. The most appealing to date are those of Talcott Parsons (1954), who has taken social structural theory as far as it can go in this direction, and Arthur Wolf (1966), who in desperation to explain his own observations on the particular problems occuring in certain Taiwanese marriages has, in effect, returned from a social structural theory to Westermarck and his explanation of the development of mutual sexual repugnancies.

Conversations with Melford Spiro concerning his observations that there is a total lack of marriage between age mates in Israeli kibbutzim and Wolf's published observations on Taiwan have prompted me to examine in detail both the anthropological and psychoanalytic literature on incest. Dissatisfied with what has been so far attempted in structural theories generally, I seek here to forward my own explanation of the psychological mechanisms that make incest prohibitions generally effective whether or not they are institutionalized as part of a system of kinship.

I contend that incest prohibitions are related specifically to a general psychological phenomenon I term "affective dissonance." This paper is an attempt to present my assumptions in brief rather than extended form. The evidence from Israel and Taiwan goes counter to the usual structural analysis, and supports affective dissonance as an explanatory concept.

CHILDHOOD CLOSENESS AND SEXUAL AVOIDANCE

Spiro, in his study of Israeli kibbutzim (1954, 1958), has remarked upon the spontaneous emergence of a nonverbalized, socially unobserved, but behaviorally operative, sibling incest taboo among children of the same age brought up together from birth in the special collective children's quarters. These age group domiciles for children are supervised by special nurses. An intensity of involvement occurs among the children. Age mates take on many of the emotional attributes of siblings even though they are never so classified by the community. There have been no reported cases within kibbutz communities of any intermarriage by young adults brought up within the same age group, yet there is no appreciable social sanctioning against such marriages (see also Yonina Talmon 1964). The families comprising the kibbutz have come together from widely diverse sources and are unrelated by any kinship ties; nor is there any social structural sense within the community that would make age mates feel themselves to have become part of a kinship pattern.

Arthur Wolf (1966) describes a patterned form of marriage among Taiwanese in which for economic reasons a female child is brought into a family to become, at an appropriate age, the spouse of a son. In tracing through what occurs in these marriages, Wolf establishes rather compelling evidence that some form of sexual avoidence is at work. Continuing sexual interest and compatibility rarely occurs between such individuals. In attempting to explain this phenomenon, he has reexamined various theories of incest avoidance and is impelled to espouse a psychological rather than institutional approach to the subject. He returns to Freud's *Totem and Taboo* and the argument that the child's emotional resistance to the possibility of sexual relations with a childhood associate is a normal "reaction formation" to a repressed impulse. Freud does not deny the continuing effect of sexual attractions developed in infancy, but points out how they are not normally manifest in adult behavior and indeed are repressed. Wolf also refers to Robin Fox (1962) who bases his reasoning about sexual avoidance on the absence of satisfactory climax of the type of sexual excitement experienced in childhood. Such experience results instead in such a sense of frustration that the insufficiency of satisfaction in the childhood experience is, in effect, a form of negative conditioning against a specific interest in an individual who may have aroused such interest in childhood. Similar to this line of reasoning is the point of view of Frank Beach (1951) who notes how male mammals do not copulate satisfactorily in an environmental setting previously associated with some form of punishment or negative conditioning. Wolf reasons along lines suggested by these observations that it is somehow the socialization experience of the containment of impulses that remains a strong experience of childhood as an atmosphere in which children in the primary family learn to be constrained toward one another, seeking from them either aggressive or sexual release. Whatever the specific experience, Wolf argues that the conditions of intimate childhood association are in themselves a sufficient cause for the development of an emotional resistance to sexual relations. Wolf defends Westermarck's theory that in effect attributes this resistance to habituation. But the reasons for incest Wolf examines, from reaction formation to repugnance, do not explain why "habituation" prevents sexual arousal.

AFFECTIVE DISSONANCE AND INCEST AVOIDANCE

In another article (1975) written as a critique of Mary Douglas's (1966) theory of taboos against pollution, I expressed briefly my dissatisfaction with the overly rational approach of Leon Festinger's (1957, 1962) theory of cognitive dissonance used to explain conscious rationalization of behavior and attitudes. Festinger has posited a strong need in all humans (be it generalized from his own culture) to resolve what he terms "cognitive dissonance." In his theory, the tension produced by inconsistency in perception produces a need for resolution by altering what one sees or believes into a more consistent pattern. I criticized this theory from the standpoint of my understanding of Japanese religious beliefs and myths as they are found in expositions of Shinto. Japanese mythology is full of glaring conceptual cognitive inconsistencies and incongruities. It is diffuse and imprecise. Japanese are not emotionally disturbed by such lack of clarification, nor do they characteristically use categorization in a way so general in Western thought. Western thinkers find it difficult to give credit to thought that eases away needs to define, to catalog, or to categorize. In Japanese culture, juxtaposed inconsistencies in thought and behavior are easily maintained consciously without emotional discomfort; individuals can countenance within their own consciousness both inconsistencies and ambiguities—to the degree that they are not affectively aroused——either enraged or made anxious by the cognitive content they are contemplating. There is no culturally induced need for Japanese to repress inconsistent thoughts. Moreover, the measure of tolerance of inconsistency or ambiguity in any other culture is not to be judged as antithetical to intellectual capacities for handling complex and differentiated cognitive patterns. There is an essential affective dimension underlying all cognitive structures. For the Japanese, it is only in those areas of the culture where differentiation is important, such as in ranking and status, that one finds Japanese concerned with maintaining consistency in cognitive ordering. It is precisely in these areas that emotions are aroused by inconsistencies or incongruities. Therefore, I generalized that it is not dissonance in cognitive patterns per se which necessitates resolution or consistency in human psychological structures; dissonance is a concern when there is affective arousal. In regard to incest, I have come to the conclusion that some form of affective dissonance is somehow automatically at work in every society as part of intimate family relationships to prevent sexual arousal. How does it work?

TOWARD A THEORY OF AFFECTIVE DISSONANCE

An affective dissonance theory suggests that there are sometimes dysfunctional, perceptual, automatic nervous system dissonances between anxiety and sexuality, erotocism and dependency, and so on. Specifically as it relates to sexual stimulation, the theory also suggests that satisfactory genital sexuality may itself depend on correctly balanced perceptual-autonomic body states. There is a sexual arousal, for instance, that may occur when proper blending of visual sexual stimuli and affective arousal relates to a sense of strangeness or even to some arousal of aggressiveness. Such forms of sexual stimulation may be incompatible with the usual types of affectionate states deeply conditioned toward particular individuals by continuous contact during childhood. Childhood erotic wishes may become buried and unconscious and be unrealizable without the total rearousal and reexperience of other, nonretrievable components of a cognitive and affective childhood pattern. This inaccessibility of a total childhood pattern, in neurotic conditions as examined by psychoanalysis, leads to an emphasis on fantasy rather than real sexual relationships in the erotic inner life of some individuals.

Erotic attachment of the mother is a normal stage in maturational development in mammals, including humans. It is some form of interference with maturation which strengthens and preserves the immature eroticism that characterizes many neurotic conditions. The grooming of the body and other acts of licking and care of erogenous areas of the infant are common to many mammalian species. Rats have shown a disturbed capacity for adult copulation when they were not properly groomed by their mothers at particular periods of infancy. Animal research seems to be fully in accord with psychoanalytic formulations concerning the necessity for properly facilitative, affectively satisfying mothering experiences in childhood. That is to say, the bodily intimacy of proper mothering around the pleasurable experiences derived from organs of intake and excretion, somehow are experientially necessary for fully satisfactory adult mutual sexual experiences.

Harlow's (1964) experiences with primates and other experiments with mammals suggest maternal grooming behavior in infancy is experientially necessary for the appearance of adequate sexual behavior. Deprived of such behavior, the adult animal cannot perform adequately. In humans the intensive erotic reciprocity between mother and child during the earliest stages of the child's own erotic development may well be a "grooming" prerequisite for heterosexual development. The continuous affective ties with the mother during psychosexual development may carry residual components of the earlier experiences, but the psychosexual development of the individual and the transmutation taking place in his schemata gradually changes the nature of his experience of the mother.

Only when a maternal or sororal relationship has been eroticized by a psychologically regressive mother or by some childhood breakthrough of incestuous sexual play between siblings would a strong, conscious continuity of unresolved erotic wishes remain into adulthood.

A mother who attempts genital stimulation of her son for her own satisfaction would have to be extremely aberrant and sexually disturbed, since the sexual satisfaction to be obtained from an infant or a small child would be in no way comparable to that obtained from an adult male. It is therefore most unusual for a small child to experience the mother's active sexuality directed toward him for her own direct genital gratification. While there is greater possibility that a child senses the mother's unsatisfied sexual needs and that she receives some indirect sexual gratification from sensual contact with him, this situation does not lead us to overt incest, but rather to a covert unconscious unresolved quality in their continuing relationship.

Parsons, in his attempt to relate psychoanalytic theory to a structural analysis, starts with what he terms the "progressive" and "regressive" features of human eroticism as they relate to social structure. Parsons (1954) draws heavily on Lévi-Strauss's (1956, 1969a) structural analysis of kinship and marriage. For example, insofar as a person in marrying out of his own family unit is performing a reciprocal obligation involving the social group or collectivity as a superordinant unit, he is no more free to choose than is an individual worker free to choose a job without regard to how it affects the superordinant industrial organization. In other words, the person is constrained directly and indirectly by group organization itself. In this sense, the occurrence of incest would be a socially regressive act, and the individual would perforce have to maintain a subadult or infantile identity. Automatically operative incest taboos looked at from this perspective serve to propel maturing individuals out of their nuclear families, both toward outside adult roles and into the formation of new nuclear social units. Lévi-Strauss does not attempt to look at these processes in terms of the psychological structures involved.

Turning to the psychological extension of this trend of analysis, Parsons, however, accepts Freud's broadened definition of eroticism (not direct physical sexual behavior) as essential to explaining the nature of affective ties within the primary family. In the early developmental stages, eroticism is not organized around genital gratification. Early eroticism is diffuse and more located in skin and oral regions. The human child, having experienced early body contact care over an extended period, sometimes finds it difficult to resolve the intense attachment that builds up toward the person playing the maternal role. This person also acts as an agent of the culture both in exercising socializing disciplines and in providing forms of essential need gratification. The socializing agent is in a position to frustrate the child, but to be effective, he or she must not lose control of the child's affectional involvement. Affective needs and periodic gratification form the motivation matrix in which increasingly disciplined socialization takes place. Parsons notes that erotic gratification is a particularly sensitive source of conditioning in the Pavlovian sense. Any direct sexual seduction in the childhood experience would be disruptive to general personality formation as would be passive experience of undue hostile and aggressive behavior. Parsons notes that it is important that the mother, as the earliest socializing agent, must have her own regressive sexual needs as well as her aggressive impulses under spontaneous control. This is so because she enters into a stronger erotic reciprocity with the child than does the father. If she cannot control her own regressive needs, either sexual or aggressive, the mother-child system may get stuck on one of the earlier psychosexual levels, or in some form of neurotic interaction hindering adult maturation. For instance, an overprotective mother, by over-reciprocating a child's dependency needs, may encourage him to an extent that she keeps the child from growing up. Her own needs may have her continue nurturant practices beyond the time that they are properly conducive to further psychosexual maturation. A hostile mother can cause avoidance behavior generalized to women harmful to the heterosexuality of both male and female children.

"Regression" might be seen then, from a social-structural sense as well as a psychological sense, as a slipping back into earlier social patterns on the part of the mother to seek gratification. Thus incestuous feelings, especially in a mother-son relationship, whether overtly genital or covert, diffuse, and unconscious, are an essential part of a social as well as a psychological inability to grow up. The social structural aspects of Parson's explanations relate incest taboos to hypothesized automatic operative sanctioning systems that move the individual toward proper adult status and role behavior. Psychological problems resulting from some form of culturally prevalent incomplete socialization may so occur within the primary family as to hinder the complete transmutation of the diffuse erotic dependent feelings of childhood into more focused genitalized adult heterosexual interests.

Unfortunately, Parsons's social structural explanation does not cover certain differences observed between culture groups. For example, Parsons is unable to be convincing when he discusses the latency period as a temporary repression of erotic needs for both sexes. The evidence from cross-cultural work well suggests that there are considerable differences in the degree of continuous random sexual play allowed during the prepubescent period. The relationship between this diffuse sexual play and the instituting of sexual taboos needs to be better elucidated since in these cultures such taboos are equally operative. Parsons's exposition does not undertake to explain taboos on sibling incest; it works much better in elucidating the nature of the mother-child relationship during early childhood.

What is missing in Parsons's theory is some further explanatory principle to include both the dynamics of the automatic repression found *in siblings* as well as in mother-child incest taboos. In my concept of affective dissonance, I start from the premise that it is the nature of the physiological structuring which underlies psychological patterning to maintain cognitive-affective harmony and to repress dissonant affective feelings, which could cause a disruption of a necessary intimate, dependent relationship. A conscious breakthrough of disruptive sexual fantasies would cause an overwhelming level of discomfort, tension, and internal conflict.

AMBIVALENCE AS A FORM OF AFFECTIVE DISSONANCE

An affective dissonance theory must further explore the relationship between the forms of repression that are involved in resolving dissonance between childhood and adult affectional ties, and interests and situations of emotional ambivalence felt toward the same person. Ambivalence usually refers to positive and negative emotions such as love and hate toward the same person. One emotion may slightly predominate and the other feeling is repressed with the expenditure of considerable energy. Ambivalent affectional expectations are not necessarily related to different levels of maturation, although this may well be, as in the instance where an adult son may experience a positive present relationship with a parent, but still be unconsciously resentful toward the parent as a former disciplinarian. He may indeed have displaced resentments about authority to other relationships while maintaining a positive conscious affiliation to the initial source of such resentments. In such a way he may resolve a potential affective dissonance. Affective dissonance is, therefore, involved in ambivalence, but is not limited to situations of ambivalence.

Affective dissonance does not of necessity involve the positive-negative affective polarity of ambivalence. In sexual matters, the dissonance may be between two positive feelings: one is directly sexual, the other more diffusely affectionate, that is, based on long familiarity in which sexual interest, if ever present, has been subordinated to other more diffuse general affectional bonds. The word "ambivalence" is inappropriate and does not apply to such situations in which sexual arousal would cause affective dissonance with other positively valenced attitudes. Ambivalence implies attitudes in which positive and negative valences are in some form of irresolution.

Ambivalence requires a positive-negative opposition, whereas affective dissonance includes also situations of dissonance related to possibly incompatible levels of maturation within the schemata of an individual involving similar emotions such as those found in erotic attachment. The dissonance may be in respect to reconciling levels of maturation or, as in an incest taboo, in conflict between a nongenitalized attachment and one involving genital arousal.

AFFECTIVE DISSONANCE AND THE MATURATION OF COGNITIVE SCHEMATA

The concept of affective dissonance is in accord with Piaget's theory of cognitive development. For example, Ulric Neisser (1962) discusses Piaget's theory of the development of cognitive schemata or organized perceptions as they integrate cognitive and affective states resulting from the assimilation of environmental stimuli. In their very development schemati cause loss of earlier memory. Neisser's analysis is a valuable modification of Freud's theory of repression as related to amnesia. It negates the idea that all amnesia results from repression and suggests rather that progressively developing emotional and cognitive patterns render more primitive the schemata no longer available as their elements are incorporated into more developed perceptions. Childhood incestuous feelings disappear when more mature genitalized sexual schemata develop. Some wishes, however, may remain as unresolved residues not accessible to consciousness. They are not consistent with developed self-concept.

For example, a male child's witnessing parental coitus, which occurs with some frequency in many cultures, is a passive experience that does not prepare him to take on the experience of active genital activity with the mother. Such experience usually takes place at a time of pregenital primacy in erotic organization and, therefore, is not necessarily "fixating." There is not, necessarily, traumatic rigidification leading to immature sexual functiong. Further maturation usually occurs so that infantile desires are replaced by more satisfactory active heterosexual objects in one's cognitive schemata.

There are many situations in which one cannot bring to consciousness feelings that would be disruptive to an ongoing day-by day pattern of intimate human needs and responses, whether intrafamilial or more general. That is to say, a sense of self in intimate relationships demands some degree of appropriate repression of inconsistency in maintaining a tolerable form of patterning.

One cannot at times attain some forms of cognitive objectivity because one cannot afford to experience the underlying affective dissonance that would result, simply because some well-established cognitive patterns conflict with one another. Primary family relationships are the most intense and affect arousing, being the least objectively perceived.

Affectional schemata develop over time. There is indeed "habituation," which comes to define strongly a close relationship. Such a relationship would be completely shattered by any errant erotic arousal. A deep, complex relationship would have to be totally reordered not only affectively but perceptually to accommodate the immediate urgency of sexual gratification. An individual's self-concept could be totally disrupted as could his perception of the other person. Then, too, habituation may dull a type of sexual arousal that depends on the excitement of strangeness—an exploratory element found characteristic in the sexual life of some individuals, at least. Knowledge of a person is dissonant with abrupt interest in a new sexual object; well established schemata leave very little accommodation for elements of surprise—or new experiences.

EXOGAMY AND PROJECTION

The more intensely intimate family roles are experienced, the less possible it is for dissonant sexual desires to break into conscious awareness. The early primary family experiences are the ones out of which all other *consistent* patterns related to human beings grow. As often discussed in psychoanalytic literature, the human psychic apparatus has the potential of splitting off conflictual affect-laden attitudes originating in response to the same person, and displacing them to different individuals. The human being also can project "evil" outside the social group so that either the primary group or some social group membership may be maintained more harmoniously. Sexual feelings are not "negative," but they too can be disruptive and are "transferred" or projected outside the immediate kin group. In this manner, "projection," as are other mental mechanisms, is called into play to resolve potentials for affective dissonance and helps explain some reasons for the psychological attraction of exogamous unions.

CULTURE-SPECIFIC PROBLEMS OF POTENCY RELATED TO AFFECTIVE DISSONANCE

A theory of affective dissonance, which at the same time concerns itself with how cognitive schemata are developed in the context of patterns of emotional consistency, is seen as supplementary to, rather than in conflict with, other features of psychoanalytic theory. It relates to what is described in psychoanalytic theory as forms of "transference" phenomena in sexual difficulties.

The fantasies that adults have of their childhood prepubescent sweethearts in Western culture are quite regressive and childish in tone. When strongly maintained, they represent fixations on childhood sexuality which may interfere with making a more mature shift of genitalized object cathexis to other adults. In other words, the underlying fixation on a regressive childhood eroticism can inhibit a more genitally organized adult sexual performance. Childhood liaisons are only very rarely actualized by marriage in adulthood. It is not only that individuals who are blood relatives and have intimate childhood associations are sanctioned away from adult liaisons, but that such indirectly or directly eroticized childhood companions, not related by kinship ties, are experienced as part of an affective configuration that cannot be integrated into adult heterosexual interests and obligations. Wolf's (1966) description of difficulties experienced in the marriages of Chinese women, who were adopted into a family as small girls explicitly for the purpose of marriage of one to the sons, demonstrates this process.

To illustrate further: cases of relative or complete impotency in marriage often involve a transference to the wife of sexualized attitudes held toward mother or sister. Individuals who have strong unconscious residual incestuous ties to a mother or sister can become disturbed in their potency with women who are cognitively equated on an unconscious level with a still sexually cathected childhood object.

In Japan, for example, there is characteristically a muted and infrequent sexual relationship between a man and his wife. The wife is culturally expected to take on a maternal role, progressively replacing her husband's mother. Many Japanese men find themselves more potent with female professional entertainers, on whom they do not depend for other forms of gratification, and for some a mistress becomes necessary for full genital satisfaction. I suggest also that the widespread appearance of the mistress in Latin American cultures may have some psychological basis beyond the usual explanation that it derives from the nonreciprocal sexual status relationship within the social structure. Mexican psychoanalysts report (personal communication) complex sexual disturbances between man and wife occurring after the birth of a child. The father finds himself unconsciously competing with his own child who is being gratified in his pregenital erotic relationship with the mother. The man cannot relate sexually in a positive way to his wife; therefore, interpersonal disharmony develops over unsatisfied wishes and the man takes another woman as a mistress. At the same time, the wife psychodynamically seems to retreat from genital interests in her husband and devotes herself with single-minded intensity to her infant.

THE PSYCHOCULTURAL PATTERNING OF DEVIANCE AS RELATED TO INCEST BEHAVIOR

There are individuals in all cultures who exhibit deviant behavior. That some few individuals do not develop the repressions found in most does not negate any psychological theory that has to encompass both normative and deviant patterns. The reasons for the breakthrough of deviant behavior can be varied. There may even be particular psychological or psychocultural regularities to explain certain types of incest when they occur occasionally.

When one examines peculiarities of the psychosexual history of individuals within a culture who commit sibling or parent-child incest, one finds that some cases, at least, can be explained because there was little direct, sustained, positive contact between father and daughter in early childhood. Isolated areas, such as the Ozarks of the United States, the northern Gaspé peninsula in French Canada, conduce to incestuous sexual liaisons. Some cases reported in the psychological literature citing life histories of prostitutes indicate a hostile, brutal father who forced incest on the daughter in a turbulent liaison. Such a relationship can remain sexual without becoming affectionate or positive, but the girl acquires a lifelong hostility toward men in general, and sexuality often becomes symbolically an exploitative relationship.

It is difficult for children who have experienced childhood incest to reconcile this experience with the normative heterosexual behavior of adults. There are unresolved dissonances in the experience of sexual behavior not occurring within socially sanctioned limits in a satisfactory way. Thus the psychological study of incest behavior becomes part of a more general approach to sexual psychopathology. It is not only a question of the individual, but how affectively and cognitively based self-consistencies are continually maintained in interaction with supporting or sanctioning social attitudes experienced primarily within the family.

Another deviant pattern found in reported incest cases in the psychoanalytic literature on pedophilia involves a passive, psychologically childlike father who, in effect, plays at a form of childhood sibling incest with his own or another child, while his wife symbolically represents a deceived adult. The girl's passive fantasies coincide with the childhood fantasies still dominanting the erotic life of the father who prefers sexual play with a nonthreatening child to that with a threatening adult. In some such cases, passive regressive fantasies on the part of a mother are also involved. These fantasies cannot as directly be realized by sexual congress with a man. There are instances reported where father-daughter incest, therefore, is unconsciously fostered by a mother as a means of achieving a vicarious experience of a childlike incestuous relationship with her own father.

The complexity of the human's capacity for vicarious experience in the imagination permits no simple direct explanations of the psychological states that occur in reported cases where an incest taboo is broken. An affective dissonance theory of incest, however, does not in any way suggest the inappropriatness of erotic feelings in a mother-child relationship. On the contrary, basic satisfaction of pregenital erotic experiences with the mother prepares the child for further psychosexual growth. It is only maturationally inappropriate genitalization of the relationship by the mother, either symbolically or indirectly, that results in aberrant psychosexual development.

Therapists working with delinquents in prison settings have reported (through personal communication) the frequent occurrence of sexualized fantasy concerning the mother that is relatively close to consciousness. In such cases, the mother is invariably very sexually active with several men. This suggests that a child's witnessing his mother's promiscuity results in a lesser repression of the adult mother's sexuality. The mother's frank sexuality is a continually stimulating reality to the growing baby. Even in such cases a son continues to demonstrate a need to maintain some level of repression. Moreover, it must be stressed that in such circumstances, the relative accessibility to consciousness of incestuous wishes is related also to the experienced degree of attachment to the mother and sense of rejection by her. The more giving the mother, or warm the relationship, even though she be sexually promiscuous, the more deeply repressed is the son's awareness of sexual interest toward her. That is, those young men who experience an essentially giving, nurturant, maternal relationship, display deeper repression of their incestuous fantasies, whereas those individuals who have not been rewarded or who have actually been rejected in the maternal relationship, have greater difficulty in repression and these sexual fantasies are more apt to come to the surface of consciousness. The consequent affective dissonance on the part of both mother and child would in most instances be so overwhelming as to be unbearable should an incestuous situation occur. Delinquent youth in most instances even go to great extremes to maintain an illusory affectively based "consistent" picture of a "giving" mother.

CONCLUSIONS

In summary, in developing a psychocultural theory using the concept of affective dissonance, both psychological and social structural forces must be considered in determining why a society inhibits or periodically allows for the appearance of unsanctioned in-

cest behavior. The data from Israel and Taiwan show the spontaneous development of sexual inhibitions in most children despite
the absence of social sanctions. While Parson's dual use of the concept of regression, as developed in the social structural theory of
Lévi-Strauss and in his adaptation of the psychoanalytic theory, is
a positive step forward, he, in effect, also recognized that the secret
of the incest taboo is not to be found in further analysis of social
structure per se.

The avoidance of affective dissonance helps explain the difficulty
experienced in reconciling the day-by-day, intimate affective sibling
associations of childhood, with consciously tolerable adult heterosexual interests. The cognitive schemata of the adult supercede
those carrying the experiences of childhood eroticism. Adult sexual
interests comprise schemata with an affective cognitive pattern of a
different nature than those formed around childhood affectional
associations.

The psychological mechanism of repression works very well in
most instances to prevent the direct appearance of incest behavior
within the primary family, but reference to that mechanism by itself tells us nothing. The reason for the incest taboo as an internal
force is to be found in further understanding of the nature of man's
affective structure as it develops in internally consistent patterns
and how infantile and adult sexual or erotic experiences are trans-
muted into adult froms of psychosexual maturation in such a way
that certain features of close relations may become affectively dissonant to the experience of sexual arousal or sexual interest. How
cathexis of objects occurs is suggested in psychoanalytic theory of
development, but the actual physiopsychological mechanisms operative in affective dissonances have not as yet been sufficiently explored either by considering them in terms of conditioning theory
or by direct recourse to concepts of ambivalence, transference, or
repression. I believe that a more unified approach combining theories of cognitive and affectional maturation await systematic exploration. Current generalizations in psychology about cognitive
dissonance have missed the point. Evidence from cultures that do
not become emotionally concerned about cognitive consistency
forces a more systematic reappraisal of *affective* dissonance in cross-
cultural comparative terms.

REFERENCES

MAJOR REFERENCES ON INCEST THEORY IN ANTHROPOLOGY

ABERLE, DAVID F., et al. 1963. The Incest Taboo and the Mating Patterns of Animals. *American Anthropologist* 65 (2):253–265.

BEACH, FRANK A. 1951. Instinctive Behavior: Reproductive Activities, *Handbook of Experimental Psychology* (S. S. Stevens, ed.). John Wiley and Sons.

BETTELHEIM, BRUNO. 1962. *Symbolic Wounds: Puberty Rites and the Envious Male.* Collier Books.

COULT, ALLAN. 1963. Causality and Cross-Sex Prohibitions. *American Anthropologist* 65 (2):266–277.

DE VOS, GEORGE A. 1975. The Dangers of Pure Theory In Social Anthropology. *Ethos* 3 (1):77–91.

DE VOS, GEORGE, and HIROSHI WAGATSUMA. 1966. *Japan's Invisible Race, Cast in Culture and Personality.* University of California Press.

DOUGLAS, MARY. 1966. *Purity and Danger: An Analysis of Concepts of Pollution and Taboo.* Praeger.

———. 1972. Self-Evidence, *Proceedings of the Royal Anthropological Institute of Great Britain and Ireland,* p. 27.

FESTINGER, LEON. 1957. *The Theory of Cognitive Dissonance.* Stanford University Press.

———. 1962. Cognitive Dissonance. *Scientific American* 207 (4):93–102.

FOX, J. ROBIN. 1962. Sibling Incest. *British Journal of Sociology* 13:128–150.

FREUD, SIGMUND. 1950. *Totem and Taboo* (James Strachey, trans.). Routledge and Kegan Paul.

HARLOW, H. F. 1964. Early Social Deprivation and Later Behavior in the Monkey. *Unfinished Tasks in the Behavioral Sciences* (A. Abrams, et al., eds.), pp. 154–173. Williams & Wilkins.

The Holy Bible. 1925. *Leviticus.* World Publishing Company.

HOMANS, GEORGE C., and DAVID M. SCHNEIDER. 1955. *Marriage, Authority, and Final Causes.* The Free Press.

LÉVI-STRAUSS, CLAUDE. 1956. The Family, *Man, Culture and Society* (H. L. Shapiro, ed.). Oxford University Press.

———. 1963. *Totemism.* Beacon.

———. 1969a. *The Elementary Structures of Kinship.* Beacon.

———. 1969b. *The Raw and the Cooked.* Harper and Row.

MALINOWSKI, BRONISLAW. 1929. *Sexual Life of Savages.* G. Routledge and Sons.

90 ▪ GEORGE A. DE VOS

MONEY-KYRLE, ROGER ERNIE. 1968. *The Meaning of Sacrifice*. Johnson reprint.

MURDOCK, GEORGE PETER. 1949. *Social Structure*. Macmillan Co.

NEISSER, ULRIC. 1962. Culture and Cognitive Discontinuity, The Anthropological Society of Washington, *Anthropology and Human Behavior*, pp. 54–71.

PARSONS, TALCOTT. 1954. The Incest Taboo in Relation to Social Structure and the Socialization of the Child. *British Journal of Sociology* 5:102–115.

———. 1955. Family Structure and the Socialization of the Child, *Family, Socialization and Interaction Process* (T. Parsons and R. F. Bales, eds.). The Free Press.

PIAGET, JEAN. 1930. *The Child's Concept of Physical Causality*. Kegan Paul.

———. 1954. *The Construction of Reality in the Child*. Basic Books.

RADCLIFFE-BROWN, A. F. and DARYLL FORDE, eds. 1950. *African Systems of Kinship and Marriage*. Oxford University Press.

SCHWARTZ, THEODORE. 1975a. Cargo Cult; A Melanesian Religious Type Response to Culture Contact, *Responses To Change* (George De Vos, ed.). Van Nostrand.

———. 1975b. Cultural Totemism, *Ethnic Identity: Cultural Continuities and Change* (George De Vos and Lola Romanucci-Ross, eds.), pp. 106–132. Mayfield Publishing Co.

SLATER, M. K. 1959. Ecological Factors in the Origin of Incest. *American Anthropologist* 61:1042–1059.

SPIRO, MELFORD E. 1954. Is the American Family Universal? *American Anthropologist* 56:839–846.

———. 1958. *Children of the Kibbutz*. Harvard University Press.

TALMON, YONINA. 1964. Mate selection in Collective Settlements. *American Sociological Review* 29:491–508.

WARNER, W. LLOYD. 1937. *A Black Civilization. A Social Study of an Australian Tribe*. Harper.

WEINBERG, KIRSON S. 1963. *Incest Behavior*. Citadel Press.

WESTERMARCK, EDWARD. 1921. *The History of Human Marriage*. Macmillan and Co.

WOLF, ARTHUR. 1966. Childhood Association, Sexual Attraction and the Incest Taboo: A Chinese Case. *American Anthropologist* 68:883–898.

WOLFF, PETER. 1960. *The Developmental Psychologies of Jean Piaget and Psychoanalysis*. International Universities Press.

Aloofness and Intimacy of Husbands and Wives:

A Cross-Cultural Study

JOHN W. M. WHITING and BEATRICE B. WHITING

Males and females—their temperaments, their relationship to one another, and their relative status—have been of major interest to Margaret Mead. In *Sex and Temperament* (1935) and later in *Male and Female* (1949) she convincingly demonstrated the importance of culture in determining similarities and differences in the behavioral styles of men and women of different societies. Her research has always been comparative but based on her own intensive field research in other cultures. We intend in this essay to test some of the hypotheses that she has generated over the years, as well as some of our own, regarding the male and female roles. Ethnographic reports on a world sample of cultures provide our data. Since these data were collected by ethnographers with other interests, our measures cannot be as subtle as those used by Margaret Mead; but we have tried to choose measures that are both valid and meaningful.

JOHN W. M. WHITING is professor of social anthropology in the Departments of Anthropology and Social Relations at Harvard University.
BEATRICE B. WHITING is professor of education and anthropology in the Department of Human Development, Harvard School of Education, at Harvard Unisity.

We have chosen the relationship between husband and wife as our focus in studying males and females. We do this because the family and family life are described in the ethnographic literature on most societies and thus comparable data are likely to be available. More important, however, is that a husband and wife are also father and mother to their children, and their relationship to one another is a crucial feature of the learning environments that shape the behavior of men and women of the next generation.

Again, partly for practical and partly for theoretical reasons, we have chosen to use as our measure whether or not a married couple ordinarily sleep in the same bedroom. Since both the floor plan of houses and the occupants of a household are described, it is not difficult to determine husband and wife living arrangements with a minimum of inference and with reasonably high reliability. Theoretically, since young children almost universally sleep in the same bedroom as their mother, the presence or absence of the father in this intimate space should have a strong influence on their conception of the nature of males and females.

METHODOLOGY

The standard cross-cultural sample (Murdock and White 1969) was chosen as the basis for testing our hypothesis. This set of 186 cultures was carefully chosen to maximize the independence of societies and to represent reasonably the languages, subsistence levels, and types of social organization of the known cultures of the world. Judgments as to rooming arrangements as well as to numerous other variables to be used in this study were available on a substantial number of societies in this sample.

In determining whether or not husband and wife were roommates, a combination of codes were used: the Palfrey House code of percent polygyny and rooming arrangements,[1] the Barry and Paxson code (1971) on sleeping proximity, and the Murdock and Wilson code (1972) on household composition.

Polygynous societies usually have alternative rooming patterns. In such societies the first wife ordinarily lives for some time monog-

1. These judgments were made by the staff of the Laboratory of Human Development (Palfrey House) and were used for a study of residence patterns (Whiting and D'Andrade 1959) and of initiation rites (Whiting 1964). The judgments were made by Roy D'Andrade, David Beswick, and Emily Huntington.

amously with her husband before he takes a second wife. Furthermore, it is rare, even in societies where polygyny is highly valued,
for every man in the course of his marital history to have a second
wife. If, as is often the case, husband and wife share a bedroom as
long as they are monogamous but sleep apart if they are polygynous, such a society could be classified in either the rooming apart
or rooming together category. For this study we have arbitrarily
chosen the rooming arrangement reported for the monogamous alternative if less than 30% of the families are polygynous. If, however, more than 30% are polygynous, the polygynous alternative
was used to classify the culture. The decision was made from judgments by the Palfrey House staff as to husband and wife rooming
arrangements both for the monogamous and for the polygynous
alternatives.

Since this study focuses on the effect of rooming arrangements
upon the child, the female-based family rather than the male-based
family was used to calculate the percent of polygyny. Two women
married to the same man would constitute two female-based polygynous families but only one male-based polygynous family. The
use of the married women as a base yields a higher percentage value
of polygyny than the use of the male head of household as a base.
This is particularly true in societies in which having more than one
wife is a privilege limited to a few chiefs. Such is the case for the
Trobriands where only 3% of the adult males are polygynously
married but 39% of the females between 15 and 45 years of age are
members of a polygynous family. For purposes of this study it is
even more significant that more than a third of the children are
brought up in pologynous families.

Barry and Paxson coded "the nighttime sleeping proximity of
mother and father to infant" (1971:467, col. 1). Their code required evidence as to the whereabouts of the infant as well as the
mother and father; in contrast, the Palfrey House code made separate judgments for each diad. The Palfrey House code has been used
for overlapping cases. Of the 76 societies for which there were scores
by both teams, there was 92% agreement as to whether or not a
husband and wife sleep in the same room. This degree of intercoder reliability seemed quite acceptable; therefore, the Barry and
Paxson coding was used for those societies of the standard sample
not coded by the Palfrey House staff. Finally, 9 cases were not rated

by either the Palfrey House staff or Barry and Paxson but were rated by Murdock and Wilson (1972) as having households in which husbands and wives sleep apart.[2]

The resulting number of coded societies then totals 159. They are distributed over the world as follows: Africa 40, Eurasia 34, Insular Pacific 25, North America 32, and South America 28.

Examples of rooming arrangements reported for the sample will serve to elucidate the code. A familiar pattern for modern industrial societies but one that is also found in many of the simple societies such as the Copper Eskimo is described by Jenness: among these Eskimos, "every inmate has . . . a definite place on the sleeping platform. The woman sleeps in the corner beside her lamp, and the little children lie between her and her husband. Outside of him sleep the older children and any guest whom they may happen to entertain (1923:85). This common arrangement, which was described for 92 societies (57% of the sample), occurs in societies with monogamy or limited polygyny in which members of the nuclear family share a bedroom.

Although co-wives do not ordinarily sleep in the same bedroom, this does sometimes occur. There are 20 examples of this arrangement in our sample (12%). The Kwoma of New Guinea (J. Whiting 1941) are a society in which 55% of adult females are polygynously married. Their houses are rectangular gabled structures with thatched roofs and sides. At one end there is an open porch that serves as kitchen, dining room, and parlor. At the other end there is a room with a small door and no windows that serves as a bedroom for a man, his wives, and their children. The husband sleeps on a raised platform. His wives and the children sleep on mats on the earthen floor.

As suggested above, it is more common for each wife in polygynous families to have her own bedroom. The husband may room with each wife in turn, he may have a bedroom of his own, he may sleep in a hut with his older sons, or he may sleep in a men's clubhouse. It is not unusual for several of these patterns to occur in the same society. The Kikuyu of Kenya have a sequence of rooming arrangements that is typical for many of the societies in subsaharan Africa (B. Whiting Field Notes 1972). When he is first married, a man builds a small wattle and daub house with a pyramidal

2. Other categories in the Murdock-Wilson code could not be used because of the ambiguity between household and bedroom.

thatched roof. He ordinarily shares this with his wife until she has born a second child. At this point he feels the bedroom is too congested and he sets about building a second house that, if he can afford the bride price, he shares with a second wife until he is displaced by her children. By this time the sons of his first wife may be old enough—6 or 7—to leave their mother's bedroom. Then the father builds a third hut that he shares with his sons.

Societies with more than 30% female-based polygyny in which co-wives sleep in separate bedrooms were classed as rooming apart, whether the husband rotates, has a hut of his own, or sleeps in the men's clubhouse. There are 40 societies (24%) in our sample that fall in this category.

Finally, there are a small number of monogamous or limited polygynous societies in which husband and wife have separate sleeping quarters. Nine of the societies (5%) in our sample are reported to have this pattern. The Rajput of Khalapur who have rooming arrangements similar to the Senapur of our sample serve to illustrate this arrangement. "In Khalapur a man generally slept in the men's quarters which he shared with his brothers and other male relatives. This was built near the cattle corral so that he could guard his livestock against theft and predation." It is here also that he spends most of his leisure time chatting and gossiping with other men. Although the men sometimes eat in the women's house, they eat in private rather than with their wives and children and more commonly they eat in the men's quarters. "The dual household arrangement thus effectively separates the men from the women and young children and prevents an intimate relationship between these two groups" (Whiting and Whiting 1975).

ROOMING APART AND POLYGYNY

It is obvious from our coding rules that there will be a strong positive association between rooming apart and polygyny. It would be wrong to assume, however, that polygyny can be taken as an index of rooming apart. Such an assumption would misclassify two of the categories described above—the 20 polygynous societies in which co-wives and their husband share a bedroom and the 9 societies with monogamy or limited polygyny where husbands and wives have separate sleeping quarters. The former have been classified as husband and wife rooming together, the latter as husband and wife rooming apart.

ROOMING ARRANGEMENTS AND HUSBAND-WIFE INTIMACY

In many parts of the world the monogamous nuclear family in which the husband and wife room together is, as a consequence of modernization, replacing traditional domestic arrangements. This is particularly true in societies where polygyny and rooming apart is traditional. In a study of such change among the Yoruba of Nigeria, Robert LeVine, Nancy Klein, and Constance Owen (1967) compared a traditional with an elite group of fathers. "The traditional family tends to be patrilocal, polygynous, and embedded in a residentially localized extended kin group; the elite have isolated, nuclear, monogamous families" (1967:238). LeVine interviewed ten fathers from each group with regard to their relation to their wives and family and found striking differences. Nine of the ten men from the traditional group said they never eat with their wives and children, whereas only one of the ten men from the elite group made this claim. Nine of the men of the elite group said that they had fed or diapered their infants, whereas only two men of the traditional group reported doing so. Finally, all ten men of the traditional group thought that it was not a good idea for a man to be present at childbirth whereas only four of the elite group reported this attitude. All of these differences are statistically significant.

In our study of the children of six cultures (Whiting and Whiting 1975) we found similar contrast. Fathers in the four rooming together cultures eat with their family, interact more with their children, and are more likely to attend their wives in childbirth than are the two societies in which husbands and wives room apart.

To discover whether these findings are generally true, we tested them on our cross-cultural sample. A judgment on eating arrangement was made by the Palfrey House staff on 77 societies in our sample and it was found that in a significant number of societies men and women who room together eat together. In 43 of the 51 (84%) cultures where the husband and wife are roommates, a married man ordinarily eats with his wife and family; whereas this pattern occurs in only 7 of the 26 cultures where husband and wife room apart. The phi value of this association is .57 (p < .001).

In many societies there are spaces set apart that are designated for men's use. The "house tamberan" of New Guinea—forbidden to women, the salaam of the Middle East and North Africa, the man's sleeping platforms of North India, and the men's huts in subsaharan Africa provide places where men can gather to gossip with other men and, in some cases, also eat and sleep. Men may attend these places regularly or only occasionally. We were interested in discovering whether men who share rooms with their wives are less likely to spend time in exclusively men's groups than are those who room apart. Scores on the presence or absence of these special areas designated for men were made by the Palfrey House staff on 55 of the societies in our sample. Exclusive men's "houses" are present in 18 of the 25 (72%) societies where husbands and wives sleep apart but in only 12 of the 36 societies (33%) where they are roommates. The phi value of the association is .38 (p < .009).

Another estimate of the domestic behavior expected of a husband and father is provided by Barry and Paxson. One of their scales entitled "Role of Father" (1971: 472, col. 14) estimates the amount of interaction between a father and his children. Their five-point scale is so dichotomized that societies scored as "regular, close relationship, or companionship" and "frequent close proximity" were given a positive value while those scoring "occasional," "rare," and "no" close proximity were given a negative value. Separate judgments were made for father-infant and father-child relationship but they were so highly correlated that to present them both would be redundant. The relation of a father to his children during infancy was chosen as the variable to relate to the rooming arrangements score. Fathers have a close relationship with their infants in slightly more than half (26 of 49) of the societies in which husband and wife are roommates but in only one quarter (5 of 20) of the societies in which a married couple sleeps apart. The phi value of this association is .27 (p < .02).

Whether or not a husband is expected to be in attendance when his wife is giving birth serves as another available measure of husband-wife relations. In some societies it is considered dangerous to the woman, in others polluting to the man, for him to be present when his wife is in labor. By contrast, in other societies the husband is expected to be present and even to help deliver the baby. Ratings were made on this variable by the Palfrey House staff on 44 societies in the sample. The husband is permitted to be present in 2 of the 23 societies in which husband and wife sleep in separate rooms and in 11 of the 34 societies in which they room together. The phi value of this relationship is .28 (p < .04).

The condoning of wife beating provides another index of the

relation between husband and wife. Palfrey House ratings on 39 overlapping cases showed no association between wife beating and rooming arrangements. It is associated rather with independent versus extended households. Wife beating tends not to occur in the latter household type which apparently means that there is safety in numbers. Patricia Draper (in press) has presented evidence corroborating this in her discussion of the increase in the frequency of wife beating among the !Kung Bushmen when they move out of their closely spaced camp groups and settle in nuclear households near Herero villages.

Taken together there seem to be two patterns governing the relationship of a man to his wife and children—one in which he is intimate and the other in which he is aloof. In the former he eats and sleeps with his wife and children, gossips with them at the evening meal, helps his wife care for their infant children, and is present and helps her at childbirth. In other words, he is highly involved in the domestic life of his family. In the societies in which the man stays aloof from his wife and children and uninvolved in domestic affairs, he spends his leisure time gossiping with other men and usually eats and sleeps with them as well. He seldom helps his wife with infant care and stays away from his wife while she is giving birth.

Since all of the above measures were available on only a limited number of societies in the sample, it was not expedient to construct an aloofness-intimacy scale. Instead the rooming arrangement score was taken as an index of such a scale.

ASSOCIATION OF HUSBAND AND WIFE ROOMING ARRANGEMENTS WITH ENVIRONMENTAL VARIABLES

The question arose in our minds as to why in some societies husbands and wives are roommates and are more intimate and domestic while in other societies husbands remain more aloof. Practical considerations seem one obvious explanation. Since in those societies where husband and wife room apart two apartments are required, one would expect that for purely economic reasons rooming together would be generally preferred. In fact, 70% of our sample room together. An additional fact in support of the economy hypothesis is that 36 of the 43 societies in which a husband and wife have separate bedrooms are situated in tropical climates where heating is not a problem and the extra sleeping space generally consists of a simply constructed thatched hut.

But pragmatics explains neither why 25% of the societies do build at least two bedrooms for each married couple nor why there are more than 40 societies (58%) in tropical climates that do not bother to build separate sleeping quarters. In other words, economy explains some but only a part of the variance.

The permanency of residence seems to be another important factor. If a society is nomadic or seminomadic, especially if materials for housing have to be transported, building two houses instead of one evidently poses a problem that is usually avoided. Only 10 of the 63 societies of our sample (16%) that are nomadic or seminomadic (coded B, S, or T in column 1, Murdock and Wilson 1972) have separate bedrooms for husband and wife; whereas 38 of the 93 societies (41%) with permanent settlements (coded P or I by Murdock and Wilson) have such a rooming arrangement. The phi value for this association is .27 (p < .001).

Before considering other functional explanations for rooming arrangements, the possibility that they are the result of historical process should be explored. To do this the distribution of the two types of rooming arrangements have been plotted on regional maps (see appendix, maps 1–6). If, for reasons to be presented later, it is assumed that the arrangement whereby a married couple room apart is a cultural invention that occurred relatively late in the history of mankind, it would be expected that their distribution would show clusters indicating where the pattern might have been invented and then spread by diffusion or migration. It can be seen from the maps that such clusters do indeed occur. There is a large one in subsaharan Africa, one in India, one in Melanesia and New Guinea, and one in the northeastern part of South America. In addition to these four clusters, there are six isolated societies in which husband and wife room apart. They are highland Gheg of Albania, the Rwala Bedouins of Arabia, the Chukchee of Siberia, the Yurok and Pomo of California, and the Mapuche of Chile.

Even the most avid historical determinist would have to admit that the pattern of husband and wife sleeping apart was invented more than once. The assumption that the Ghegs, Rwala Bedouins, and the clusters in Africa and India all were historically connected would not account for the appearance of this pattern among the

Chukchee, the Yurok and Pomo, the cluster in South America, or the Mapuche. This suggests at least five independent inventions and still leaves the functional question unanswered. Can the conditions for such an invention be specified? Can it be explained why the invention spread widely in some parts of the world and remained isolated instances in others?

An explanation can be sought at two levels—the sociocultural and the psychological. We propose that husbands and wives will room apart in those societies where warriors are needed to protect property and that rooming apart has the psychological effect of producing hyperaggressive males.

Before exploring the sociocultural conditions that produce the need for warriors, it is expedient to detail the psychological consequences of contrasting rooming arrangements. In her brilliant chapter in *Male and Female* on "Womb-Envying Patterns," Margaret Mead laid the groundwork for the psychological hypothesis that we have adopted. Her description of the Iatmul, a society situated on the banks of the Sepik River in New Guinea, illustrates her concept of womb-envying patterns. This society, though not in our sample, would be classified as rooming apart. Although she does not indicate where husbands and wives sleep, she reports that there are several small men's houses in each village as well as "one large men's house or more, built with the effort of several clans" which is taboo to women and in which "all the important events of the men's elaborate ritual, war making, and debating go on" (1949: 93–94). She describes the little boys as "surprisingly feminine, willowy, giving very little premonition of the bombast and high, headstrong behavior that will characterize them as adults. Their identification has been, inevitably, first with women" (1949:95). Later they are initiated into the men's cult where they are taught to "depend for their sense of manhood on a phantasy structure of bamboo flutes, played within leaf hedges imitating man made wombs. . . . [There men] are not peaceful shepherds but bold fierce head hunters . . . capable of magnificent anger" (1949:103–104). The Iatmul, as Mead describes them, exemplifies what we have called sex identity conflict. This hypothesis is derived from Freud's theory of the mechanisms of defense. It holds that a boy who is brought up in a household in which his mother seems to control all the resources will envy her status, covertly practice her role, and as a consequence develop what we have called a feminine optative identity. If, when he grows up, he discovers that his childhood view of the relative power of males and females was distorted and that in other than the domestic sphere men rather than women control resources, he is placed in a dilemma—do I want to be female or male? This sex identity conflict, the theory holds, can be resolved by behaving in a hypermasculine manner. Furthermore, the greater the contrast between the perception of the relative power of men and women in the domestic sphere and in the sphere of economics and politics, the stronger will be the conflict and the more elaborate the defensive solution.[3]

That sex identity conflict produces hyperaggressive males has been shown in several studies. The relatively high rate of murder and assault in the two father-aloof societies in our study of six cultures (Whiting and Whiting 1975) was interpreted as partially determined by sex identity conflict. This interpretation is further supported because the children in these two cultures behave in a more aggressive-authoritarian and a less intimate-sociable manner than children of comparable sex and age in the other four cultures where their mothers and fathers sleep in the same bedroom.

In a cross-cultural study of the antecedents of crime, Bacon, Child, and Barry (1963) reported a significant association between personal crime and mother-child households. There was no association between the composition of the household and theft. Since their definition of personal crime included murder, assault, and witchcraft, which they interpreted as the intent to murder by magical means, their finding also supports the hypothesis that aloofness between husband and wife is positively related to aggressiveness. Only 22 of their societies overlapped with the sample used in this study. The personal crime score correlated positively ($r = .21$) but not significantly with the rooming apart score.

Another finding that supports the major hypothesis of this study is that aloofness between husband and wife is associated with warlikeness. Polygynous societies are more likely to place a high value on military glory than are societies with other household types (J.

3. Studies supporting the sex-identity conflict hypothesis include D'Andrade 1973, Longabaugh 1973, Carlsmith 1973, Harrington 1970, Munroe, Munroe, and Whiting 1973, Herzog 1973, Munroe and Munroe 1973, Burton and Whiting 1961, and B. Whiting 1965.

Whiting 1969). These findings are based on a scale of military glory developed by Slater and Slater (1965). In this scale, items indicating a high value placed on military glory included seeking death in battle, a belief that warfare is the principle road to worldly glory, and that military virtues such as valor, recklessness, and fighting skill are important. The association of this scale with polygyny (phi $= .28$, $p < .01$) was interpreted as supporting the sex identity conflict hypothesis. The association between the military glory score and rooming arrangements on the 34 overlapping cases was positive ($r = .21$) but not statistically significant.

Another consequence of rooming apart is of interest. Whiting and D'Andrade (1959) found on a cross-cultural sample of 47 societies no instance of an adolescent boy sharing the bedroom with his mother and sisters when his father and mother room apart; whereas he does sleep in the same bedroom in more than half the societies in which his mother and father room together. This finding was interpreted as a response to incest taboos. It is also important that the young man in rooming apart societies usually moves in with his father and older brothers, or enters a bachelor group and lives with them. The Masai "Morans" (junior warriors) are an example of such an arrangement. They move into a "manyatta" (special living quarters for young men) and spend their time protecting the family herds and making retaliatory rustling raids on the herds of neighboring tribes. The rooming apart pattern thus is conducive to the formation of "fraternal interest groups" which have been shown by recent studies to be associated with feuding (Van Velsen and Van Wetering 1960, Otterbein 1970, Ember 1974, and Divale 1974).

That the practice of sleeping apart is associated with a high value placed on military glory, with hyperaggressive males, and with "fraternal interest groups" lends support to the hypothesis that the custom may have been invented and have diffused as a concomitant of the need for warriors, which in turn may be related to the presence or importance of a substantial capital investment that needs to be protected. If this assumption is correct, then the husband aloof pattern should occur more commonly among farmers and herdsmen than among hunters, gatherers, and fishermen since the former have more property to protect. Herds and gardens involve a greater capital investment than a foraging terrain or fishing grounds.

To test the above hypothesis the ratings made by Murdock and White (1969) as to the major base of subsistence were used. The results are presented in table 1. As can be seen, the hypothesis is confirmed. Only one gathering society (the Pomo of California) and two fishing societies (the Yurok of California and the Callinago of the Caribbean) have the pattern of rooming apart. If our interpretation is correct, the remaining 38 societies have little need to train their sons to be warriors.

TABLE 1
THE ASSOCIATION BETWEEN SUBSISTENCE TYPE
AND HUSBAND AND WIFE ROOMING ARRANGEMENTS

Capital investment	Husband-Wife Rooming arrangements		Percent apart
	Together	Apart	
Low			
Hunting	12	0	0
Gathering	13	1	7
Fishing	14	2	12.5
High			
Herding	7	6	43
Horticulture	10	3	23
Shifting Agriculture	26	19	42
Advanced Agriculture	22	16	42
phi = .156, p < .001*			

* Association between low vs. high capital investment and rooming together vs. rooming apart.

Husbands and wives sleep apart in 6 of the 14 herding societies. All of these societies are either nomadic or seminomadic, which should make such an arrangement less probable.

The interaction between climate and herding as a determinant of rooming arrangements is of interest. Of the 6 herding societies situated in the tropics, all but 1, the Tuareg of North Africa, have a rooming apart pattern, whereas of the 8 herding societies situated in colder climates, only one—the Chukchee of Siberia—have this pattern.

That only 3 of the 13 societies practicing horticulture have the sleeping apart pattern requires some comment. All save one of the societies with this type of subsistence in the sample are situated in the insular Pacific. Husbands and wives sleep apart in none of the 8 societies that are on small islands of which they are in sole possession. The sleeping apart pattern is present in 2 of the 4 horticulture societies situated in the larger islands of New Guinea and Melanesia which are occupied by two or more groups. Although inter-island raiding certainly occurred between the occupants of the small islands in Polynesia and Micronesia, their insularity, if our hypothesis is correct, may have served as a protection, but this is a posthoc interpretation.

Perusal of the list of societies coded as having agriculture, either of a simple or advanced nature, as a subsistence base is also enlightening. Many of these are American Indian groups who also depend to a large extent upon hunting and gathering, have seminomadic settlement patterns and, of course, dwell in a cold climate. In none of the 9 societies that fit this pattern do the husband and wife sleep apart.

Also in the lists of agricultural societies are those complex stratified societies that have developed a constabulary and/or a professional army as an alternative means of protecting property. If our hypothesis is correct, husbands and wives should room together in these societies. To test this hypothesis the scale of cultural complexity developed by Murdock and Provost (1973)[4] was used. Any society receiving a score greater than 30 on their 40-point composite scale of complexity was considered complex. Of the 21 societies in our sample rated as complex by this criterion, only 2, the Hausa of northern Nigeria and the Senapur of north India have the sleeping apart pattern.

The relationship between rooming arrangements, subsistence patterns, and cultural complexity for the five major regions of the world is summarized in table 2. As can be seen, husbands and wives seldom sleep in different bedrooms except in middle level societies. Of the 48 societies with such a rooming arrangement, only 3 occur with a hunting, gathering, or fishing economy, and only 2 occur where the societies are judged to be at a high level of complexity. It is also clear from table 2 that rooming apart is most likely to occur in Africa where there is the greatest concentration of societies at the middle level of development. The association is in the predicted direction for all the regions with the exception of North America, although it only reaches statistical significance for Africa ($p < .001$) and Eurasia ($p < .05$).

---

4. This scale represents the sum of the following ten 4-point scales for which 4 represents the most complex value: writing and records, fixity of residence, agriculture, urbanization, technological specialization, land transport, money, density of population, political integration, and social stratification.

TABLE 2
THE DISTRIBUTION OF SUBSISTENCE TYPES BY REGION

	Simple		Middle level		Complex		% Middle Level	% Apart	phi*
	Together	Apart	Together	Apart	Together	Apart			
Africa	4	0	5	27	3	1	80%	70%	.33 (p < .001)
Eurasia	6	0	13	7	12	1	51%	20%	.13 (p < .05)
Oceania	2	0	14	5	2	0	82%	22%	.06 (n.s.)
North America	25	2	2	0	1	0	10%	6%	−.01 (n.s.)
South America	10	1	10	4	1	0	54%	19%	.06 (n.s.)

N = 159.

* The association between middle level vs. simple and complex and rooming together vs. apart.

If one assumes from the above evidence that rooming apart occurred relatively late in the history of mankind, it is interesting to speculate as to possible mechanisms that might have led to its invention. First, it is unlikely that there were in the distant past ethnopsychologists who understood the hypermasculine defensive syndrome. It also seems unlikely that the knowledge that better warriors could be produced by adopting the rooming apart pattern was discovered entirely by blind trial and error. The sexual division of labor practiced by middle level societies today suggests a possible mechanism. Transhumant herdsmen such as the Samburu (J. Whiting Field Notes 1968) leave the women, young children, calves, and a few milking cows in high country during the dry season while the men and junior warriors take the rest of the herd into the lowlands. It is in the lowlands that conflict with neighboring tribes occurs. Herds must be protected from rustling raids and counter raids must be carried out. The Samburu believe that they would be considerably hampered in these activities if they had to protect their families as well as their herds. Middle level gardeners also leave their wives and children behind when they are acting as sentinels or carrying out retaliatory raids.

The widespread belief that contact with women is dangerous or weakening for a warrior before battle is another mechanism that may have induced those middle level societies who most frequently engaged in war to adopt the rooming apart pattern.

The increase in polygyny with agriculture may be another reason for the rooming apart pattern in middle level societies. In rudimentary agriculture, especially when it was introduced as an adjunct to herding, women are the main gardeners. When women play an important role in gardening and agricultural products are an essential part of the diet, it is expedient for a man to marry more than one wife and the rooming apart pattern is likely to be adopted.

It is our interpretation of history that when, as a consequence of transhumance, sentinel duty, and the sex taboo on warriors before going to battle, the rooming apart pattern was adopted, it had unanticipated consequences of inducing sex identity conflict in the sons—a result that was adaptive as long as all young men in each generation had to become warriors.

That the rooming apart pattern was given up when the culture became sufficiently complex also needs to be explained. One interpretation is that rooming together is the most convenient form for family life and it will be assumed when the need for rooming apart is no longer present. Another possible explanation is that in middle level agricultural societies women rather than men are likely to be chiefly involved in gardening. This makes polygyny advantageous and increases the likelihood of rooming apart. With the advent of the plow, which is utilized by all of the complex societies of our sample except the Hausa, men rather than women take over the responsibility for food production and polygyny loses its advantage. Again it is only the Hausa among the complex societies of our sample where more than 30% of the families are polygynous. Such a decrease in the utility of polygyny could be another mechanism that might impell a reversion to monogamy. The effect of modernization in East Africa as well as many other parts of the world clearly attests to the shift toward monogamy and rooming together.

In sum, then, it is seldom customary for husbands and wives to room apart. They do so only under special circumstances: when the climate is benign and, as a consequence, building extra bedrooms is not very costly; when they live a settled life and thus do not have to move camp frequently; and when they have a substantial capital investment to protect and inadequate help from the state.

The production of junior warriors, however, is not the only or perhaps even the most important consequence of a husband and wife sleeping in separate bedrooms. From our evidence it is probable that the husband who does not sleep with his wife remains aloof from her and the children in other spheres of domestic life. It is likely that he does not eat with them, that he does not help with the care of young children, that he does not help his wife give birth. It is also probable that he spends most of his time in the company of other men in some space that is not frequented by women. This aloofness is also transmitted to children. The social behavior of children brought up in cultures with the rooming apart pattern is less intimate and more aggressive than that of children brought up in cultures in which the fathers are more involved in domestic affairs.

REFERENCES

BACON, MARGARET K., IRVIN L. CHILD, and HERBERT BARRY, III. 1963. A Cross-Cultural Study of Correlates of Crime. *Journal of Abnormal and Social Psychology* 66:291–300.

BARRY, HERBERT, and LEONORA PAXSON. 1971. Infancy and Early Childhood: Cross-Cultural Codes 2. *Ethnology* 10:466–508.

BURTON, ROGER V., and JOHN W. M. WHITING. 1961. The Absent Father and Cross-Sex Identity. *Merrill-Palmer Quarterly of Behavior and Development* 7:85–95.

CARLSMITH, LYN. 1973. Some Personality Characteristics of Boys Separated from Their Fathers During World War II. *Ethos* 1:466–477.

D'ANDRADE, ROY G. 1973. Father Absence, Identification, and Identity. *Ethos* 1:440–455.

DIVALE, WILLIAM TULIO. 1974. Migration, External Warfare, and Matrilocal Residence. *Behavior Science Research* 9:75–134.

DRAPER, PATRICIA. In press. !Kung Women: Contrasts in Sexual Egalitarianism in the Foraging and Sedentary Context, *Toward an Anthropology of Women* (Rayna Reiter, ed.). Monthly Review Press.

EMBER, CAROL R. 1974. An Evaluation of Alternative Theories of Matrilocal Versus Patrilocal Residence. *Behavioral Science Research* 9:135–150.

HARRINGTON, CHARLES. 1970. *Errors in Sex-Role Behavior in Teen-Age Boys.* Teachers College Press.

HERZOG, JOHN D. 1973. Initiation and High School in the Development of Kikuyu Youth's Self-Concept. *Ethos* 1 (4):478–489.

JENNESS, DIAMOND. 1923. Physical Characteristics of the Copper Eskimos. *Report of the Canadian Arctic Expedition 1913–18*, vol. 12, pt. B. F. A. Acland.

LeVINE, ROBERT A., NANCY H. KLEIN, and CONSTANCE R. OWEN. 1967. Father-Child Relationships and Changing Life-Styles in Ibadan, Nigeria, *The City in Modern Africa* (H. Milner, ed.). Praeger.

LONGABAUGH, RICHARD. 1973. Mother Behavior as a Variable Moderating the Effects of Father Absence. *Ethos* 4:456–465.

MEAD, MARGARET. 1935. *Sex and Temperament.* William Morrow & Co.

———. 1949. *Male and Female.* William Morrow and Co.

MUNROE, ROBERT L., and RUTH H. MUNROE. 1973. Psychological Interpretation of Male Initiation Rites: The Case of Male Pregnancy Symptoms. *Ethos* 1:490–498.

MUNROE, ROBERT L., RUTH H. MUNROE, and JOHN W. M. WHITING. 1973. The Couvade: A Psychological Analysis. *Ethos* 1:30–74.

MURDOCK, GEORGE P., and CATERINA PROVOST. 1973. Measurement of Cultural Complexity. *Ethnology* 12:379–392.

MURDOCK, GEORGE P., and DOUGLAS R. WHITE. 1969. Standard Cross-Cultural Sample. *Ethnology* 8:329–369.

MURDOCK, GEORGE P., and SUZANNE WILSON. 1972. Settlement Patterns and Community Organization: Cross-Cultural Codes 3. *Ethnology* 11:254–295.

OTTERBEIN, KEITH F. 1970. *The Evolution of War.* HRAF Press.

SLATER PHILIP E., and DORI A. SLATER. 1965. Maternal Ambivalence and Narcissism: A Cross-Cultural Study. *Merrill-Palmer Quarterly of Behavior and Development* 11:241–59.

VAN VELSEN, H. H. E. THODEN, and W. VAN WETERING. 1960. Residence, Power Groups, and Intra-Society Aggression. *International Archives of Ethnology* 49:169–200.

WHITING, BEATRICE B., 1965. Sex Identity Conflict and Physical Violence: A Comparative Study. *American Anthropologist* 67 (6), part 2.

WHITING, JOHN W. M. 1941. *Becoming a Kwoma.* Yale University Press.

———. 1964. Effects of Climate on Certain Cultural Practices, *Explorations in Cultural Anthropology* (Ward H. Goodenough, ed.), pp. 511–544.

———. 1969. The Place of Aggression in Social Interaction, *Collective Violence* (James F. Short, Jr., and Marin E. Wolfgang, eds.). Aldine-Atherton.

WHITING, JOHN W. M., and ROY G. D'ANDRADE. 1959. A Cross-Cultural Study of Residence from Infancy Through Marriage. Paper presented at the annual meeting of the American Anthropological Association, Mexico City.

WHITING, BEATRICE B. and JOHN W. M. 1975. *Children of Six Cultures: a Psycho-Cultural Analysis.* Harvard University Press (in press).

APPENDIX

The following maps illustrate the location of societies in the major regions of the world. Husband and wife rooming arrangements are indicated as follows: Apart ▪, together ●. The maps are adapted from Murdock and White 1969. The numbers are those assigned by them for the standard sample.

Map 1. Africa

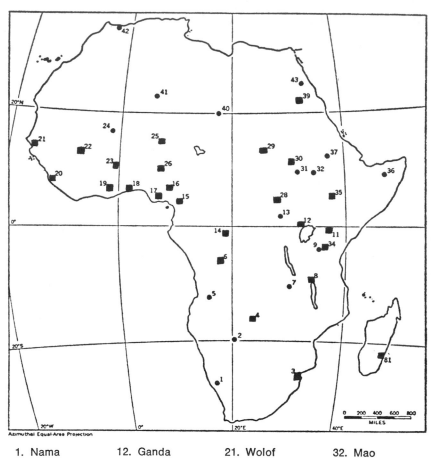

1. Nama	12. Ganda	21. Wolof	32. Mao
2. !Kung	13. Mbuti	22. Bambara	34. Masai
3. Thonga	14. Nkundo	23. Tallensi	35. Konso
4. Lozi	Mongo	24. Songhai	36. Somali
5. Mbundu	15. Banen	25. Fulani	37. Amhara
6. Suku	16. Tiv	26. Hausa	39. Nubians
7. Bemba	17. Ibo	28. Azande	40. Teda
8. Nyakyusa	18. Fon	29. Fur	41. Tuareg
9. Hadza	19. Ashanti	30. Otoro	42. Riffians
11. Kikuyu	20. Mende	31. Shilluk	43. Egyptians
			81. Tanala

Map 2. West Eurasia

46. Rwala	51. Irish	54. Russians	59. Punjabi
48. Ghog	52. Lapps	57. Kurd	64. Burusho
50. Basques	53. Yurak	58. Basseri	65. Kazak

Map 3. East Eurasia

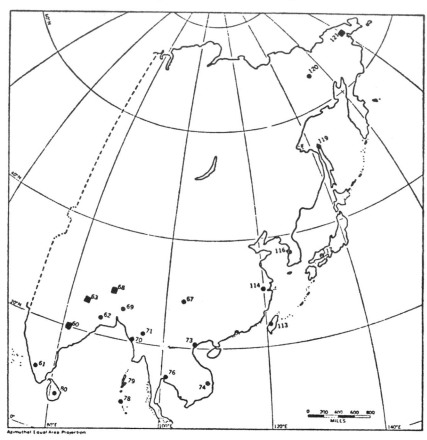

60. Gond	69. Garo	78. Nicobarese	116. Koreans
61. Toda	70. Lakher	79. Anda-	117. Japanese
62. Santal	71. Burmese	manese	119. Gilyak
63. Khalka	73. Vietnamese	80. Vedda	120. Yukaghir
67. Lolo	74. Rhade	113. Atayal	121. Chukchee
68. Lepcha	76. Siamese	114. Chinese	

Map 4. Insular Pacific

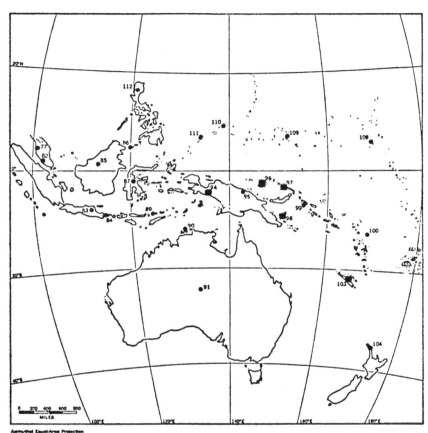

77. Semang	87. Toradja	97. New Ireland	106. Samoans
82. Negri	09. Alorese	98. Trobriand-	108. Marohalleso
Sembilan	90. Tiwi	ers	109. Trukese
83. Javanese	91. Aranda	99. Siuai	110. Yapese
84. Balinese	94. Kapauku	100. Tikopia	111. Palauans
85. Iban	95. Kwoma	103. Ajie	112. Ifugao
86. Badjau	96. Manus	104. Maori	

Map 5. North America

122. Ingalik	131. Haida	139. Kutenai	147. Comanche
123. Aleut	132. Bellacoola	140. Gros Ventre	148. Chiricahua
124. Copper	133. Twana	141. Hidatsa	Apache
Eskimo	134. Yurok	142. Pawnee	149. Zuni
126. Micmac	135. Pomo	143. Omaha	150. Havasupai
127. Saulteaux	136. Yokuts	144. Huron	151. Papago
128. Slave	137. Paiute	145. Creek	152. Huichol
129. Kaska	138. Klamath	146. Natchez	153. Aztec
130. Eyak			160. Haitians

Map 6. South America

156. Mickito	164. Carib	171. Inca	178. Botocudo
157. Bribri	165. Saramacca	172. Aymara	179. Shavante
158. Cuna	166. Mundurucu	173. Siriono	180. Aweikoma
159. Goajiro	167. Cubeo	174. Nambicuara	181. Cayua
161. Callinago	168. Cayapa	175. Trumal	184. Mapuche
162. Warrau	169. Jivaro	176. Timbira	185. Tehuelche
163. Yanomamo	170. Amahuaca	177. Tupinamba	186. Yahgan

Dream Concepts of Hausa Children:

A Critique of the "Doctrine of Invariant Sequence"
in Cognitive Development

RICHARD A. SHWEDER and ROBERT A. LEVINE

With her report on the developmental waxing of animistic thinking among the people of Manus (in contrast to the developmental
waning of animism in the West) Margaret Mead (1932) initiated an
extant intellectual tradition in which the claims to universality of
developmental theories are evaluated in the light of cross-cultural
evidence. We hope this essay can be said to have some degree of
legitimate lineage connection to that eponymous ancestral study in
the Admiralty Islands of nearly half a century ago.

RICHARD A. SHWEDER is assistant professor of human development in the Department of Behavioral Sciences, Committee on Human Development, at the
University of Chicago. ROBERT A. LEVINE is professor of anthropology, psychiatry, and human development at the University of Chicago.
The data presented in this article were collected as part of the research program of the Child Development Research Unit, Ahmadu Bello University,
supported by a grant from the Carnegie Corporation of New York to that university, by a grant from the United States Office of Education to the Early Education Research Center, University of Chicago, and by a Research Scientist
Development Award (5-K02-MH-18, 444-10) from the National Institute of
Mental Health to LeVine. We are also indebted to Douglass R. Price-Williams
for advice in designing the study, to Musa Abdullahi for interviewing the children along the lines described in LeVine and Price-Williams (1974), and to
Paul Brinich for the initial codings of the data.

INTRODUCTION

The "doctrine of invariant sequence" is the sine qua non of the cognitive-developmental approach to socialization. Less a true doctrine than a special definition of cognitive development (as a directed process of conceptual change regulated by the logical orderings inherent in concepts), less a dogma than the hypothesization of logically necessary culturally invariant temporal sequences in the way children change their minds, the "doctrine of invariant sequence" has nonetheless provoked considerable controversy and has been described as "the most interesting and often debated aspect of the cognitive-developmental approach" (Hoffman 1970: 265).

From an anthropological perspective the controversial nature of the "doctrine of invariant sequence" is apparent; the "doctrine" restricts the role of cultural determinants to amplifying or dampening the *rate* of conceptual change, and rejects as minimal the influence of cultural determinants on either the nature of conceptual interpretations at any point in a sequence, or the overall direction of their movement.

Kohlberg, a leading exponent of the "cognitive-developmental approach" aptly summarizes the "doctrine of invariant sequence" as follows: "understanding cognitive stages depends upon a logical analysis of orderings inherent in given concepts," and "the existence of cognitive stages implies an invariance of sequence in development, a regularity of stepwise progression regardless of cultural teaching or circumstance. Cultural teaching and experience can speed up or slow down development but it cannot change its order or sequence" (1969:355, 1966:6).

It is the purpose of this essay to evaluate the sense and validity of the "doctrine of invariant sequence" with special reference to a study presented by Kohlberg (1969) as exemplary of the cognitive-developmental approach, namely, his cross-cultural comparative inquiry into children's understandings of the events in their dreams. Our critical discussion of the role of a logical analysis for the ontogeny of understanding is supplemented with data on changes in the dream-event understandings of sixty Hausa children in Nigeria. We judge these data to be particularly relevant because the changes that take place between the initial and ultimate dream-event understandings of Hausa children do not proceed along the single, invariant temporal ordering so fundamental to cognitive-developmental accounts. The essay concludes with some tentative suggestions for an approach to conceptual change which emphasizes rational criteria beyond the capacity of logic to describe, criteria having to do with the applicability and relevance of forms of understanding.

A COGNITIVE-DEVELOPMENTAL ACCOUNT OF DREAM-EVENT UNDERSTANDINGS: LOGICAL PRIORITIES AND TEMPORAL PRECEDENCES

Kohlberg (1966, 1969) has presented a "cognitive-developmental" account of changes in the way children understand the events in their dreams. It is to his credit to have recognized the *possibility* that while adults around the world are not in accord in their understanding of dream-events, an untutored consensus is arrived at by children in diverse cultures. Presumably uninstructed in their culture's interpretation of dreams, or insensitive to its teachings, American, Canadian, Swiss, Formosan (and, as we shall see, Nigerian) children alter their initially inadequate working hypotheses about the nature of dream events, and come to believe that the events in their dreams are internally located and inherently private "appearances" (instances of "mental imagining").

A universal "spontaneously" evolved childhood understanding of dream-events is a fascinating albeit only partially documented phenomenon. The cognitive-developmental account of changes in children's understandings of dream-events, however, goes much further. On the basis of a logical analysis of relevant dream-event attributes (e.g. their "reality," "sharability," and "location") cognitive-developmental theorists such as Kohlberg prescribe *the* temporal order in which understandings of these attributes must be acquired.

The "doctrine of invariant sequence," this hypothesized existence of a logically necessary culturally invariant temporal sequence in a child's changing understanding of concepts, is the distinctive characteristic of cognitive-developmental accounts. With special reference to changes in children's understandings of dream-events Kohlberg has stated that "the steps [in arriving at the notion that dream-events are unreal, inherently private, and internally located, etc.] represent progressive differentiations of the subjective and the objective which logically could not have a different order" and "the observed sequence is one which corresponds to an inner logic of the concept of reality itself" (1969:359).

Kohlberg's formulation of the "doctrine of invariant sequence" in this context is consistent with Piaget's presentation. Piaget emphasizes the "originality" of the child's convictions about dream-events "in defiance of personal circumstances, experiences, and overheard conversations" (1929:32) and suggests that the confusion in the child's mind between signs and things signified must be clarified before the child is in a position to distinguish what is internal from what is external (Piaget 1929:121).

The cognitive-developmental prescription of necessary temporal orderings in development (the "doctrine of invariant sequence") leans heavily on the philosophical notion of a relationship of logical priority between activities or attributes. One activity or attribute is logically prior to a second if it would be logically impossible for an instance of a second activity or attribute to occur without an instance of the first occurring, the converse not being so (see Black: 1962). For example, in the sense just defined, "knowing a rule" is logically prior to "deliberately breaking a rule." One may "know a rule" without "deliberately breaking the rule" but it is logically impossible to "deliberately break a rule" without "knowing the rule" (see Alston:1971). The relationship of hierarchical inclusion among attributes is a special case of logical priority. For example, the concept "colored" is logically prior to the concept "red" in the sense that all "red" things are "colored" but not all "colored" things are "red" (see Hamlyn 1971).

Once the notion of a "logical priority" is understood, the "doctrine of invariant sequence" is easily summarized. If there is logical priority among activities or attributes, there *must* be temporal precedence. One must "know a rule" *before* one can "deliberately break it"; one must understand the concept "colored" *before* one can understand the concept "red" (cognitive-developmental theorists would presumably distinguish between having the *concept* "red" and effectively using visual stimuli within a certain range of hue, intensity, and saturation as *discriminative cues*).

Kohlberg reasons this way in his study of children's understandings of dream-events. He lists several attributes relevant to a description of the untutored consensually agreed upon understanding of dream-events arrived at by children in all cultures. He analyzes the "logical priorities" among the attributes (which he believes describes the "inner logic of the concept of reality") and prescribes the temporal order in which they must occur. Three of the attributes discussed by Kohlberg appear in this study: (1) "reality"—are the dream-events unreal (cases of seeming) or real (cases of being)?; (2) "visibility"—are the dream-events inherently private or capable of public perception?; (3) "location"—are the dream-events internally located or located outside the dreamer's body?

The order in which I have listed these attributes follows Kohlberg's analysis of their "logical priorities." For example, he states, "it is apparent that internality (location of the dream experience inside the body) presupposes unreality (recognition that the dream is not a real object) since a real object could hardly be in the body" (1969:359). As a consequence, the temporal sequence of changes in a child's understandings of dream-events "logically could not have a different order" (1969:359). The child must understand that dream-events are unreal before understanding they are accessible only to his perception; this second understanding must be acquired before the understanding that dream-events happen inside the body. To the query "Why could there not be a culture in which children understand the concept "internally located" before understanding the concept "unreal" the answer is simply "because such an ordering violates logical necessity" (see Nagel:1961).

THE "DOCTRINE OF INVARIANT SEQUENCE" AND CHILDREN'S UNDERSTANDING OF DREAM-EVENTS: A CRITICAL EVALUATION

"If there is logical priority then there must be temporal precedence" is an assertion that can be scrutinized with only certain kinds of evidence. The converse claim, "if there is temporal precedence then there must be logical priority," does not follow from the original assertion. Thus positive evidence of invariant temporal sequence is not relevant. No one denies that an invariant sequence of change may have a nonlogical source (e.g. the invariant occurrence of oral eroticism prior to phallic eroticism in psychosexual development).

Negative evidence, however, (e.g. from the investigation of Hausa children to be reported in this essay) *is* relevant. The outcome of Kohlberg's "logical analysis" of dream-event attributes is a prescription for a single invariant temporal order in which certain dream-event understandings must be acquired. Hausa children *do not* follow the prescription. Therefore, we must either question the adequacy of the logical account or reject the original assertion, *or both.*

THE ADEQUACY OF THE LOGICAL ACCOUNT

The outcome of an analysis of logical priorities is the elaboration of a set of "criteria for demonstrating a certain form of understanding," that is, "criteria for properly being said to have the concept in question" (Hamlyn 1971). As Hamlyn points out, no one would be convinced that a child understood the concept "red" if he did not also understand the logically prior concept "colored." "Uncolored-red" is a logically impossible concept. We can assess the adequacy of Kohlberg's particular analysis of "the inner logic of the concept of reality" (which he then applies to dream-events) by asking whether it entitles us to reject certain understandings of experience, and hence certain understandings of dream-events, *as logically impossible.*

In Kohlberg's analysis, the distinction between the real and the unreal (between things that are and things that seem to be) is logically prior to the distinction between the inherently private and the potentially public (between things that lack and things that have the potential for perceptual sharing). In turn this distinction is logically prior to the distinction between the internally located and the externally located (with reference to the body). One must have private access to the internally located; what is privately accessible must be unreal.

Kohlberg's analysis might be said to entitle us to accept as logical the following four ways of describing one's experiences:

1. as external perceptions (real, public accessibility, externally located)
2. as mirages (unreal, public accessibility, externally located)
3. as hallucinations (unreal, private accessibility, externally located)
4. as fantasies (unreal, private accessibility, internally located)

One might even describe Kohlberg's view of the necessary temporal order of changes in children's understandings of dream-events in terms of these four modes of describing experience in general. Children first understand dream-events as external perceptions, then as mirages, then as hallucinations, and finally as fantasies.

Kohlberg's analysis might also be said to entitle us to dismiss as illogical the following four ways of describing one's experiences:

5. as internal perceptions (real, public accessibility, internally located)
6. as internal sensations (real, private accessibility, internally located)
7. as private perceptions (real, private accessibility, externally located)
8. as shared fantasies (unreal, public accessibility, internally located)

But is this the case? Are these last four ways of describing one's experiences any less *logical* than the first four? Internal perceptions (e.g. of intrasomatic events during surgery) and internal sensations (e.g. the pain in one's own stomach about which others may be informed but which they certainly cannot experience [see Ducasse 1961]) are obviously not illogical. No one could reasonably claim that you fail to understand the pain inside your gut because you talk about it as "real." The same can be said for private perceptions and shared fantasies. There are no logical grounds for distinguishing a hallucination (e.g. hearing voices) from a private perception of auditory stimuli. After all, the perceiver may have an entirely unique, and "never to occur again" auditory capacity. Similarly, as unlikely as it might seem, no one can deny on logical grounds the possibility of the existence of a species whose fantasies were pictorially displayed on a small screen located just behind the retina and visible through the pupil from the outside (an internal screen that rapid eye movements during dreaming seem to suggest is imagined by our sensory apparatus).

Thus the rational basis of dream-event understandings seems to reside less in the logic or illogic of certain forms of experiential understanding and more in the evaluation of the differential *applicability* of each form of understanding to *recognized* evidence about the conditions under which dreams are experienced. We return to this point later.

THE LOGICAL ANALYSIS OF CONCEPTS AND THEIR ACQUISITION

The question of logical analysis and concept acquisition has been the subject of philosophical exchanges (Alston 1971, Hamlyn

1971. Hanson 1961, Nagel 1961, Toulmin 1961, 1969, 1971a) whose influence on our thinking we gratefully acknowledge without implicating their authors in our position.

We reject the cognitive-developmental assertion "if there is logical priority there must be temporal precedence" for the following reasons:

1. Logical relations among concepts are simultaneously occurring relations. If an understanding of these concepts is to be acquired at all, nothing in their logical relatedness implies they must be acquired in a particular temporal order, or for that matter in sequence at all. They may be acquired simultaneously and all at once in final form; they may be acquired dialectically and partially in a kind of intermittent piecemeal fashion.

Stated differently, a logical analysis elaborates the "criteria for demonstrating a certain form of understanding" (Hamlyn 1971) at a single point in time. It has nothing to say about sequences of understandings, and such past understandings (or lack of understanding) are irrelevant to present evaluations of "having a concept." On the basis of a logical analysis (and using Hamlyn's example) one might be entitled to claim at a *single point in time* that a child could not possible understand the concept "red" unless he also understood the concept "colored." But, one would not be entitled to doubt a child's understanding of the concept "red" at some designated point in time on the basis of the child's lack of understanding of the concept "colored" at the immediately preceding point in time. Conversely, one could not claim that a child who understood "red" *must* have understood "colored" at the point in time immediately preceding such an understanding.

2. An *invariant* temporal sequence cannot be prescribed on the basis of a logical analysis because many possible logical orderings are inherent in a concept. As Nagel has remarked (1961) "many concepts can be analyzed in several alternative ways so that the particular set of logical priorities attributed to such concepts depends on which other concepts are taken as primitive."

3. The "doctrine of invariant sequence" is incompatible with experimental evidence on the "psychology of reasoning." The inferential process of the logically untrained individual is dominated by extralogical considerations. Wason and Johnson-Laird (1972), in a series of experiments, have shown how difficult it is for individuals

(with a deductive competence) actually to make purely formal deductions, "how unnatural to think in terms of the truth-functional relations among abstract propositions."

As Wason and Johnson-Laird (1972) point out, it is the content (and the meaning) of what one thinks about and not the canons of any propositional calculus which are decisive for how one thinks. Their subjects display a significant tendency wherever possible to give causal or temporal interpretations to conditional statements. Two logically equivalent conditional statements, such as "if prices increase, the firm goes bankrupt" and "prices increase only if the firm goes bankrupt" (they are logically equivalent in the sense that they are falsified only by an increase in prices without the bankrupcy of the firm) lead to different deductions on the basis of their causal-temporal connotations (1972:73). Asked to reason about abstract materials (hence materials difficult to relate in terms of causative or temporal hypotheses) subjects assume that conditional statements imply their converse, have difficulty with negatives, and are biased towards verification instead of disconfirmation. The authors argue that "even with fully-fledged assertions individuals do not naturally engage in truth-functional thought. They are always ready to leave the logical requirements of the task behind and try to establish some meaningful connection between events" (1972: 81). They conclude from their research that everyday reasoning depends on rational criteria that logic is incapable of characterizing adequately.

A NIGERIAN EXHIBITION OF THE "LOGICALLY IMPOSSIBLE"

Among Hausa children there are alternative sequences by which children change their understandings of dream-events. Initially Hausa children believe the events in their dreams to be real occurrences, potentially capable of public perception, which take place outside their bodies (i.e., external perceptions). Although they come to believe the events in their dreams to be unreal appearances, located inside their bodies, to which only they have potential perceptual access (i.e. fantasies) there is no single transitional route to this ultimate childhood understanding. Betwixt their initial "realism" and subsequent "subjectivism," one set of children comes to believe that dream-events are real, potentially visible experiences that happen inside their bodies (i.e. internal perceptions); another set of children believe the dream-events are unreal appearances that are invisible to others but have locations outside the body (i.e. hallucinations).

The existence of this type of variance is unintelligible from the cognitive-developmental point of view, a point of view from which the first Hausa transitional type (i.e. dreams understood to be internal perceptions) is simply "logically impossible" (Kohlberg 1969:359). Its documented occurrence calls for a kind of explanation with less emphasis on "logic" and more emphasis on the evaluation of the differential applicability of forms of understanding in relationship to particular experiences (some of which may be culturally variable) and particular criteria for application (some of which may also be culturally variable). This negative evidence from Nigeria is presented below.

SAMPLE

Children were sampled from the central ward of a Hausa market town in northwestern Nigeria.[1] Interviews were conducted with sixty children of both sexes distributed over the ages five to thirteen as follows (Age/Number of Subjects) 5/4, 6/16, 7/11, 8/7, 9/6, 10/8, 11/2, 12/5, 13/1.

PROCEDURE

Children were asked a series of questions concerning their dreams by an indigenous interviewer speaking the native tongue. From the point of view of this study, the following questions are relevant:

1. Do you ever have dreams at night?
2. Tell me a dream you had.
3. Did that (described action or event) really happen?
4. Was the dream in your room or inside you?
5. If I had been there, could I have seen the thing or action dreamt?
6. Whom do you sleep with?
7. Could he (she) have seen your dream?

1. For additional contextual material and another study conducted with approximately the same sample of children, see LeVine and Price-Williams (1974).

Forty-seven children gave answers complete enough to judge the *reality, visibility,* and *location* attributes of their understanding of dream-events. Thirteen additional children gave answers complete enough to judge their understanding of one or two of these attributes.

RESULTS

Intercoder reliability for the children's answers to questions about the *reality, visibility,* and *location* of dream-events averages .92 (Phi). Analyzed individually, each of the three attributes is significantly related to age. As they grow older, Hausa children understand dreams to be unreal cases of mental imagining ($r = .64$, $n = 56$, $p = < .001$), which are inherently private ($r = .60$, $n = 56$, $p = < .001$), and located inside the dreamer's body ($r = .38$, $n = 53$, $p = < .01$).[2]

Table 1 presents the findings on the temporal sequencing of changes in understandings of dream-events. Of eight conceivable kinds of ways of understanding experience in terms of its reality, public accessibility, and location, six occur in Hausa children's understandings of the events in their dreams. Examples from the interviews, of each type of understanding, are given below.

The dream-event as an external perception: (Do you ever have dreams at night?) Yes. (Tell me a dream you had.) I dreamt that a hyena came to our room; when I saw it I began to cry. (Did that really happen?) Yes. It is true that hyena came to our house. (Was the dream in your room or inside you?) The dream is outside. (If I had been there could I have seen the hyena?) You could have been able to see the hyena. (Whom do you sleep with?) I sleep with my mother and my younger brother. (Could your mother have seen the hyena?) My mother could not see it *because she is asleep.*

The dream-event as a mirage: (Do you ever have dreams at night?) Yes. (Tell me a dream you had.) I dreamt my younger sister fell into a well and died. (Did that really happen?) No, because I still see her. (Was the

2. The Hausa children in our sample were also asked about the origin of their dreams (i.e. where do dreams come from?). Only thirty-eight of the children responded to this question. The others "did not know." Of those who "did know," however, older children understood their dream to have an internal origin (e.g. it came from the heart or the eyes instead of the bush or the night); ($r = .53$, $n = 38$, $p = < .001$). Preserving a reasonable sample size was our main consideration in dropping this attribute from our analysis of transitional types.

dream in your room or inside you?) The dream was inside the room. (If I had been there could I have seen your sister dying?) Yes. (Whom do you sleep with?) I sleep with my sister Ladidi. (Could Ladidi have seen your sister dying?) Yes.

The dream-event as an internal perception: (Do you ever have dreams at night?) Yes. (Tell me a dream you had.) I dreamt that both my mother and father were not at home and it was a dark night. Then I heard at the back door a frightening noise, and got frightened and ran away. Then I woke up. (Was it true that you ran away?) Yes. (Was the dream in your room or inside you?) The dream was inside me. (If I had been there could I have seen you running?) No. (Why?) Because you would be asleep. (Whom do you sleep with?) My mother. (Could your mother have seen your dream?) No she could not have seen it because she was asleep. (Suppose she was not asleep?) Then she would have seen it.

The dream-event as a hallucination: (Do you ever have dreams at night?) Yes. (Tell me a dream you had.) A fairy tried to take a car and kill someone, then he tried coming to me but I ran away. (Did that really happen?) No. (Was the dream in your room or inside you?) Inside the room. (If I had been there could I have seen the fairy?) No. (Whom do you sleep with?) Ali. (Could Ali have seen the fairy?) Ali would not be able to see the fairy because the fairy disappears on sight.

The dream-event as an internal sensation: (Do you ever have dreams at night?) Yes. (Tell me a dream you had.) I dreamt I went to an unknown town with my mother. I touched some goods which belonged to the police force and those goods cost two shillings. My mother had only one shilling and so she entered a house and borrowed a shilling. The next day she collected the money and from there I woke up. (Did that really happen?) Yes. (Was the dream in your room or inside you?) Inside me. (If I had been there could I have seen your mother borrowing the money?) No. A man sees his dream alone. (Whom do you sleep with?) Salisu. (Could Salisu have seen your dream?) Salisu could not have seen it because I was the only one that saw it.

The dream-event as a fantasy: (Do you ever have dreams at night?) Yes. (Tell me a dream you had.) Yesterday at Birning Gwari, on our way back from Kaduna I stepped on a grave in an attempt to go and urinate. When we came home I dreamt that the man in the grave came out to hit me and was chasing me around. (Did that really happen?) No. The dead body did not come out. (Was the dream in your room or inside you?) Inside me. (If I had been there could I have seen the dead man chasing

TABLE 1

DREAM-EVENT UNDERSTANDINGS AMONG FORTY-SEVEN HAUSA CHILDREN

	Type of Understanding*							
	External perception 1	Mirage 2	Internal perception 3	Hallucination 4	Internal sensation 5	Fantasy 6	Private perception 7	Shared fantasy 8
Dream-events are unreal?	0	1	0	1	0	1	0	1
Dream-events are inherently private?	0	0	0	1	1	1	1	0
Dream-events are internally located?	0	0	1	0	1	1	0	1
Number of subjects	18	4	9	7	1	8	0	0
Average age (years: months)	6:2	7:0	7:2	8:7	9:0	10:4	—	—

* 0 = No
  1 = Yes

you?) No. You cannot see it because it is just a dream which results from the fear I had when I stepped on the grave. (Whom do you sleep with?) I sleep with Takur and Zayyanu. (Could Takur have seen the dead man chasing you?) Takur would not be able to see the dead body because I am the only one who stepped on the grave and as a result of fear dreamt about the dead man.

The youngest group (average age: 6 years, 2 months) typically understands dream-events to be real occurrences that are visible to others and externally located (i.e. external perceptions). The oldest group (average age: 10 years, 4 months) typically understands dream-events to be unreal cases of mental imagining that are inherently private and internally located with regard to the dreamer's body (i.e. fantasies).

The most frequent transitional type of understanding occurs in nine children who understand dream-events to be real, potentially open to public access, and located inside the body (i.e. as internal perceptions). These children treat dream-events as if they were intrasomatic stimuli *potentially* visible if one could "look through the eyes of the dreamer" or open him up as in an operation.

One reasonable interpretation of the results in table 1 postulates the existence of two alternative temporal sequences by which Hausa children change their minds about the events in their dreams. At approximately age six, children understand dream-events to be real, public, and external (i.e. external perceptions). At age seven, they change their minds about *either* the reality or the externality of these events but not both. They view dream-events as either mirages or internal perceptions. By age nine, dream-events are understood to stand in a relation of privileged access to the dreamer (i.e., they are understood as either hallucinations or internal sensations). By age ten, dream-events are understood as unreal, inherently private, and internally-located (i.e. as fantasies). The two developmental sequences are presented in figure 1.

There are certain general observations to be made about dream-event understandings among Hausa children which may account for our findings. In a culture where children sleep alone it is likely they will disconfirm their belief in the reality of dream-events before they disconfirm their belief in their external location. The reality of certain kinds of dream-events is easily disconfirmed by

Approximate Age

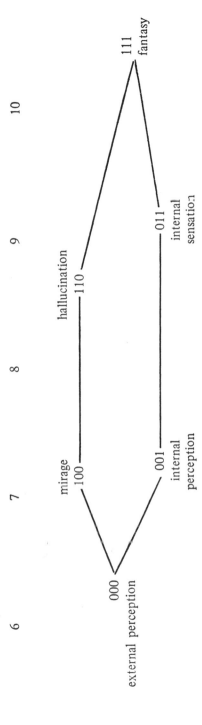

The questions: Unreal*?/Private?/Internal?

The answers: 0 = No
               1 = Yes

FIG. 1.   Alternative Temporal Sequences in Hausa Children's Understanding of **Dream-Events**

waking experience (e.g. one of our subjects dreamt her sister drowned in a well yet was awakened by her in the morning). The external location of dream-events is not so easily disconfirmed especially if no one witnesses their lack of public occurrence.

The difficulty of access to evidence disconfirming the externality of dream-events is somewhat attenuated for Hausa children. They typically have numerous roommates who have the uncanny potential not to see the purported events in the dream. It seems likely in a culture with crowded sleeping quarters such as Hausa that some children receive massive disconfirmation of their initial understanding that dream-events take place outside their bodies before they remember dream-events whose reality can easily be questioned. As we have seen (table 1), several Hausa children in fact come to understand their dream-events as real, publically accessible, yet internally located (as internal perceptions).

DISCUSSION

The existence of considerable variability in the routes by which Nigerian children *change their minds* about dream-events is not surprising. As far as we know no study has ever shown a single invariant sequence of changes in dream-event understandings. Kohlberg (1966, 1969) drops between 30% and 40% of "aberrant" subjects from his analysis of *transitional* invariance, and Laurendeau and Pinard (1962:103–104, 114) explicitly mention the considerable variation observed in the transitional period between "realism" and "subjectivism." This period includes "all the possible steps between the total reification of the dream, attenuated by unskillful attempts at interiorization, on the one hand, and the almost complete subjectivation of the phenomenon together with a residual expression of realism on the other," for example, the form of understanding in which the dream is understood to be "like a story, like a little play" happening inside the child's head, potentially visible to anyone who could open the head to have a look (is this an internal perception reminiscent of our Hausa subjects or a shared fantasy?). What *is* surprising is how little *theoretical* interest has been taken in this undeniable variability. We believe any satisfactory account of the evolution of dream-event understandings must render this variability intelligible not invisible.

Throughout this essay we have been skeptical of the view that changes in children's understandings of dream-events must follow a single and logically determined order. The principle of the "doctrine of invariant sequence" ("if there is logical priority there must be temporal precedence") and Kohlberg's analysis of the "inner logic of the concept of reality" both seem questionable to us. Documentation of transitional variability in dream-event understandings among the Hausa makes us that much more doubtful. But, so does the initial "realism" of children from diverse cultures.

How are we to interpret the agreement between six-year-old Hausa children and four-year-old American children that the events in their dreams are external perceptions (real, capable of public perception, and externally located)? This seems to us remarkable; the agreement is not made intelligible by suggesting, as do cognitive-developmentalists, that these children lack relevant distinctions that can only appear in a logically determined, nested order. For if six-year-old Hausa children did not distinguish real/unreal, public/private, external/internal, one would expect free variation in their responses; they should fail to comprehend the distinction and thus randomly produce responses. Cognitive-developmental theory fails to explain how it is that lacking, for example, the distinction between real and unreal, young children should understand dream experiences as characteristically *any* one pole of an absent distinction, and why, given that they do respond so characteristically, it is *that* one pole and not the other that is preferred. Either young children understand their dream experiences *and* everyday waking perceptions to be neither real nor unreal (which tells us very little about how they do understand them but is at least consistent with the notion of "lacking a distinction") or, as we think more likely, they distinguish by some criteria the real and unreal but have no good reasons to view dream-events as anything but real.

We believe these "good reasons" for applying one form of understanding and not another, these criteria for evaluating the differential *applicability* of concepts to experience have received too little attention in the study of cognitive development. Toulmin's philosophical investigations of "rationality" (1971b, 1972) are germane in this regard. He argues that an account of understanding has less to do with the creation of logical systems, the avoidance of inferential errors, and the formally coherent interdefinition of concepts, and more to do with "the manner and circumstances in which a person is prepared to change or modify his ideas," "the criteria of reference by which choices are made between rival ways of understanding." He believes that concepts and forms of understanding most typically co-exist in conceptual populations or aggregates (i.e. they are very loosely integrated and more often independent) from which choices among potentially relevant members are made with reference to very ungeneralized (local) intellectual problems, contexts, and criteria of relevance.

With regard to dream-events, it seems to us the choice among evolutionary history of the species or the cultural history of the rival forms of understanding is subject to diverse constraints. All knowledge available to the organism, whether preadapted in the group, or postadapted in the life history of the individual, begins with external perception. There may well be a preparation of homo sapiens to understand experiences as external perceptions until such an understanding is shown to be deficient. The informational conditions under which such an evaluation of "deficiency" is likely to be made include the instability over authoritative observers of the effect associated with a phenomenon, that is, its lack of reliability and the consequential difficulty in finding consensual validation for one's judgments about experience (see Jones and Nisbett 1972, and Kelley 1967). Certain other kinds of understandings may be differentially selected against or amplified by one's culture. Schooler and Caudill (1964) for example, in a comparative study of symptoms among schizophrenics in Japanese and American mental hospitals, have commented upon the significantly higher incidence of "hallucinations" among those committed as insane in America, a fact they hypothesize *may* be related to American cultural concerns about "clear-sightedness" and the "accurate perception of reality." Japanese may be able to have "hallucinations" without being quite so readily committed as "mad."

We are raising as an issue the question of the explanatory adequacy of a particular form of understanding in the face of certain kinds of evidence (some of which is and some of which is not culturally variable), certain criteria for what counts as relevant evidence and certain standards for what counts as an adequate explanation (again some of which are and some of which are not culturally variable). For example, certain kinds of evidence are made more intelligible by certain kinds of understandings. In the face of knowledge that dream-events are not perceived by those who should have been in a position to perceive them, certain understandings of the dream-events (e.g. they are mirages) are simply inadequate.

Our position with regard to children's changing understandings of dream-events is as follows:

Children come to know what it is they mean by any particular form of understanding, and come to reject their initial understanding of dream-events piecemeal and in relation (among other things) to evidence that their way of construing dream-events is inadequate. The specific orderings of changed understandings that do occur reflect the children's differential access to evidence disconfirming their working hypotheses. Some kinds of disconfirming evidence may ultimately be presented to children in all cultures, but at the very least there is no reason to believe all relevant disconfirming evidence is universally presented to children in the same *order* either within or across cultures. Cross-cultural or intracultural variability in the *order* in which disconfirming evidence is presented to children may have no influence on the understanding of dreams ultimately arrived at, but such variability in the order of evidence presentation will be related to the routes by which children achieve this understanding.

In summary, the understanding that dream-events are fantasies may be the most adequate understanding "spontaneously" available to the child in the face of certain universal facts about waking experience, that is, untutored in the entailments of adult dream concepts and the subtleties of their application to everyday experience.[3] But the child's sequence of understandings in arriving at this relatively more adequate of childhood understandings depends heavily on the order in which these overwhelming facts of everyday experience (e.g. the sister who did not drown in the well) are encountered.

Our position places primary emphasis on the adequacy of childhood understandings given access to certain kinds of evidence. As far as we know, no study has ever shown a single invariant se-

3. There is no reason to view ultimate childhood understandings of dream-events as adequate in any absolute sense as anyone must realize who ponders how mental phenomena (which by ultimate childhood definition are inherently private and lack extention in space) can be *located* anywhere (whether internally or externally).

quence of changes in dream-event understandings, but if such an invariant sequence had been reliably documented we would have looked for an invariance *in the order* in which evidence disconfirming of one aspect or another of children's initial dream-event understandings had become available to them, and not for a logically necessary overall direction to conceptual change.

At this time we are not in a position to carry our general observations any further. In the context of our critique, however, the existence of alternative ways of changing one's mind about dream-events among Hausa children, and, as discussed above, its *possible* relationship to aspects of these children's culturally influenced experience (i.e., Hausa sleeping arrangements) should, at the very least, (1) disenchant us from too heavy a reliance on a logical analysis in an account of children's changing understandings of concepts, (2) emphasize the importance of careful studies of these changing understandings in relation to relevant evidence encountered by a child from his *cultural* as well as noncultural experience, and (3) encourage studies of cross-cultural variations (or lack of variation) in the criteria on the basis of which children change their minds.

William James put nicely one the themes of this essay and we will let him have the last word (as quoted by Durkheim 1960:409).

"the enormously rapid multiplication of theories in these latter days has well-nigh upset the notion of any one of them being a more literally objective kind of thing than another. There are so many geometries, so many logics, so many physical and chemical hypotheses, so many classifications, each one of them good for so much and yet not good for everything, that the notion that even the truest formula may be a human device and not a literal transcript has dawned upon us."

REFERENCES

ALSTON, WILLIAM P. 1971. Comments on Kohlberg's "From Is to Ought," *Cognitive Development and Epistemology* (Theodore Mischel, ed.), pp. 269–288. Academic Press.

BLACK, MAX. 1962. The Analysis of Rules, *Models and Metaphors; Studies in Language and Philosophy* (Max Black, ed.), pp. 95–139. Cornell University Press.

DUCASSE, CURT. 1961. In Defense of Dualism, *Dimensions of Mind* (Sidney Hook, ed.), pp. 85–89. Collier Books.

DURKHEIM, EMILE. 1960. Pragmatism and Sociology, *Essays on Sociology and Philosophy* (Kurt H. Wolff, ed.), pp. 386–436. Harper and Row.

HAMLYN, D. D. 1971. Epistemology and Conceptual Development, *Cognitive Development and Epistemology* (Theodore Mischel, ed.), pp. 3–24. Academic Press.

HANSON, N. R. 1961. The Stratification of Concepts, *Dimensions of Mind* (Sidney Hook, ed.), pp. 211–213. Collier Books.

HOFFMAN, MARTIN L. 1970. Moral Development, *Carmichael's Manual of Child Psychology* (Paul H. Mussen, ed.), pp. 261–349. J. Wiley.

JONES, EDWARD E., and RICHARD E. NISBETT. 1972. The Actor and the Observer: Divergent Perceptions of the Causes of Behavior, *Attribution: Perceiving the Causes of Behavior* (Edward E. Jones, et al., eds.), pp. 79–94. General Learning Press.

KELLEY, HAROLD H. 1967. Attribution Theory in Social Psychology, *Nebraska Symposium on Motivation* (David Levine, ed.), pp. 192–240. University of Nebraska Press.

KOHLBERG, LAWRENCE. 1966. Cognitive Stages and Preschool Education. *Human Development* 9:5–17.

———. 1969. Stage and Sequence: The Cognitive-Developmental Approach to Socialization, *Handbook of Socialization Theory and Research* (David A. Goslin, ed.), pp. 347–480. Rand McNally and Co.

LAURENDEAU, MONIQUE, and ADRIEN PINARD. 1962. *Causal Thinking in Children.* International Universities Press.

LeVINE, ROBERT A., and DOUGLAS R. PRICE-WILLIAMS. 1974. Children's Kinship Concepts: Cognitive Development and Early Experience Among the Hausa. *Ethnology* 13:25–44.

MEAD, MARGARET. 1932. An Investigation of the Thought of Primitive Children, with Special Reference to Animism. *Journal of the Royal Anthropological Institute* 62:173–190.

NAGEL, ERNEST. 1961. Psychology and the Analysis of Concepts in Use, *Dimensions of Mind* (Sidney Hook, ed.), pp. 208–210. Collier Books.

PIAGET, JEAN. 1929. *The Child's Conception of the World.* Harcourt, Brace and Co.

SCHOOLER, CARMI, and WILLIAM CAUDILL. 1964. Symptomatology in Japanese and American Schizophrenics. *Ethnology* 3:172–178.

TOULMIN, STEPHEN. 1961. Concept-Formation in Philosophy and Psychology, *Dimensions of Mind* (Sidney Hook, ed.), pp. 191–203. Collier Books.

———. 1969. Concepts and the Explanation of Human Behavior, *Human Action* (Theodore Mischel, ed.), pp. 71–104. Academic Press.

————. 1971a. The Concept of "Stages" in Psychological Development, *Cognitive Development and Epistemology* (Theodore Mischel, ed.), pp. 25–60.

————. 1971b. From Logical Systems to Conceptual Populations, *Boston Studies in the Philosophy of Science, Volume VIII* (Roger C. Buck and Robert S. Cohen, eds.), pp. 552–564. D. Reidel Publishing Co.

————. 1972. *Human Understanding, Volume 1.* Princeton University Press.

WASON, P. C., and P. N. JOHNSON-LAIRD. 1972. *Psychology of Reasoning.* B. T. Batsford Ltd.

Resilience in Cognitive Development

JEROME KAGAN

Each scientific discipline, during successive eras in its growth, is loyal to one member of a set of opposed assumptions that typically form the axioms of the discipline. Holton (1973) has called these polarized premises *themata*. Debate over whether matter is particulate or wavelike, whether the universe is steady-state or expanding, or whether growth is continuous or discontinuous are among the themes that scientists have debated in the past and will continue to discuss in the future because, as Bohr wisely noted, the propositions are likely to be complementary rather than incompatible.

This paper considers the evidence bearing on a pair of opposed themata that have given direction to the empirical study of human psychological development. One proposition holds that the experiences of infancy produce a set of dispositions that have a continuous influence throughout life, implying that some of the effects of early experience are not malleable to change. The opposed position is

JEROME KAGAN is professor of human development in the Department of Psychology and Social Relations at Harvard University. This research was supported in part by Grant number HD-04299, and Contract number Ph 43-65-640 from the National Institute of Child Health and Human Development, Grant number GS-33048, Collaborative Research on Uniform Measures of Social Competence, National Science Foundation, and a grant from the Spencer Foundation, Chicago, Illinois.

that the infant is resilient and the effects of early experience—which can be dramatic—are reversible under proper environmental conditions. The debate centers on the degree of modifiability of psychological structures established early in life. There is unequivocal support for the view that the experiences of the young infant have a powerful contemporary effect on his behavior, temperament, and knowledge. This hypothesis is unchallenged. But it is less clear how stable these early structures are, especially if the environment should change in a serious way. Stated in the interrogative, how resilient—or responsive to change— are the cognitive structures and behavioral dispositions shaped during the first three years of life.

Although the infant is influenced by his environment from the moment he is born, the equally popular assumption that the effects of those early experiences can extend long into the future does not, at the moment, have unequivocal support. Hence we should ask why many psychologists, parents, and educators have been reluctant to examine the validity of that second statement. In addition to the obvious influence of psychoanalytic theory and the persuasive animal data, there are additional reasons, both phenomenological and philosophical. Each person feels a compelling sense of continuity and connectedness when he reflects on the experiences of his early childhood. This sense of the past's contribution to the present derives from man's need to regard his life as coherent and his past decisions as part of a rationally causal chain. A second, more speculative, basis for believing in the extended power of early experience could be a derivative of one of the central maxims of Western Protestantism—preparation for the future. Application of that maxim to child rearing would lead parents to award validity to the idea that if children are treated optimally during the early years, the healthy attitudes, talents, and behaviors established during that first era should provide protection against possible traumas during adolescence and adulthood. Proper early familial treatment, like early vaccination, might inoculate the child against vulnerability to future distress. Finally, faith in the permanent influence of early experience is in accord with the commitment to political egalitarianism that is so strong in Western Protestant democracies. If society treats children properly during the opening years there is at least the hope that the distress, incompetence, and hopelessness that prevent full political participation by all adult citizens could be eliminated and a truly egalitarian society established.

I recently interviewed a 14½-year-old girl who spent most of the first 30 months of her life in a crib in a small bedroom with no toys and a sister one year older than herself. The mother, who felt unable to care for her fourth child, restricted her to the bedroom and instructed her 8-year-old daughter to care for the child. When she was removed to a foster home at 2½ years of age, she was severely malnourished, retarded in weight and height, and so retarded psychologically that she was untestable. She has remained with the same foster family for the last 12 years. At present her full scale IQ is 88; she performs normatively on a wide battery of cognitive tests and her interpersonal behavior is not seriously different from that of an average rural Ohio adolescent.

Koluchová (1972) has recently reported a similar developmental history for twin Czechoslovakian boys who were placed in total isolation by their stepmother and father from 18 months to 7 years. Most of the time the boys were in a small unheated closet, but they were often locked up for long periods in the cellar of the house. The boys were never allowed outside the house and were inhumanly treated. When the children were removed from the home at age 7 they were physically ill, psychologically untestable, and displayed extreme surprise and fear to common events like automobiles and toys. This extreme behavior, which resembled that of Harlow's surrogate-reared monkeys, gradually abated in the hospital environment. The boys were sent to a children's home for six months and then to a foster home. When the boys were tested at 11 years of age—only a few years after their emergence from the isolated environment—their full scale Wechsler IQ scores were 95 and 93, and the physician noted that they appeared above average for their age.

THE GUATEMALAN STUDY

I recently observed infants and children living in an isolated, subsistence farming village called San Marcos in the highlands of northwest Guatemala. As a result of parental treatment, frequent illness, lack of experiential variety, and mild malnutrition the one-year-olds were quiet, nonsmiling, minimally alert, motorically flaccid and temperamentally passive. This profile of characteristics is in sharp contrast to the modal profile of middle class American infants who are highly vocal, smiling, alert, and active. Experimental and observational procedures designed to assess level of cognitive development among these Indian infants revealed that, relative to the Americans, they were 3 to 12 months behind the latter depending on the cognitive system studied.

The Guatemalan infants were markedly less attentive than the Americans to visual and auditory events, and this difference was greater at one year that it was at 5 months (Kagan and Klein 1973). The Guatemalan infants were retarded relative to the Americans in their tendency to reach for an attractive object that they watched being hidden, and not one of a group of 12 infants revealed facial surprise following a sequence in which he watched an object being hidden under a cloth but saw no object when that cloth was removed. These observations suggest a retardation of about 4 months in the display of behavioral signs diagnostic of what Piaget has called object permanence.

A third source of data came from observations of stranger anxiety. Each of sixteen infants between 8 and 20 months was observed following the first exposure to a strange male. The first age at which obvious apprehension or crying occurred was 13 months, suggesting an approximate lag of 5 months between the Guatemalan and American infants. Information on nonmorphemic babbling and the onset of meaningful speech also supported a diagnosis of slower growth, for there was no marked increase in frequency of babbling or vocalization between 8 and 16 months among twelve infants observed at home. Comparable observations in American homes reveal a significant increase in babbling and the appearance of morphemic vocalization for some children. Furthermore, meaningful speech usually appears first at 2½ years, about 12 to 18 months later than the time of average display of initial words in American children. These data, together with the extremely depressed and withdrawn appearance of the Guateman infants, suggest that for a small set of universal competences displayed by all children during the first two years of life, the Indians were significantly late in attaining these abilities. Since more than 90 percent of the infants were homogeneously passive, nonalert, and quiet, it is unlikely that the recovery of intellectual functioning to be reported was the result of the selective mortality of a small group of severely retarded infants.

The home environments. It is believed that the restricted experiences of the Guatemalan infants were responsible for their slower rate of growth. During most of the first year, the infant is tightly clothed and restricted to the inside of a windowless hut about 75 feet square, constructed of bamboo walls and a roof of thatched grass. The dirt floor contains an open fire, some wood, a straw mat, and a few clay receptacles. Ears of corn, cups, and pots hang from the walls and roof. The light level inside the hut at noon is low and approximates the level outside at dusk. The infant spends approximately a third of his time on his mother in a sling, a third sitting or lying on a straw mat, and the final third sleeping in his hammock. The infant has no conventional toys with which to play, and adults are minimally interactive with him. Time-sampled observations of infants in the home revealed that play or vocalization directed at the baby by others (parents, relatives, or older children) occurred less than 10 percent of the time, in contrast to 25 to 40 percent of the time in American homes. As a result, the babies were generally very quiet.

By 13 to 16 months, however, when the baby becomes mobile and is allowed to leave the hut, he encounters the greater variety inherent in the outside world. He engages an environment that includes domestic animals, other children, trees, rain, clouds, and makes the accomodations those experiences require. The 8- to 10-year-old is assigned tasks and responsibilities, such as helping the father in the field, caring for infants, cooking, cleaning, and carrying water. During the postinfancy years the child becomes increasingly alert and active and it is relevant, therefore, to ask if these older Guatemalan children, who were slow in attaining the universal competences of infancy, are different from less isolated Guatemalan or urban Western children with respect to some of the universal cognitive competences of preadolescence.

THE COMPETENCE OF OLDER CHILDREN

Tests designed to assess cognitive processes believed to be part of the natural competence of growing children were administered to samples of Guatemalan and American children. We tried to create tests that were culturally fair, recognizing that this goal is, in the extreme, unattainable. We assumed, along with many psychologists, that perceptual analysis, recall and recognition memory, and inference are among the universal cognitive abilities of children (even though they do not exhaust that set), and our tests were designed to evaluate those processes.

Recall memory for familiar objects. The ability to organize experience for commitment to long-term memory and to retrieve that information on demand is a basic cognitive skill. It is generally believed that the form of the organization contains diagnostic information regarding cognitive maturity for, among Western samples, both number of independent units of information as well as the conceptual clustering of that information increase with age.

A twelve-object recall task was administered to the Indian children of San Marcos and to children from a Ladino village seventeen kilometers from Guatemala City whose infant experience was not as restricted. The eighty subjects from the Ladino village were 5 and 7 years old, equally balanced for age and sex. The fifty-five subjects from San Marcos were between 5 and 12 years of age (26 boys and 29 girls).

The twelve miniature objects to be recalled were common to village life and belonged to three conceptual categories: animals (pig, dog, horse, cow); kitchen utensils (knife, spoon, fork, glass); and clothing (pants, dress, underpants, hat). Each child was first required to name the objects and if the child was unable to he was given the name. The child was told that after the objects had been randomly arranged on a board he would have 10 seconds to inspect them, after which they would be covered with a cloth, and he would be required to say all the objects he could remember.

Table 1 contains the average number of objects recalled and the number of pairs of conceptually similar words recalled—an index of clustering—for the first two trials. The maximum clustering score for a single trial was 9 points. All the children showed a level of clustering beyond chance expectation (which is between 1.5 and 2.0 pairs for recall scores of 7 to 8 words), recall scores increased with age for children in both village (F ranged from 11.2 to 27.7, p < .05), and there was no significant difference in performance between the two samples. Indeed, the San Marcos children performed slightly better than the Ladino youngsters.

No 5- or 6-year-old in either village and only twelve of the forty 7-year-olds in the Ladino village were attending school. School for the others consisted of little more than semiorganized games. Moreover, none of the Indian children from San Marcos had ever left

TABLE 1
MEAN NUMBER OF OBJECTS AND PAIRS RECALLED

	Ladino village			
	Trial 1		Trial 2	
Age	Recall	Pairs	Recall	Pairs
5	5.2	2.1	5.4	2.1
7	6.7	3.3	7.8	3.7

	Indian village			
	Trial 1		Trial 2	
Age	Recall	Pairs	Recall	Pairs
5–6	7.1	3.4	7.8	3.8
7–8	8.6	3.4	8.3	3.6
9–10	10.3	4.9	10.3	4.3
11–12	9.6	3.4	10.1	3.6

the village, and the 5- and 6-year-olds typically spent most of the day within a 500-yard radius of their homes. Hence, school attendance and contact with books and a written language do not seem to be prerequisites for clustering in young children.

The recall and cluster scores obtained in Guatemala were remarkably comparable to those reported for middle class American children. Appel *et al.* (1971) presented twelve pictures to Minneapolis children in Grade 1 (approximately age 7), and fifteen pictures to children in Grade 5 (approximately age 11) in a single trial recall task similar to the one described here. The recall scores were 66 percent for the 7-year-olds and 80 percent for the 11-year-olds. These values are almost identical to those obtained in both Guatemalan villages. The cluster indexes were also comparable. The American 7-year-olds had a cluster ratio of 0.25; the Indian 5- and 6-year-olds had a ratio of 0.39.[1]

Recognition memory. The robust performance on recall was also found on a recognition memory task for thirty-two photos of faces, balanced for sex, child versus adult, and Indian versus Caucasian, administered to thirty-five American and thirty-eight San Marcos children 8 to 11 years of age. Each child initially inspected thirty-two chromatic photographs of faces, one at a time, in a self-paced procedure. Each child's recognition memory was tested by showing him thirty-two pairs of photographs (each pair was of the same sex,

1. The cluster index is the ratio of the number of pairs recalled to the product of the number of categories in the list times one less than the number of words in each category.

age, and ethnicity), one of which was old and the other new. The child had to state which photograph he had seen during the inspection phase. Although the American 8- and 9-year-olds performed slightly better than the Guatemalans (82 versus 70 percent) there was no significant cultural difference among the 10- and 11-year-olds (91 versus 87 percent). Moreover, there was no cultural difference at any age for the highest performance attained by a single child. These data are in accord with those of Kagan *et al.* (1973) and Scott (1973).

The favored interpretation of the poorer performance of the younger children in both recognition memory studies is that some of them did not completely understand the task, and others did not activate the proper problem-solving strategies during the registration and retrieval phases of the task.

It appears that recall and recognition memory are basic cognitive functions that seem to mature in a regular way in a natural environment. The cognitive retardation observed during the first year does not have any serious predictive validity for these two important aspects of cognitive functioning for children 10 to 11 years old.

Perceptual analysis. The Guatemalan children were also capable of solving difficult Embedded Figures Test items. The test consisted of twelve color drawings of familiar objects in which a triangle had been embedded as part of the object. The child had to locate the hidden triangle. The test was administered to the rural Indian children of San Marcos, as well as to less isolated Indians living close to Guatemala City (labeled Indian$_1$ in figure 1), Ladino villages, and two groups from Guatemala City.

The Guatemala City middle class children had the highest scores and, except for San Marcos, the rural children the poorest. The surprisingly competent performance of the San Marcos children results, we believe, from the more friendly conditions of testing. This suggestion is affirmed by an independent study in which a special attempt was made to maximize rapport and comprehension of instructions with a group of rural isolated children before administering a large battery of tests. Although all test performances were not facilitated by this rapport-raising procedure, performance on the Embedded Figures Test was improved considerably. It is important to note that no 5- or 6-year-old was completely incapable of solving some of these problems. The village differences in mean

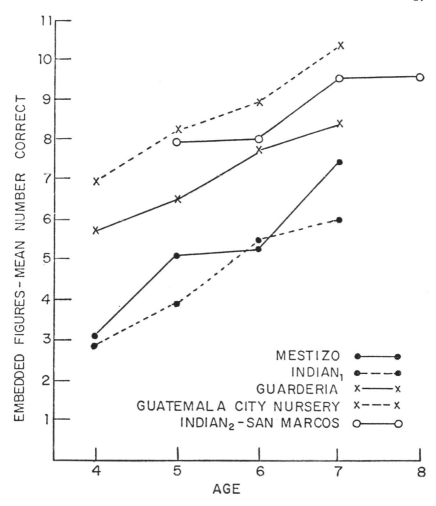

FIG. 1. Mean number correct on the Embedded Figures Test

score reflect the difficulty that the rural children had with three or four of the harder items. This was the first time that many rural children had even seen a two-dimensional drawing and most of the 5-, 6-, and 7-year-olds in San Marcos had no opportunity to play with books, paper, pictures, or crayons. Nonetheless, these children solved seven or eight of the test items. As with recall and recognition memory, the performance of the San Marcos child was comparable to that of his age peer in a modern urban setting.

Perceptual inference. The competence of the San Marcos chil-

dren on the Embedded Figures Test is affirmed by their performance on a test administered only in San Marcos and Cambridge
and called Perceptual Inference. The children (60 American and
55 Guatemalan, 5 to 12 years old) were shown a schematic drawing
of an object and asked to guess what that object might be if the
drawing were completed. The child was given a total of four clues
for each of thirteen items, where each clue added more information. The child had to guess an object from an incomplete illustration, to make an inference from minimal information (see figures 2
and 3).

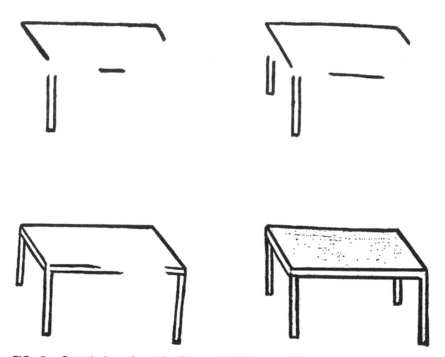

FIG. 2.   Sample item from the Perceptual Inference Test

There was no significant cultural difference for the children 7 to
12 years old, although the American 5- and 6-year-olds did perform
significantly better than the Indian children. In San Marcos, performance improved from 62 percent correct on one of the first two
clues for the 5- and 6-year-olds to 77 percent correct for the 9- to
12-year-olds. The comparable changes for the American children
were from 77 to 84 percent (see figure 4).

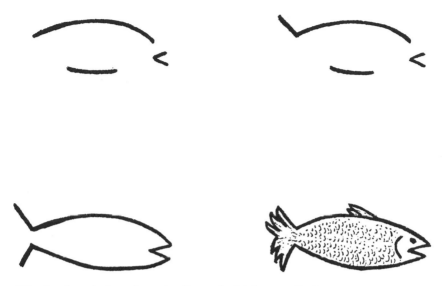

FIG. 3. Sample item from the Perceptual Inference Test

Familiarity with the test objects was critical for success. All the San Marcos children had seen hats, fish, and corn and these items were rarely missed. By contrast, many American children failed these items. No San Marcos child not attending school, and therefore unfamiliar with books, correctly guessed the book item; whereas most of those in school guessed it correctly. As with memory and perceptual analysis, the retardation seen during infancy did not predict comparable retardation in the ability of the 11-year-old to make difficult perceptual inferences.

Conceptual inference. The San Marcos child also performed well on questions requiring conceptual inference. In this test, the child was told verbally three characteristics of an object and required to guess the object. Some of the examples included: what has wings, eats chickens, and lives in a tree; what moves trees, cannot be seen, and makes one cold; what is made of wood, is used to carry things, and allows one to make journeys. There was improved performance with age; the 5- and 6-year-olds obtained an average of 9 out of 14 correct, and the 11- and 12-year-olds obtained 12 out of 14 correct. The San Marcos child was capable of making inferences from both visual and verbal information.

This corpus of data implies that slower attainment of selected

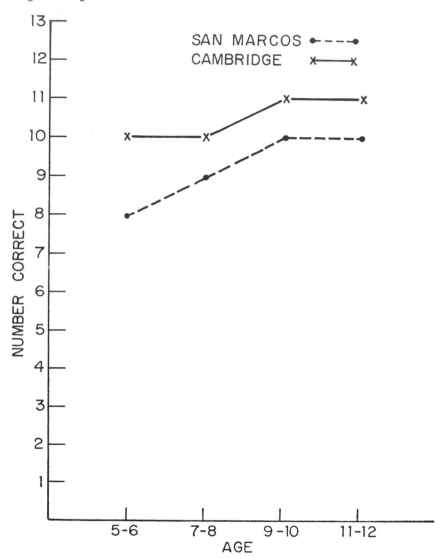

FIG. 4. Number correct on the Perceptual Test

universal competences of infancy does not have any important implications for the competences of the preadolescents with respect to perceptual analysis, perceptual inference, recall, and recognition memory. Indeed, the Guatemalan 10-year-olds performed at a level comparable to those of American middle class children.

The suggestion that basic cognitive competences emerge at different times and that the child retains the capacity for actualization of the basic human competences until a late age is not substantially different from the earlier conclusions of Dennis and Najarian (1957). Although the forty-nine infants 2 to 12 months of age living in poorly staffed Lebanese institutions were seriously retarded on the Cattell developmental scale (mean developmental quotient of 68 compared with a quotient of 102 for a comparison group), the 4½- to 6-year-olds who had resided in the same institution all their lives performed at a level comparable to American norms on a memory test (Knox Cubes) as well as on Porteus mazes and the Goodenough Draw-a-Man-Test.

Of more direct relevance is Dennis's (1973) recent follow-up study of sixteen children who were adopted out of the same Lebanese institution between 12 and 24 months of age—the period durin which the San Marcos infant leaves the unstimulating environment of the dark hut—with an average developmental quotient of 50 on the Cattell Infant Scale. Even though the assessment of later intellectual ability was based on the culturally biased Stanford-Binet IQ test, the average IQ, obtained when the children were between 4 and 12 years old, was 101, and thirteen of the sixteen children had IQ scores of 90 or above (Dennis 1973).

This finding is in substantial agreement with a recent follow-up study of sixty-five 4½-year-old children who had spent their first 2 to 4 years in an institution in which an exclusive relation between an infant and one caretaker was actively discouraged. Of the original group of sixty-five, fifteen were now living with their natural mothers, twenty-four had been adopted, and twenty-six were still living in the institution. There was no difference among the three groups at 4½ years of age on Wechsler IQ scores (the IQ means ranged from 100 to 115). Although the institutionalized children had been retarded in language development when they were 2 years old, they were not retarded with respect to British norms at 4½ years. "No evidence of cognitive retardation, verbal or otherwise, was found in a group of 4-year-old children institutionalized since early infancy. . . . As far as reversibility of the ill effects of institutionalization is concerned, cognitive retardation was reversed even within the institution between ages 2 and 4" (Tizard and Rees 1974:97, 98; see also Rheingold and Bayley 1958).

ANIMAL INVESTIGATIONS

More dramatic support for the notion that psychological development is resilient comes from recent experimental studies with animals. Several years ago Harlow's group demonstrated that although monkeys reared in isolation for the first six months displayed abnormal and often bizarre social behaviors they could, if the experimenter were patient, solve the complex learning problems normally administered to feral-born monkeys. The prolonged isolation did not destroy their cognitive competence (Harlow, Schiltz, and Harlow 1969). More recently, Suomi and Harlow (1972) have shown that even the stereotyped and bizarre social behavior shown by 6-month isolates can be altered by placing them with female monkeys three months younger than themselves over a 26-week therapeutic period. "By the end of the therapy period the behavioral levels were virtually indistinguishable from those of the socially competent therapist monkeys" (Suomi and Harlow 1972:491; see Gomber and Mitchell 1974 for a similar result).

Even imprinting toward a nonnatural object in a laboratory context seems to be reversible. In a laboratory context Hess attempted to imprint ducklings to human beings. For twenty continuous hours newly hatched ducklings were exposed to adults and, before long, followed the adults. The ducks were then given a female mallard that had hatched a clutch of several ducklings several hours before. After only an hour and a half of exposure to the female, the human imprinted ducklings followed the female on her first exodus from the nest. The laboratory imprinting had been reversed (Hess 1972). This phenomenon is analogous to changes in the object of primary attachment among primates. Rhesus monkeys were raised from birth with cloth surrogates, their mothers, or a peer monkey for three to ten months. Then all the monkeys were separated from these objects of primary attachment and gradually exposed to spayed, adult female dogs. Initially most of the monkeys were fearful, but this behavior disappeared quickly and after seven hours all monkeys approached the dogs and eventually clung to them. Soon the monkeys displayed the classic signs of attachment—clinging and following. The initial attachment had been changed (Mason and Kenney 1974).

These dramatic alterations in molar behavior are in accord with replicated reports of recovery of visual function in monkeys and cats deprived of patterned light soon after birth (Wilson and Riesen 1966, Baxter 1966, Chow and Stewart 1972). Kittens deprived of light for one year recovered basic visual functions after only ten days in the experimenter's home (Baxter 1966); kittens who had one or both eyes sutured for nearly two years were able to learn pattern discriminations with the deprived eye only after moderate training (Chow and Stewart 1972). Even complex cognitive functions can recover following removal of frontal cortex in young monkeys. In a recent dramatic study, rhesus monkeys were given bilateral, orbital prefrontal lesions during the first, fourth, or eighth week of life and compared with age-matched, unoperated controls at 1 to 1½ years and gain at 2 years. The monkeys were tested on spatial delayed response, visual pattern discrimination, spatial delayed alternation, and object discrimination reversal. The task most sensitive to the lesion, spatial delayed alternation, requires the animal to alternate his responses to the right and left food wells on succeeding trials with a 5-second delay between trials. The operated monkeys were seriously impaired when tested at 1 and 1½ years of age, regardless of when the operation had been performed (1, 4, or 8 weeks). But when they were 2 years old, they had recovered that competence and were not significantly different from the unoperated controls. The investigators suggested that this result was because of maturation of other cortical regions during the second year of life (Miller, Goldman, and Rosvold 1973).

If the extreme behavioral and perceptual sequellae of isolation and brain ablation in monkeys and cats can be altered by such brief periods of rehabilitative experience or time for recovery, it is not difficult to believe that the rural Guatemalan infant is capable of as dramatic a recovery over a period of nine years. These data do not indicate the impotence of early environments, but rather the potency of the environment in which the organism is functioning. There is no question that early experience seriously affects kittens, monkeys, and children. If the first environment does not permit the full actualization of psychological competences, the organism will function below his ability as long as he remains in that context. But if he is transferred to an environment that presents greater variety and requires more accomodations, he seems more capable of exploiting that experience and repairing the damage wrought by the first environment than some theorists have implied.

CONCLUSIONS

The total corpus of information implies that the young animal retains an enormous capacity for change in early patterns of behavior and cognitive competence, especially if the initial environment is seriously altered. The data offer no firm support for the popular belief that certain events during the first year can produce irreversible consequences in either human or infrahuman infants. If one limits the discussion to universal cognitive competences, in contrast to culturally specific skills, it appears that a slower rate of mastery of the universal abilities during the first two years places no serious constraints on the eventual attainment of many of the competences of preadolescence. For most of this century developmental psychology has been friendly toward the pole of the irreversibility-reversibility theme that posited irreversible effects of early experience. The extreme form of that position is as unlikely as the opposite pole that assumes complete capacity for resilience of all dispositions at any age. The purpose of this paper has been to persuade the receptive reader to move just a little closer toward the latter view. The first messages written on the *tabula rasa* may not necessarily be the most difficult to erase.

REFERENCES

APPEL, L. F., R. G. COOPER, N. MCCARRELL, J. S. KNIGHT, S. R. YUSSEN, and J. H. FLAVELL. 1971. The Developmental Acquisition of the Distinction between Perceiving and Memory. Unpublished Manuscript.

BAXTER, B. L. 1966. Effect of Visual Deprivation during Postnatal Maturation on the Electroencephalogram of the Cat. *Experimental Neurology* 14:224–237.

CHOW, K. L., and D. L. STEWART. 1972. Reversal of Structural and Functional Effects of Longterm Visual Deprivation in Cats. *Experimental Neurology* 34:409–433.

DENNIS, W. *Children of the Creche.* Century-Crofts. 1973.

DENNIS, W., and P. NAJARIAN. 1957. Infant Development under Environmental Handicap. *Psychological Monographs* 71, no. 436.

GOMBER, J., and G. MITCHELL. 1974. Preliminary Report on Adult Male Isolation-reared Rhesus Monkeys Caged with Infants. *Developmental Psychology* 10:298.

HARLOW, H. F., K. A. SCHILTZ, M. K. HARLOW. 1969. The Effects of Social Isolation on the Learning Performance of Rhesus Monkeys, *Proceedings of the Second International Congress of Primatology* (C. R. Carpenter, ed.), Vol. I. Karger.

HESS, E. H. 1972. Imprinting in a Natural Laboratory. *Scientific American* 227:24–31.

HOLTON, G. 1973. *Thematic Origins of Scientific Thought.* Harvard University Press.

KAGAN, J., R. E. KLEIN, M. M. HAITH, and F. J. MORRISON. 1973. Memory and Meaning in Two Cultures. *Child Development* 44:221–223.

KAGAN, J., and R. E. KLEIN. 1973. Cross-Cultural Perspectives on Early Development. *American Psychologist* 28:947–961.

KOLUCHOVÁ, J. 1972. Severe Deprivation in Twins: A Case Study. *Journal of Child Psychology and Psychiatry* 13:107–111.

MASON, W. A., and M. D. KENNEY. 1974. Redirection of Filial Attachments in Rhesus Monkeys: Dogs as Mother Surrogates. *Science* 183:1209–1211.

MILLER, E. A., P. S. GOLDMAN, and H. E. ROSVOLD. 1973. Delayed Recovery of Function Following Orbital Prefrontal Lesions in Infant Monkeys. *Science* 182:304–306.

RHEINGOLD, H. L. and N. BAYLEY. 1959. The Later Effects of an Experimental Modification of Mothering. *Child Development* 30:363–372.

SCOTT, M. S. 1973. The Absence of Interference Effects in Preschool Children's Picture Recognition. *Journal of Genetic Psychology* 122: 121–126.

SUOMI, S. J., and H. F. HARLOW. 1972. Social Rehabilitation of Isolate-reared Monkeys. *Developmental Psychology* 6:487–496.

TIZARD, B., and J. REES. 1974. A Comparison of the Effects of Adoption, Restoration to the Natural Mother, and Continued Institutionalization on the Cognitive Development of 4-year-old Children. *Child Development* 45:92–99.

WILSON, P. D., and A. H. RIESEN. 1966. Visual Developments in Rhesus Monkeys Neonatally Deprived of Patterned Light. *Journal of Comparative and Physiological Psychology* 61:87–95.

Theorizing about Socialization of Cognition

MICHAEL COLE and SYLVIA SCRIBNER

INTRODUCTION

Speculation and disagreement about the influence of cultural environment on the development of the mind has characterized the social sciences since their inception in the nineteenth century. Within both anthropology and psychology, it has been possible to find defenders of the idea that children raised in nontechnological societies fail to develop "higher order" mental skills; it is just as easy to find adherents of the position that all apparent differences mask underlying, universal equivilences (see Boas 1911, LeVine 1970, Mead 1964, Scribner and Cole 1973).

While we have also engaged in such discussions (Cole and Bruner 1971, Cole and Scribner 1974) we have grown increasingly uneasy about the nature of the debate. When asked to summarize our current knowledge about the "socialization of the intellect" by editor Schwartz, we found that conceptual problems surrounding the na-

MICHAEL COLE is associate professor of ethnographic psychology and director of the Laboratory of Comparative Human Cognition at the Rockefeller University, New York. SYLVIA SCRIBNER is a senior research associate in the same laboratory.
We wish to thank the Carnegie Corporation for support in the preparation of this paper. The comments of Daniel Wagner and Ted Schwartz on an earlier draft of this paper are also gratefully acknowledged.

ture of data and its relation to theory prevented us from providing more than a catalogue of facts for which there was no agreed-upon interpretation by anthropologists and psychologists currently working on this question. Consequently, we have decided to examine the presuppositions that anthropologists and psychologists bring to the enterprise, the observations they are led to make, and the kinds of inferences about "socialization of the intellect" that have become accepted within each discipline. We point out some weaknesses inherent in current formulations, and offer a framework designed to produce a common ground for future explorations of this question.

As an illustration of the difficulties that concern us, we have chosen a brief interchange between Margaret Mead and Jerome Kagan which took place at the convention of the American Association for the Advancement of Science in the fall of 1972.

Professor Kagan had just completed a report on psychological research in Guatemala. Working with young infants on a task that assessed their responses to stimulus novelty, Kagan had found that rural Guatemalan children were several months retarded in the "cognitive function of activation of hypotheses" at around one year of age. Working with older children, using recall of familiar objects, recognition memory, an embedded figure test, and other standard procedures for assessing cognitive development in the United States, Kagan asserted that there were only minimal differences between Guatemalan and American children by the age of 8 or 9 years. Taken together, the pattern of results led Kagan to conclude that "infant retardation seems to be partially reversible and cognitive development during the early years more resilient than had been supposed (Kagan and Klein 1973:957)."

Following Professor Kagan's presentation, Professor Mead took the floor to comment (we quote from memory): "Why has it taken psychologists so long to discover what anthropologists have known all along?" To which Kagan replied, "I guess we're a little slow."

It seemed to us at the time, and seems so still, that in the laughter which followed this charming interchange, an important point was overlooked. In a very basic sense, Professors Mead and Kagan were talking past each other. Not only had Kagan failed to discover what Mead already knew, they did not (as anthropologist and psychologist respectively) know the same things. They were only, on this occasion, expressing their shared opinion that Guatemalan peasants are mentally competent. Unexplored were possible, even probable disagreements about the suitability of the data for such a conclusion and the implications of other research showing that performance among Guatemalan or similar peoples were not up to "American standards" on tasks very like the ones that Kagan used. The crucial problem arises just from the fact that data do exist which seem to point to conclusions antithetical to Mead's and Kagan's. Such data have been gathered by both anthropologists (Gladwin 1970) and psychologists (Greenfield and Bruner 1969) who conclude that there exist fundamental differences in the thought processes of people socialized into different cultures, differences that are related directly to such theoretical constructs as "level of cognitive development." How are such data and conclusions to be interpreted?

We believe the general failure of anthropologists and psychologists to share the same definitions, facts, and theoretical constructs is a fundamental impediment to our understanding of the relation between culture and the development of cognitive processes; all the more so because this failure often goes unnoticed. Because they share a common interest and a common terminology, psychologists and anthropologists tend to make the assumption that they share a common topic of inquiry—each in his own way pursues the link between social experiences and cognition. We believe this assumption is unfounded on both sides of the equation: anthropologists and psychologists do not mean the same thing when they speak of cognitive "consequences"; they do not agree on the characteristics of culture that are potential "antecedents"; and they distrust each other's method for discovering the links between the two. As long as these underlying differences remain "unnoticed," there is little hope that they will be overcome. In this paper, we examine some of the basic differences between the two disciplines as they have been expressed in theory and practice and consider whether and how they might be resolved. While we are concerned with the differing interpretations of both culture and cognition, our major attention is directed to the way in which the two disciplines treat cognition. For reasons that we hope become clear in the course of the discussion, we believe that unless there is some agreement on what "cognitive consequences" we are studying, there are no guidelines for deciding what aspects of culture are relevant to the search for "critical socializing" experiences.

The disagreements between anthropologists and psychologists on the nature of cognition and how it is to be studied are interrelated in many complex ways, but we find it useful to consider them in terms of three dichotomies: (1) emphasis on content or process in defining cognition; (2) choice of naturally occurring or contrived situations as contexts for data collection; and (3) reliance on observational or manipulative research techniques. Some investigators cross over from one pole to another, but, in general, anthropologists emphasize content, natural occurrences, and observation, while psychologists stress process, contrived situations, and experimental control. As we shall see, the way in which the investigator defines cognition influences his choice of research method and, in turn, his choice of method determines the data he collects and thus the inferences he can make about the nature of cognition. Although we are presenting these choices as dichotomies because they are often posed that way in partisan discussion, we hope to show that the oppositions are more apparent than real and that both approaches can be integrated in the research enterprise. In the final section we describe and criticize our early attempts at an anthropological-psychological integration and suggest directions that might be taken in future research.

AN EXAMPLE

How the differing approaches work out in practice can be illustrated by the hypothetical responses of psychologists and anthropologists to an actual piece of cross-cultural research on cognition. We have chosen for this example a recently published study by Daniel Wagner (1974) in Mexico entitled, "The Development of Short-term and Incidental Memory: A Cross-Cultural Study."

Wagner's task required his subjects to recall the position of one of 7 familiar items in a linear array. The location of the to-be-recalled item varied from trial to trial. The items (pictures on cards) were shown one at a time for two seconds each, and then turned face down. After all 7 had been presented, a duplicate of one item in the row was shown to the subject and he (she) had to point to its location. At two seconds per item, and taking into account the time required to turn over the cards, the longest interval between presentation and recall test was about 20 seconds, the shortest about 3 seconds.

We selected this work for several reasons. First, it is a technically fine piece of research (Cole was present when the work was begun and knows how carefully and painstakingly Wagner chose his stimulus material, worked on his instruction, trained his assistant, and observed each data collection session). Second, the research was carried out among Mayan people living in Yucatan not far from Kagan's site in Guatemala and it investigated memory, one of the "basic cognitive functions" Kagan studied.[1] But Wagner's conclusions seem diametrically opposed to Kagan's:

Higher-level mnemonic strategies in memory may do more than "lag" by several years—the present data indicate that without formal schooling, such skills may not develop at all (Wagner 1974:395).

This conclusion is based on several facts, two of which suffice for this discussion. (1) Overall recall of the target item improved almost entirely as a function of number of years of education, not as a function of age (subjects ranged in educational experience from 1 to 15 years, in age from 7 to 35 years). (2) Analysis of the function relating time-of-delay between presentation and test to amount recalled showed the pattern of results associated with application of rehearsal strategies (Wagner's referent for "higher level mnemonic strategies") *only* for those subjects (adults or children) who attained more than the fifth grade in school.

INTELLECT: CONTENT VS. PROCESS

Developmental psychologists might find Wagner's results interesting for a variety of reasons. Age and educational experience are hopelessly confounded in the United States. Wagner provides evidence that the traditional developmental function seen in the work

---

1. While Kagan's own research might seem the most appropriate vehicle for this discussion, several factors, including those given in the text, argue against making his data the focal point of the presentation. Paramount is that while we share Kagan's belief in mental competence of Guatemalan peasants, we do not believe that this conclusion follows from the published reports (Kagan and Klein 1973, Kagan, Haith, and Morrison 1973). Since classification of our interpretation would require a lengthy discussion located almost entirely within the domain of psychological theory and data analysis, we have chosen a less controversial study to illustrates paradoxes that are interdisciplinary in scope.

of Hagan (1971) and Flavell (1970) on mnemonic development may be more of an "educational development" than a maturational one.

Cross-cultural psychologists would add Wagner's results to the growing list of instances where formal schooling seems to affect intellectual performance (cf. Cole and Scribner 1974, for a review). They would also look carefully at the procedures and groups used to derive hypotheses as to why formal education makes a difference in Wagner's work and not Kagan's. Kagan did not vary independently the age, educational level, and urbanization of his subjects. Does his finding of "no difference" in memory skills have to do with marked effects of schooling? Is the difference to be associated with the age of his subjects (his oldest children were 11–12 years old while Wagner's effect occurred at the age/education level that averaged 14–15 years and 8 years of education)? Do performance differences have to do with the different tasks Kagan and Wagner used to diagnose memory skills,[2] or differences in the cultures of Yucatecan and Guatemalan Maya?

There are clearly a great many questions psychologists might raise about this research and its interpretation. But there is one question they are unlikely to deal with: no matter how different their theoretical persuasions, most psychologists will take it for granted that this research is, more or less adequately, "measuring" population variations in memory *processes*. They will share the basic assumption that it is possible, in principle and in fact, to examine memory processes across diverse social groups with relatively little concern for the content of what is being remembered.

We do not mean to imply that psychologists do not put a good deal of time and care into selecting their experimental material. Especially in recent years, stung by accusations of ethnocentrism and cultural bias, investigators have exercised considerable ingenuity in devising what they consider to be "culturally fair" materials and in assuring that materials are equally "familiar" to the cultural groups being compared (see Glick 1975 and Berry 1969, for interesting discussions on comparability in cross-cultural experimenta-

2. It is unlikely that the nature of the tasks is the locus of apparent differences in these authors' conclusions. We have recently completed a series of studies in Yucatan, including a free recall study quite similar to the one used by Kagan, but found education-dependent results parallel to those obtained by Wagner (Sharp and Cole 1974).

tion). But this very effort contains within it the notion that the content of the intellectual task can be neutralized and in some sense held "consant" across groups so that performance differences can be assumed to reflect differences in "pure process."

To be sure, present-day psychological investigators are showing that for many intellectual tasks there is a relationship between the nature of the task material and the operations that are brought to bear on it (Price-Williams, Gordon, and Ramirez 1969, Irwin and McLaughlin 1970, Cole *et al.* 1971). In *practice,* however, most psychologists still tend to interpret performance with a given set of materials as revealing some fixed set of "content-free" processes within the subject population (cf. Berry and Dasen 1974). This is what they *mean* when they talk about cultural variations in cognition.

But psychologists are by no means alone in finding it difficult to deal with content-process relationships in cognition. Anthropological theorizing about cognition in some ways presents a mirror image to what we have just described. Many anthropologists will criticize the Wagner experiments because Wagner attempts to come to conclusions about the memory of Yucatec Mayans using material that is artificial, meaningless or of no "interest" to the Mayans (despite his use of materials intended to have the opposite characteristics). A fair test of memory, they may argue, requires that each cultural group be tested with materials and tasks that are meaningfully organized within that society. While this argument recognizes the legitimacy of investigating process when content is taken into account, in *practice,* most anthropologists tend to ignore possible process variations and attribute to differences in "content" all observed cultural group differences. If the Iatmul display a prodigious memory for totemic names (Bateson 1958) and the Swazi for cattle transactions (Bartlett 1932), they make the assumption that the "memories" of Iatmul and Swazi are the same; they just remember different things. What the majority of anthropologists mean by cultural variations in cognition are differences in thinking or memory *content.*

Levy-Bruhl remains the classic example of the ambiguity with which terms referring to cognition—terms like "thought" and "perception"—are handled in anthropological literature. What are we to conclude when he asserts that:

primitives perceive nothing in the same way we do. The social milieu which surrounds them is different, the external world they perceive differs from that which we apprehend (1966:30).

or

primitives perceive with eyes like ours, but they do not perceive with the same minds (1966:31).

Here, and in many places in his writing, Levy-Bruhl oscillates between an insistence that he is talking only about "collective representations" (culture-wide belief systems or thinking *content*, in the context of this discussion), and examples that imply that he is talking about specific cognitive *processes* operating within individuals.

This slipping from content-to-process was roundly criticized by Boas (1911) many years ago; he pointed out that one cannot legitimately infer psychological processes directly from an examination of culture-wide beliefs and attitudes. Because Levy-Bruhl's conclusions have been widely repudiated, it might appear that Boas's caution was taken to heart by succeeding generations of anthropologists and that we are beating a dead dog. But consider this statement from a leading contemporary anthropologist whose views on cognition appear to be the direct antithesis of Levy-Bruhl's: "Both science and magic require the same sort of mental operations and they differ not so much in kind as in the different types of phenomena to which they are applied" (Levi-Strauss 1966:13). Here again, what is stressed are differences in content between two thought systems ("phenomena to which they are applied") and the same unwarranted leap is made from an analysis of *cultural* systems to a generalization about individual mental processes. We agree that Levy-Bruhl's conclusions about mental processes are unfounded; but so are Levi-Strauss's.

The problem arises in part from the limitation of dealing with thought as content. But further problems are posed for psychological and anthropological theorizing because the focus on content or process influences choices for our two remaining dichotomies.

CRITICAL SITUATIONS: NATURAL VS. CONTRIVED?
Let us return to our example and the discussion of what the Wagner experiment tells us about memory development. Just as psy-

chologists assume that this experiment taps some underlying process, so they tend to assume that this *same* process is operative outside of the experimental situation. The motivation for the research, after all, is to shed light on the role of various experiences (school, literacy, technology, culture) on the development of memory skills of Yucatecans or Guatemalans in general—not just on the skills of individuals serving as subjects in a specialized experiment. We think it is safe to say, however, that attempts to reach general conclusions from this experiment represent the kind of psychological theorizing that would come under attack by anthropologists.

Robert Edgerton succinctly summarized the position of many anthropologists by saying that the roots of anthropology's anti-experimental convictions

are deep in anthropological history. . . . At heart, anthropologists are naturalists whose commitment is to the phenomena themselves. Anthropologists have always believed that human phenomena can best be understood by procedures that are primarily sensitive to context, be it situational, social or cultural (1974:63–64).

With this commitment to phenomena as they naturally occur, it is easy to understand why anthropologists might challenge the generalizability of the Wagner findings. They may be inclined to interpret the results as reflecting only differences in the way various people respond to the demands of artificially contrived situations.

For example, focusing on the performance difference between Wagner's subjects who went to school and those who did not, the anthropologist might conclude that going to school helps people to interpret the demands of nonnatural experimental tasks. In effect, this line of analysis would lead to a conclusion such as: The less educated subjects were sufficiently unfamiliar with such tasks that the instructions failed to communicate the task demands clearly. The difference in performance would then be considered a reflection of comprehension of the task, not of short-term memory skills.

This analysis might be bolstered by reference to numerous everyday, naturally occurring activities in which uneducated subjects demonstrate adequate short-term memory. For example, it might be pointed out that interpreting complex grammatical phrases with embedded clauses or carrying on a normal conversation are both contexts that require and produce short-term recall many times a day in all Yucatecan adults. Knowledge of Yucatecan culture might lead to suggestions of other contexts in which short-term recall must be at work, such as the production of complicated patterns in hammock weaving. How is the evidence from such naturally occurring situations to be squared with experimental evidence? What do we conclude if the two sources of evidence seem to conflict? Before attempting to answer those questions, we need to consider our third dichotomy.

OBSERVATION OR EXPERIMENT

In addition to stressing the need to investigate cognition in context, the anthropologist values what Edgerton describes as "unobtrusive" methods of research:

Our methods are primarily unobtrusive, non-reactive ones; we observe, we participate, we learn, hopefully we understand. . . . This is our unspoken paradigm and it is directly at odds with the discovery of truth by experimentation (1974:63–64).

Here is yet another source of anthropological attack on the generalizability of experimental results: group differences found in experiments simply reflect differences in the readiness with which individuals of differing cultural, social, and educational backgrounds enter into the "subject role" and the behaviors appropriate to this particular social encounter. The experiment, by its very nature, changes the phenomenon under investigation.

Keeping these anthropological criticisms of the experimental method in mind, let us reverse the case and consider the shortcomings of naturalistic observation as a research methodology. We will not argue here the validity of Edgerton's characterization of anthropological method, although it should be recognized that he is expressing the ideal, or perhaps the ideology, not the reality of anthropological research. Intensive interviewing of selected informants is not unobtrusive and is rarely nonreactive. Our purpose, however, is to illustrate the restrictions of the unstructured observational method for drawing inferences about individual cognitive processes. These restrictions are recognized and analyzed with unusual clarity by Bateson (1958) in his discussion of memory skills among the Iatmul. Bateson picks memory as his topic because his ethnographic work revealed that learned men among the Iatmul are veritable storehouses of totems and names that are used in debating. Adding the number of name songs belonging to each clan, the number of names per song, and the songs from other clans that some men knew, Bateson estimated that such people must carry ten to twenty thousand names around in their heads. He takes this as prima facie evidence of highly developed memory capacities.

So far, Bateson's discussion could have come straight out of Levy-Bruhl who, along with many others, claimed exceptional memory capacities for nonliterate peoples. Bateson, however, was a field worker conversant with work in the experimental psychology of memory of the period, so his analysis did not stop here.

Bateson went on to provide an early test of a *psychologically derived* hypothesis about the relation between culture and memory. Specifically, he provided convincing evidence against Bartlett's hypothesis (1932) that preliterate peoples remember by a rote process. He did this by recording the order in which informants offer mythical names on different occasions and by observing that, when asked about past events, the Iatmul do not have to describe a series of chronologically related events to give a meaningful reply. He also studied the techniques of debating and easily rejected the notion that people call in their store of names in any rote fashion. He even provided evidence about the deliberate use of mnemonic devices in debating.

But then Bateson was stuck, which he clearly recognized:

though we may with fair certainty say that rote memory is not the principal process stimulated in Iatmul erudition, it is not possible to say which of the higher processes is chiefly involved (1958:224).

He goes on to offer some hypotheses about plausible memory mechanisms underlying the Iatmul achievements, but these he cannot be sure of on the basis of ethnographic data alone. As he puts it:

I have little material which would demonstrate the methods of thought of individual natives, and therefore depend almost entirely upon the details of the culture, deducing therefrom the patterns of thought of the individuals. Ideally it should be possible to trace the same processes in the utterances of informants and in individual behavior in experimental conditions as well as in the norms of the culture (1958:229).

Bateson's work clearly illustrates the importance of ethnographic inquiry in exploring culture-thought relations. It illustrates the way in which strategic observations can rule out a hypothesized process, and it suggests situations in which remembering is an important activity. It just as clearly illustrates that a purely observational approach encounters specific limits in accounting for the way in which cultural demands influence thought processes.

As we examine these oppositions between anthropological and psychological approaches to intellect, the limitations of each approach taken by itself become apparent. It is painfully obvious that each discipline rests on a very narrow and specialized data base from which it makes overly broad and often improper generalizations. The dangers in this position were clearly specified by Nadel:

unless the relations between social and psychological enquiry are precisely stated, certain dangers, all-too-evident in anthropological and psychological literature, will never be banished. Psychologists will overstate their claims and produce, by valid psychological methods, spurious sociological explanations; or the student of society, while officially disregarding psychology, will smuggle it in by the back door; or he may assign to psychology merely the residue of his enquiry—all the facts with which his own methods seem incapable of dealing (1951:289).

The case for substantive collaboration between psychologists and anthropologists could not be made more clearly. Both groups want to extend the power and range of their theories about the intellectual consequences of differing sociocultural experiences. If each has a limited view of the problem and a limited range of techniques, some combination of resources is needed to accomplish the goal.

But can this be more than a prescription to "do good?" We think so. The dichotomies we have described are traditions that have grown up in practice but are not intrinsic characteristics of the scientific enterprise.

People in both disciplines have pointed to the weaknesses of this dichotomous thinking and have argued that there is no inherent incompatibility between content and process, observation and experiment—and by extension, anthropology and psychology.

Since we have been considering culture and memory, it is sobering to recall that the psychologist Sir Frederick Bartlett (1932), a pioneer in this field, investigated both the content and process of memory in studies conducted a half century ago. He showed how instrumental the "socially dominant interests" of the culture are in determining what individual members of the culture remember. It is no accident that Swazi have "good" memory for cattle transactions and the Iatmul for totemic names, and psychologists wishing to understand memory cannot proceed as if these relationships are arbitrary. Nadel (1951:292) made a similar point in a more general vein. In practice, he said, it is often difficult if not impossible to separate thinking-as-content from thinking-as-process. The psychologist examining any mental mechanism is of necessity examining a mechanism normally operating with material given in society and culture, and he cannot get away from such "living contents" even in the artificial isolation of an experiment. Similarly, if anthropologists are concerned with how "living contents" come into existence and change over history, they need to understand what operations ("processes") individuals bring to the material that is culturally given.

There has also been growing recognition that the dichotomy between observation and experiment is unfounded. Bateson's study of Iatmul memory skills is a fine example of the complementary nature of the two techniques in anthropological practice. The case for a complementary relation between experiment and natural observation within psychology has been argued by a distinguished investigator of comparative behavior whose own research elegantly combined the two research approaches. Schneirla (1972) urged investigators to think of field and laboratory research as basically similar, each making different aspects of behavior available for analysis. "Field work may be thought of as furnishing opportunities for investigation not initially available under laboratory conditions, to be gained through access to the complete natural phenomena . . . the laboratory may be considered as a limited and controllable field in which isolation and quantitative measurement of selected aspects of behavior can be made. Properly speaking, in terms of the logic of science, there is really no experimental method as distinct from observation" (1972:3–4).

Even after clearing away "differences in principle" we are still left with the problem of how integration can be achieved in practice. It would be helpful at this point if we could present a piece of research showing what "ethnographic psychology" actually looks like. Unfortunately we have not been able to find such a model. Our own work on culture and memory was an early attempt to combine anthropological and psychological approaches but it suffered from many of the same shortcomings we have documented here. Although this work has been described in detail elsewhere (Cole *et al.* 1971, Scribner 1974) we present it briefly to show the problems that arose as we struggled to interpret our results and the modifications in research strategy that we developed as a result.[3]

Our studies of memory among the Kpelle began with the expectation based upon anthropological folklore that nonliterates would perform better on a memory task (have more highly developed memory skills) than literates. We not only derived our hypothesis from anthropological literature but we took great care to develop our experimental materials (we were using word lists) from verbal responses given by a representative sample of Kpelle men and women on standard linguistic elicitation tasks. Even with the use of such materials, our initial studies of free recall, using the standard experimental techniques, failed to confirm the notion of "superior memory" among nonliterates. Quite the reverse. The free recall performance of Kpelle rice farmers was such that were we to make simple performance-process inferences, we would have concluded that they were virtually retarded. Furthermore, we might have been led to the conclusion that without schooling to a point where literacy is achieved, higher mnemonic skills do not develop. This would have followed because Kpelle children exposed to about eight years of school, like Mayan children, exhibited recall performances that are associated with "higher mnemonic abilities" in the psychological literature.

We did not jump to such a conclusion. We were disturbed by the discrepancy between our experimental results and the anthropological folklore which motivated them. We were inclined to share the anthropologist's skepticism about the representativeness of performance in an experimental situation and became convinced that no reasonable conclusions about group differences could be made on the basis of results of a single experimental performance. It seemed

---

3. A detailed example of a combined naturalistic and experimental approach to the study of cognitive processes is presented in the final chapter of Cole and Scribner *Culture and Thought: A Psychological Introduction* (1974) .

to us that our task, rather than our subjects' lack of ability, might be the source of poor performance. At the time we thought the solution lay in substituting for the single experiment a series of experiments in which the nature of the task requirements was systematically modified.

So we set out to modify our initial free recall task in such a way that "normal performance" (e.g. the performance we had come to expect from college sophomores) was achieved. From the psychological literature on free recall, we borrowed such manipulations as presenting concrete objects, emphasizing the organizing principles inherent in the materials, varying those principles along both taxonomic and functional lines, paying people to do well, and many others.

Although these studies produced statistically significant variations in some cases, we were far from our goal of observing really good, let alone remarkable recall. In addition to casting about for alternative experimental procedures, we began to ask ourselves about occasions when Kpelle people would be likely to have to recall lists or sets of things as a more-or-less isolated activity. We imagined a wife going off to market who, being illiterate, could not prepare a shopping list. We discovered a Kpelle game where children had quickly to recall the name of many leaves. At some point we recognized that the folk stories we had been collecting for several years were remembered products, albeit not lists of isolated "things." Our seat-of-the-pants "ethnography" of Kpelle remembering, when combined with experimentally derived results, began to produce some rather dramatic changes in performance; under a variety of conditions we began to observe organized, and in some cases, high levels of recall among noneducated Kpelle.

The set of circumstances which changed performance was quite heterogeneous: embedding to-be-recalled items in pseudofolk stories quite clearly indicated that recall was influenced by the organization of the story; associating items with concrete objects (chairs) increased organization and recall as did requiring people to recall one specified category at a time; paired associate learning was clearly influenced by the list structure to a much greater degree than free recall of the same list.

These findings led to a reformulation of the factors underlying recall performance in a range of tasks of which ours were a subsample. We were led to hypothesize that the tasks that produced good performance shared the characteristic that the potential structure of the set of materials was made explicit and the task itself induced the subject to make use of this structure.

Because of the time limitations on research projects (ours actually lasted four years, longer than most) we were not really able to test our inductive hypothesis about the locus of performance differences between educated and noneducated Kpelle. Our ideas about "providing structure" have been shown in the interim to dovetail neatly with a variety of developmental analyses of recall (Brown 1974) but we only vaguely grasped the issue when we had to "close down shop." Fortunately, one study following up these ideas has been completed by Scribner (1974). Her subjects were first required to arrive at a *stable* structuring of to-be-recalled items. Although different populations of subjects structured the materials in different ways, recall was generally good and organized in a manner consistent with the structure provided by the subjects themselves.

Our work then had led us to the point where we could specify with some confidence what features of the task and material controlled good performance. But as soon as we attempted to account for differences in performance among the Kpelle or between Kpelle adults and those of industrialized cultures, we were at a loss. Why did "schooled subjects" among the Kpelle perform so differently from those individuals who had never gone to school? Why did our devices making the structure of the material explicit work so well with traditional farmers? No matter how we analyzed our experimental tasks, we could not get from them to any understanding of the culturally determined experiences that might account for the different deployment of memory skills that we observed among the Kpelle. Nor were we much closer to bridging the gap between anthropological reports of everyday memory feats and our experimental findings. It now seems apparent to us that we cannot account for performance in our experimental tasks until we learn a great deal more about the kind of memory-requiring tasks or situations that Kpelle people (or any people) normally encounter and how the demands of the experimental task compare to the demands imposed by these everyday situations (see Scribner 1975).

For example, suppose that we sought to pursue the line of reasoning that arose during our work on free recall among the Kpelle where we imagined a nonliterate Kpelle wife going off to market. Aside from what our imaginations can tell us, we really know next to nothing about this mundane remembering occasion.

Let us suppose that Kpelle women really do check their larders and then set off for the marketplace. Do they commit the needed items to memory before leaving? Or do they wait until browsing through the seller's stalls to "be reminded" of what they need? Our psychological analysis emphasizes the difference between actively rehearsing to-be-recalled materials and using ready-made recall cues. Which activity does "remembering what groceries to buy" really entail for the Kpelle housewife?

If we are to get beneath such global variables as "urbanization" and "literacy," many more questions such as these need to be posed for a variety of situations where people seem to have to rely on "remembering" in a relatively well-defined observable manner. We need, in effect, an ethnography of a specific cognitive activity, the implications of which are then tested by a variety of observations, including experimental ones. It might turn out that the prominent economic and social activities that traditional Kpelle engage in rarely, if ever, require deliberate, before-the-fact remembering. Or it might turn out that only certain specialists, or all people only on special occasions need engage in such activities. Whichever the case, we would have to be certain to use our analysis of indigenous occasions for remembering as a point of contact between psychological and ethnographic descriptions. We only began such work in our research, and as a result, our study of culture and memory shares the limitations of other cross-cultural research of its kind.

Relatively early in our thinking on this problem we were led to remark that we found it useful to treat experiments as specially contrived situations for the manifestation of cognitive skills. In the light of our subsequent experiences and Schneirla's formulation, it seems to us now that the term cognitive *skills* was gratuitous and that experiments are best seen as specially contrived occasions for cognitive *activity*—a subset of occasions provided in every society for the development and manifestation of intellectual capacities.

In this view both the anthropologist and the psychologist are dealing with the same "stuff"—cognitive activities—and naturalistic observations and experimental observations are both part of the single enterprise of analyzing how this activity is shaped and organized by the features of the particular situation in which it occurs. For the psychologist, this poses the somewhat awesome problem of developing new techniques for studying cognitive activities as they unfold in daily life. But it poses a challenge to the anthropologist as well. There is precious little in the anthropological literature to guide a psychologist who was convinced of the importance of studying cognition in "real-life" situations. Neither an analysis of belief systems nor a sophisticated componential analysis of kinship terms is likely to carry us very far. But if the ethnographer took as his task the analysis of cognition as a *specific set of activities* engaged in on *specifiable occasions* for reasons deducible from his *social* theory, a real rapprochement is possible. If such a reciprocal approach were worked out between two scholars, or within the head of one, their *common concern would be cognitive activity in a variety of settings analyzed in varying degrees of detail.* "Cultural differences in memory" would then refer to cultural variations in the organization of different kinds of remembering tasks, the intellectual activities that these tasks require, and consequently, the kinds of "memory skills" that members of different cultural groups, or specialists within each group, could be expected to develop.

At the present time, we have only flawed or partial demonstrations of how a combined ethnographic-psychology of cognition might look. But we think that a sharp awareness of our current limitations, augmented by a clearer vision of our goal, can bridge "East" and "West," leaving both richer in the process.

REFERENCES

BARTLETT, F. C. 1932. *Remembering.* Cambridge University Press.

BATESON, G. 1958. *Naven.* Stanford University Press.

BERRY, J. W. 1969. On Cross-Cultural Comparability. *International Journal of Psychology* 4:119–128.

BERRY, J. W., and P. R. DASEN. 1974. *Culture and Cognition: Readings in Cross-Cultural Psychology.* Harper and Row.

BOAS, F. 1963. *The Mind of Primitive Man* (original edition, 1911). Free Press.

BROWN, A. L. 1974. The Development of Memory: Knowing, Knowing You Don't Know and Knowing How to Know. Unpublished paper. University of Illinois.

COLE, M., and J. S. BRUNER. 1971. Cultural Differences and Inferences about Psychological Processes. *American Psychologist* 26:867–876.

COLE, M., and S. SCRIBNER. 1974. *Culture and Thought: A Psychological Introduction*. Wiley.

COLE, M., J. GAY, J. A. GLICK, and D. W. SHARP. 1971. *The Cultural Context of Learning and Thinking*. Basic Books.

EDGERTON, R. 1974. Cross-Cultural Psychology and Psychological Anthropology; One Paradigm or Two? *Reviews of Anthropology* 1:52–65.

FLAVELL, J. H. 1970. Developmental Studies of Mediated Memory, *Advances in Child Development and Behavior* (H. W. Reese and L. P. Lipsitt eds.), vol. 5. Academic Press.

GLADWIN, T. 1970. *East is a Big Bird*. Harvard University Press.

GLICK, J. 1975. Cognitive Development in Cross-Cultural Perspective. *Review of Child Development Research* (J. Horowitz, ed.), vol. 4. Russell-Sage (in press).

GREENFIELD, P. M., and J. S. BRUNER. 1969. Culture and Cognitive Growth, *Handbook of Socialization Theory and Research* (D. A. Goslin ed.). Rand McNally.

IRWIN, M. H., and D. H. MCLAUGHLIN. 1970. Ability and Preference in Category Sorting by Mano Schoolchildren and Adults. *Journal of Social Psychology* 82:15–24.

HAGEN, J. W. 1971. Some Thoughts on How Children Learn to Remember. *Human Development* 14:262–271.

KAGEN, J., and R. E. KLEIN. 1973. Cross-Cultural Perspectives on Early Development. *American Psychologist* 28:947–961.

KAGAN, J., R. E. KLEIN, M. M. HAITH, and F. J. MORRISON. 1973. Memory and Meaning in Two Cultures. *Child Development* 44:221–223.

LEVINE, R. A. 1970. Cross-Cultural Study in Child Psychology. *Carmichael's Manual of Child Psychology* (P. M. Mussen ed.), 2:559–614.

LEVI-STRAUSS, C. 1966. *The Savage Mind*. University of Chicago Press.

LEVY-BRUHL, L. 1966. *How Natives Think*. Washington Square Press.

MEAD, M. 1964. *Continuities in Cultural Evolution*. Yale University Press.

NADEL, S. F. 1951. *The Foundations of Social Anthropology*. Cohen and West.

PRICE-WILLIAMS, D., W. GORDON, and M. RAMIREZ. 1969. Skill and Conservation: A Study of Pottery-making Children. *Developmental Psychology* 1:769.

SCHNEIRLA, T. C. 1972. Observation and Experimentation in the Field Study of Behavior. *Selected writings of T. C. Schneirla* (L. R. Aaronson, E. Tobach, J. S. Rosenblatt, and D. S. Lehrman, eds.). W. H. Freeman and Company.

SCRIBNER, S. 1974. Organization and Recall in a West African Society. *Cognitive Psychology* 6:475–494.

SCRIBNER, S. 1975. Situating the Experiment in Cross-Cultural Research. *The Developing Individual in a Changing World* (K. F. Riegel and S. A. Meacham, eds.), vol. 1. Mouton (in press).

SCRIBNER, S., and M. COLE. 1973. The Cognitive Consequences of Formal and Informal Education. *Science* 182:553–559.

SHARP, D. W., and M. COLE. 1974. The Influence of Educational Experience on the Development of Cognitive Abilities Manifested in Formal Tests. *Final Report to the National Institute of Education.*

WAGNER, D. A. 1974. The Development of Short-term and Incidental Memory: A Cross-Cultural Study. *Child Development* 45:389–396.

A Conjunctive Pattern in Middle Class Informal and Formal Education

ROBERT I. LEVY

Whenever the conditions are appropriate, we must get him to perform the acts in a successful or acceptable way. By one means or another we must get him to say "7," or to sit down with a book, or to smile, or to look at what the robins are doing. Secondly, whenever he does one of these things more or less adequately, whenever he comes up with a success, we must be sure that he is rewarded or reinforced. When he says "7," the teacher should accept this answer in an enthusiastic manner. When he spends some time in reading we should be sure that he encounters satisfaction. When he acts in a cheerful manner we should commend him or be sure that things are pleasant for him.

> John M. Stephens, *The Psychology of Classroom Learning*, 1965. Holt, Rinehart and Winston, p. 108.

Arrange learning situations so that rewards for correct performance are immediate, appropriate, and consistent.

> James M. Sawrey and Charles W. Telford, *Educational Psychology*, 1968. Allyn and Bacon, p. 179.

Assumption 10: If the child is fully involved in and having fun with an activity, learning is taking place. Many open educators eschew any attempt whatsoever to control or manipulate children's behavior. . . . [Although] the

ROBERT I. LEVY is professor of anthropology at the University of California at San Diego. He has done research in Tahiti and Hawaii, and is currently doing studies in a traditional Hindu city in Nepal.

adult, to a large extent, determines the nature of the school environment [by choosing books, equipment, resources], the child decides with which of these materials he will work, to which problems he will address himself, for how long, and with whom.

> "Open Education: Assumptions about Children's Learning," Roland S. Barth, in Charles H. Rathbone (ed.), *Open Education: The Informal Classroom*, 1971. Citation Press, p. 124.

Teaching, learning, continuities, discontinuities, and the consequences of patterning at many levels are continuing and major concerns in Margaret Mead's work. She has repeatedly considered the special problems of discontinuity involved both for adults of traditional cultures in entering into one or another version of the modern world through transformation of their own cultures or through emigration, and for the children forever entering changing modern cultures.

The condition in our society today is dramatized by the late-born child whose mother finds that nothing that she learned ten years ago about how to treat children or of what to expect from them can be applied to this newcomer, who seems even to have learned to cry with a new note in its voice, who will have to have different clothes, will display different tastes, and will weep for quite different reasons. . . . The adults in the modern world face children who are not only unlike their own past childhood, but who are actually unlike any children who have ever been in the world before (Mead 1962:23).

And in the same lecture, delivered in 1950, she noted the problem of the teacher whose task it is to prepare children

to face away from the past and toward the future. . . . Where the teacher who represents the past and tradition must accept directly and finally both what she herself has been taught and those who stood for the past, the teacher who must urge her pupils to desert or surpass their parents has to abandon the matter but, in a way, keep the manner. She comes to terms during her training, if that training is to succeed, not with her own parents as they themselves were with all their weaknesses and strengths, but with the demands which parents and teachers in the abstract have a right and a duty to make on children" (1962:28f.).

The problem of discontinuity has recently been discussed by Sylvia Scribner and Michael Cole, who argue that "the school's knowledge base, value system, and dominant learning situations and the functional learning systems to which they give rise are all in conflict with those of the student's traditional culture" (Scribner and Cole 1973:558). They suggest that many aspects of discontinuity between informal and school learning are problems to some degree for children in all cultures.

THE TEACHING-LEARNING PARADIGM

I will suggest a teaching-learning pattern that in my experience of American middle class culture and in contrast to my observations of some non-Western cultures represents a centrally significant continuity in American middle class urban informal and school education. I am concerned with a manner in which "primary learning" is presented. This manner, I believe, has consequences both for further strategies for subsequent learning (Scribner and Cole's "functional learning systems, Gregory Bateson's "deutero-learning")[1] and for ordering the learner's assumptions about the nature of things.

The pattern (and one of its recent criticisms) is suggested in the pedagogic formulas quoted at the beginning of this paper. It is, I believe, both a common middle class strategy for child rearing and in the schools a dominant actual and ideal technique. Being continuous—at least for an important segment of the middle class—it facilitates this group of children's movement through the school system, and, plausibly, the development in them of a certain set of common sense assumptions, of a certain kind of educational outcome.

The basic pattern is this. Learning is presented (1) in the form of discrete primary learning tasks (put a peg in a hole, where is the cat, spell dog, how much are two and two); (2) tasks are separated out of the flow of events as special episodes, with a beginning, an end, and some sort of a marker signaling "this is a special situation"; (3) tasks are carefully calibrated during the years when the secondary learning pattern is being established to be comfortably

1. See Gregory Bateson, "Social Planning and the Concept of Deutero-Learning" (Bateson 1972:159–176), and "The Logical Categories of Learning and Communication" (Bateson 1972:279–308). "Deutero-learning" is Bateson's term for learning to learn, or secondary learning. His argument is that the patterns of deutero-learning are produced by the shapes and phrasings of primary learning, and that these derived patterns in themselves constitute an aspect of personal values, orientation, and character.

within the perceptual-motor and cognitive capabilities of the child; (4) tasks end at a point of resolution; (5) the point of resolution is so structured that it has two digitally opposed outcomes, "success" or "failure" (that is, the point of resolution is equivalent to the point at which the "solution" is provided); (6) tasks are all amenable to "successful solution"; (7) such a solution is reached in a short period of time (within the attention span or, later, "motivational span" of the child); (8) the "solution" is rewarded (the nonreward for "failure" comes to be perceived as punishment), which reward is clearly differentiated from a secondary minor reward for "trying"; (9) the usual reward in the stage of the establishment of the learning pattern is praise associated with increased tenderness or lovingness; (10) and this reward is from a figure of major emotional importance to the child.

This pattern describes, I believe, the common sense educational strategy of a large segment of middle class homes, and is the pattern which the Neo-behaviorists have idealized as *the* paradigm for learning. The schools extend it and build on it. As the child progresses through the school system the length of each task-event is gradually increased. One has an hour to complete the task, a day, a week, a term. But it is still a discrete task, approaching a moment of resolution, involving a sure reward for moderate effort. The outcome has always been dichotomous, either "success" or "failure,"[2] but in the informal phase of establishment of the pattern in the family failure was unusual. Now, to the surprise of some children who have successfully learned the pattern, their performance more and more frequently leads to failure. They will be filtered out of academic enterprises and will search for other places where they can engage in "the strategy" with success. But most children who have learned the paradigm succeed within its terms and pass through the school system. Having left school they continue, trained, to apply their understandings, including those about learning and teaching, to the flux of the world's problems. And, as Bateson has pointed out of secondary learning, it can only be disconfirmed under extremely unusual circumstances. Random events will be seized upon for a sense of validation. Thus the pessimist

2. Learning about one's relative ranking, one's capabilities as fitted into a hierarchical scheme, is in some conflict with this pattern, and does not come easily to middle class American children. Hierarchy of capabilities is signaled in schools as a result of the summation of successes and failures, and is experienced as relatively accidental.

cognitively treasures each defeat, the optimist each victory, the learner of the paradigm each effort-following success.

PSYCHOLOGICAL CONSEQUENCES OF THE PARADIGM

The assumption that the form in which learning occurs has powerful consequences and the questions as to which aspects of form are significant and what consequences can be expected from a given aspect of form are matters of assumption and assertion. Although a body of lore about these questions has become accepted in personality theory (where assumptions, particularly about self and personal relations, are thought to be generalized from early transactions), there has been relatively little attention to these questions in academic psychology. Bateson, in 1942, commented that "learning to learn" as the acquisition of a class of abstract habits of thought was "to some extent new to psychologists" (1972:166). He found support for his ideas about learning to learn in Hull's reports of subjects' increasing proficiency in rote learning as they worked through a series of rote learning tests, and (in later papers) in Harlow's concept of "set learning." Recent emphasis in cognitive psychology on rules for generating behavioral responses and the problem, which eventually must be confronted, of how these rules are acquired[3] may be expected to provide new convergences between experimental psychology and anthropologically useful learning theory. For the present we are constrained to, one hopes, plausible speculations.

The implications of the teaching-learning paradigm for secondary learning would seem to include those aspects of American orientations or "social personality" which are related to mobility, industrialization, and rapid social change.[4] Many of these implica-

3. For example, Greeno and Bjork 1973.
4. Margaret Mead (1949) has speculated on those aspects of the child's secondary learning that are *immediate* results of culture change. In presenting "some preliminary hypotheses about the order of regularities which will be found in the character structures of those reared under continually shifting conditions of secondary culture contact, where rapid technological changes, sharp generation conflicts, and frequent new migrations prevent any stable second generation pattern from developing," she argued that "the growing child develops an approach to life, which I, stressing the habit of taking each situation as a single unit and adapting rapidly and fully to it, have called *situational*. . . . There is a tendency to reduce all values to simple scales . . . whereby the extreme incommensurables of many different sets of cultural values can be easily, though superficially, reconciled and placed in a hierarchical order. . . . The perception of the outer world becomes atomized, as the growing child is no longer presented with a coherent set of culturally interrelated experiences to guide his perception" (1949:28–29).

tions have been adaptive to these social conditions for the past few centuries, but now threaten to become seriously maladaptive to emerging social and ecological conditions.

I propose that someone who is continuously exposed to the teaching-learning paradigm would tend to acquire certain assumptions that would be felt to apply to certain major domains of experience, those that will come to be thought of as "solvable problems." Furthermore, the child's learning, in contrast to Tahitian learning experience, for example, will induce him to believe that many situations are "problems," that many problems are "solvable."

The assumptions are: Learning is performance, achievement, and mastery. Learning-achievement is possible with ordinary competence. Any "normal" person should be able to do anything. If one is not able repeatedly to learn-achieve it is a sign of some basic incompetence, and a matter of shame. George De Vos has remarked that failing at a task, a Japanese tends to state, "I couldn't do it," and an American "I didn't want to do it," both avoiding the deeper shame, respectively, of rejection of duty on the one hand, and of task performance incompetence on the other (De Vos 1973: chap. 1).

Learning-achieving is a matter of conceiving and engaging in discrete, limited tasks—the practical outlook. It is felt to be obscuring, mystical, obstructure, academic to think of wider contexts and problems, beyond the practical task unless those considerations are forced by repeated failure. Learning-achievement is for the purpose of resolutions, which are certain. The solution of a problem becomes sufficient reward and justification for the enterprise. If the solution creates problems, they can be solved by engaging in further discrete tasks. The reward involved with successful resolution is vitally important to one's emotional well being, to one's self-esteem. "Success" is the completion of the task by the discovery of the correct answer. Nature is a puzzle yielding correct answers to investigation.

From repeated learning episodes of the paradigmatic form one learns that one is competent to risk solving problems, and that thus one can gain satisfaction in problem solving. It is not the *achievement of competency* that is in itself primarily rewarded as it is in settings where, for example, certification and initiation indicate permanent changes in status, such status changes being somewhat suspect to middle class Americans who ask, "What has he done lately?" Rather the sense of competency generalized from easy and rewarded successes encourages task engagement that, however, carries a continuing risk. One learns that there are tasks in the world which one can do in such a way that one will probably be rewarded.

The content of the task is trivial, except as it is related to greater or lesser success markers. A task cannot be dropped without dysphoria until it is marked as success or failure. Failure, however, in one type of task can be compensated by success in another type, and thus the facilitation of narrow, driven, specializing people.

Individuals seem to generalize these assumptions to different extents—some narrow them to their business or professional life, some, of interest to Fromm and other social psychologists, extend these orientations to wider ranges of relationships and conceptions. I would suppose that some of the question of generality depends on the range of contexts in which this kind of teaching is presented to a child, and the nature of the other kinds of teaching-learning modes it experienced. The question of generalization is obscure, but it is within that range of phenomena that are experienced as *problems* for whatever reason that this set of strategies, interpretations, and expectations seems to be activated.

CONTRASTS TO THE PARADIGM

The features of learning on which I have been commenting, and their presumed consequences, banalities of description of the "modern American character" just before its present ongoing contemporary changes, are visible precisely because they are in some sense problematic, in that they contrast with other modes and possibilities of action. Some contrasts are familiar from the anthropological literature. "[In 'Aina Pumehana] many parents do not encourage their children to walk, and at times appear to discourage them from becoming mobile in order to reduce the possibility of injury" (Howard 1974:41). "Walking and talking are not important events from the [Maori] mother's point of view. No particular urging or encouragement is given by the mother. . . . The child learns in his own good time, and when that time comes, he will walk, and later talk" (Ritchie 1957:77). "The preschool period might be called the period of observation and imitation for the

Rājpūt child. He is considered too young to learn from instruction; very little is expected of him; and he spends most of his day observing the busy scene around him" (Minturn and Hitchcock 1966: 125).

The Tahitian individuals whom I studied seemed to me to have experienced, in their childhood—and to be perpetuating in dealing with their own children—teaching-learning patterns, and, presumably, consequently related personality and cognitive features that differed clearly from American middle class patterns (Levy 1973: chap. 13 and passim). Several aspects of the Tahitian teaching-learning pattern contrast with the paradigm I have outlined: Most learning is not presented as specially marked episodes, but occurs in the context of ongoing household and community activities. Informal teaching is largely directed to violations, to the prevention of trouble-causing behavior. The child learns many skills by observation and through overt and covert rehearsal. Many of the tasks that the child tries are too difficult. The child tries again, sporadically, until eventually he or she is able to do the task. The episodes of learning by modeling and observation are terminated when the child has had enough, is bored, tired, or defeated. The episodes of learning to prevent violations are terminated when the child desists from the activity at issue. The early episodes in learning by modeling and observation usually terminate in task "failure." Active teaching, being aversive, is oriented to punishment (specifically threat, which presumably has different consequences than other possible punishments—e.g., hitting or withdrawal of love). Active teaching is presented through a network of kin rather than (as in the early stages of the American paradigm) through one or two individuals.

I have argued (Levy 1973) that such teaching-learning forms are part of a redundant hierarchy of influences and controls that shape culturally important personal traits in similar directions. The learning from such forms contributes "common sense" to the assemblage of personal adaptive and orienting forms. Some of the implications of such teaching-learning forms which seem to contrast with the implications of the middle class paradigm presented here are the following: Learning (or achievement) is progression in the avoidance of error, that is adaptation to the corrective ("punishing" or "threatening") messages of existing social or environmental systems. In attending to limitations, to things that may make a task difficult or impossible, one includes the limits of one's personal skills and desires. One assumes that if others can learn or perform some task, then probably, someday, through some inner process of development, one will be able to and/or will want to do it oneself. The heavy drinker assumes that someday he will no longer want to drink; the adolescent boy who ignores as many village demands as possible assumes that someday he will want to have a household and to accept village tasks. This will come naturally, without need for a struggle with oneself. Learning that involves some sort of struggle or effort (an "achievement") is limited by larger situations. The ease of learning and probability of success varies as the situation varies and one has little control over the situation. In general, there is little point in struggling with a task unless it is intrinsically rewarding, or followed by clearly perceivable rewards. As new performance has in general not been rewarded, and, in fact, as it has often been punished as a disturbance, innovation and "risk taking" are sensed as dangerous. Finally, for Tahitians, messages of control, passed on through a diffuse network of socializers and structured as vague threats, become generalized as a quality of the world, imminent in "violations," which include disturbance causing innovation, change, and achievement.

Such teaching and learning techniques and their presumed psychological correlates are reported everywhere in Polynesia and Micronesia (Levy 1969). But they are certainly not specifically Eastern Oceanic. They would seem to be both naturally occurring and adaptive in certain kinds of environments.[5]

For Eastern Oceanic islanders these assumptions, presumably de-

5. I would propose tentatively that such variables as community size, degree of community differentiation, relative emphasis on steady state or change, and the quality (good or poor) of community integration, influence certain options in dealing with children, which in turn lead to orientations of adaptive importance. In relation to teaching-learning forms with significant secondary consequences, the options may include the following: children may be either relatively undifferentiated from adults or strongly contrasted to them; if they are contrasted, the child may be either a sentimental object in itself or a focus for manipulation; if it is seen primarily as a focus for manipulation it may be manipulated primarily for "fitting-in" or for "achievement." A choice must also be made between the sanctions to be applied for manipulation, perhaps ultimately between power (threats, hurt) and "love" (see Becker 1964). Some of these options are suggested by Philippe Ariès's (1962) analysis of the history of European childhood since the Middle Ages.

rived in part from the patterning of primary learning, provide a common sense basis for adaptations to environments of limited and delicately balanced resources and to a probably consequently conservative and relatively tranquil horticultural and fishing society. For the Polynesians and Micronesians common sense orientations that encourage cautious respect for their environment were as useful as the middle class Western orientations encouraging mastery through achievement and innovation were, for a while, to their bearers.

For Western middle class America (and England), new paradigms are being urged both for the school and for the family. Barth's statement above indicates the ideal of "open education." And for the family we have, for example, Lloyd deMause enthusiastically portraying a moral evolution in ways of dealing with children which is said to have culminated in the mid-twentieth century in the "helping mode."

[This] involves the proposition that the child knows better than the parent what it needs at each stage of its life, and fully involves both parents in the child's life as they work to empathize with and fulfill its expanding and particular needs. There is no attempt at all to discipline or form "habits." Children are neither struck nor scolded, and are apologized to if yelled at under stress. . . . From the four books which describe children brought up according to the helping mode, it is evident that it results in a child who is gentle, sincere, never depressed, never imitative or group-oriented, strong-willed and unintimidated by authority (deMause 1974:53–54).

This sort of thing is an attempt to transform some of the elements in the paradigm I have presented here, and is an attempt to propose one kind of postmodern man. If these programs and polemics do predict a new paradigm, only time will tell its full implications for secondary learning, and the adjustive and adaptive advantages and costs that will result.

REFERENCES

Ariès, Philippe. 1962. *Centuries of Childhood.* Alfred a Knopf.
Barth, Roland S. 1971. Open Education: Assumptions about Chil-

dren's Learning, *Open Education: The Informal Classroom* (Charles H. Rathbone, ed.). Citation Press.

BATESON, GREGORY. 1972. *Steps to an Ecology of Mind.* Chandler Publishing Company (Paperback edition, Ballantine Books, 1972).

BECKER, WESLEY. 1964. Consequences of Different Kinds of Parental Discipline, *Review of Child Development Research* (Martin Hoffman and Lois Hoffman, eds.). Russell Sage Foundation.

DeMAUSE, LLOYD. 1974. The Evolution of Childhood, *The History of Childhood* (Lloyd deMause, ed.). The Psychohistory Press.

DE VOS, GEORGE. 1973. *Socialization for Achievement.* University of California Press.

GREENO, JAMES, and ROBERT BJORK. 1973. Mathematical Learning Theory and the New "Mental Forestry." *Annual Review of Psychology* 24:81–116.

HOWARD, ALAN. 1974. *Ain't No Big Thing.* University Press of Hawaii.

LEVY, ROBERT I. 1969. *Personality Studies in Polynesia and Micronesia.* Social Science Research Institute. University of Hawaii.

———. 1973. *Tahitians, Mind and Experience in the Society Islands.* University of Chicago Press.

MEAD, MARGARET. 1949. Character Formation and Diachronic Theory. *Essays Presented to A.R. Radcliffe-Brown.* The Clarendon Press.

———. 1962. *The School in American Culture.* Harvard University Press.

MINTURN, LEIGH, and JOHN HITCHCOCK. 1966. *The Rājpūts of Khalapur, India.* John Wiley and Sons.

RITCHIE, JANE. 1957. *Childhood in Rakau.* Publications in Psychology, no. 10. Victoria University of Wellington (New Zealand).

SAWREY, JAMES M., and CHARLES W. TELFORD. 1968. *Educational Psychology.* Allyn and Bacon.

SCRIBNER, SYLVIA, and MICHAEL COLE. 1973. Cognitive Consequences of Formal and Informal Education. *Science* 182:553–559.

STEPHENS, JOHN M. 1965. *The Psychology of Classroom Learning.* Holt, Rinehart and Winston.

Time: History versus Chronicle;

Socialization as Cultural Preexperience

GEORGE DEVEREUX

Preamble. Since I feel unable to differentiate in an operationally meaningful manner between socialization and enculturation, this study was so planned as to make unnecessary a distinction between the two phenomena—assuming that they are two, rather than only one. The process of socialization/enculturation is, throughout this paper, represented by the symbol S/C.

"Cultural communication" is defined as information that cannot be obtained through—or inferred from—direct observation (sense data): it must necessarily pass from one mind to another. This specification can be clarified by means of a simple distinction between two major types of communicated information:

1. *Nomothetic information* (usually in the imperative mood): All single, nubile persons must be chaste ("That is our custom").

2. *Descriptive information* (usually in the indicative mood): All —or nearly all, or most—single nubile persons are chaste ("That is our practice").

The descriptive information could be obtained through nonverbal research (by the accumulation of sense data only) and, on the basis of the data accumulated in this manner, one could formulate the generalization: "That is our (or their) practice." But, re-

GEORGE DEVEREUX is professor of ethnopsychiatry at the École des Hautes Études en Sciences Sociales.

gardless of the amount of sense data *so* accumulated, one remains incapable of formulating the nomothetic statement, or even to evolve the notion of "custom." For it is an inherent quality of every statement in the imperative mood that it is (logically) *future-directed*. This finding remains true even if a person who had violated the custom in the past is being punished for it here and now and, possibly, for some time to come.

These brief preliminary observations indicate that the principal objective of this study is the articulation of S/C with the time dimension.

Terminology and symbols. To avoid overloading the text with repetitive specifications, the following symbols are used:

> S/C (as already noted) denotes socialization/enculturation.
> T/E denotes learning by trial and error.
> H/N denotes "here and now."
> P/E denotes preexperience.

P/E is a symbolic anticipation of a "thing" or situation that, in the absence (H/N) of any part or direct emanation (scent, etc.) of the "thing" or situation, produces a subjective experience comparable to what one would have were that "thing" or situation present H/N. This P/E subsequently enables the subject who had undergone it to cope efficiently with the "thing" or situation as, if, and when—*if ever*—it *is* present H/N. I state at once that P/E, as here defined, appears to be a purely human experience, resulting from cultural communication. Thus:

1. A mother coyote can, on perceiving a human smell, "teach" her cubs to dread that (H/N) smell and—*as a serendipity*—to avoid subsequently anything smelling that way. But she can do this only as, if, and when the scent *is* present, H/N.

2. A human mother can cause her city-bred child to avoid wolves or lions, simply by telling the child about these animals, no constituent part or trace (smell) of which is present H/N. She can even make her child fear (inexistent) bogies, and the like.

The human capacity to have P/E's appears to be directly related to the human capacity for anticipation. Köhler's ape, finding that there was a banana that he could not reach, and observing that his cage contained several boxes, seemed to "reflect," exhibited what Köhler calls a "Eureka-reaction," piled the boxes on top of each other and thus managed to reach the banana (Köhler 1927). But, unlike man, the ape cannot *anticipate* a problem and cannot figure out ("plan") in *advance* how it would eventually pile up boxes to reach a banana hung just beyond his reach, if that situation ever arose.

Two further terms also have to be elucidated.

Referral (or *relevance*): Though I may learn N/N about the 1776 American Revolution, I must be able to *refer* this information, just acquired, to the past. I may learn H/N that there will be an eclipse of the moon *x* years hence, but must *refer* this information to the future. I may learn H/N of the existence of Mount Everest, but must *refer* this information to "elsewhere" (Asia).

Pertinence: This term denotes the time and/or place at which the information acquired H/N will be "useful"—will lead to a "reward" or "positive reinforcement." Thus, when an alien is naturalized, he is asked questions about the American Revolution, that is, about facts that are clearly to be referred to the *past*. But, in terms of the theory underlying naturalization procedures, this knowledge is held to have pertinence for the *future*; it is supposed to make the former alien a better citizen.

Practically all S/C training is deemed to have future pertinence, even if it has past relevance (knowledge of the creation myth or of history), or does not refer to "here." (Hungarians are taught that they came from Turan, which is *still* located in central Asia.) Now, because most S/C training concerns matters that are *not* "present" H/N and are, moreover, held to have pertinence largely for the future, it is evident that hardly any S/C learning can be strictly of the T/E (trial-and-error) type. For, in practically all T/E learning, the "pertinence" (positive reinforcement, reward) is part of a rather *short* temporal configuration. Thus, if one seeks to train a rat to press a lever *in order* to get a pellet of food, the pellet must become available a few seconds after the level is pressed. If it does not materialize almost at once, the rat seems unable to "connect" his pressing of the lever with the appearance of the pellet of food. It will, of course, eat the pellet whenever it appears, but will not "experience" the pellet as the result or goal ("pertinence") of its previous lever-pressing activities; it will probably experience the pellet as a "chance (nonserendipity) find."

This interpretation acquires added significance in the light of the finding that most animal activities that have a remote (future) pertinence, are "instinctive." A certain female wasp paralyzes a caterpillar with its sting and then lays her eggs on it. When her eggs hatch, they will feed on the paralyzed caterpillar. But one cannot hold that the wasp planned this. For the *individual* wasp this "appy" outcome is not a reward; it is strictly a "*species serendipity.*" Similarly, many spider species weave nets that, as it turns out, are subsequently useful as traps for their prey. But, since it cannot be held that the *individual* spider intentionally wove a *hunting* net, the net's (future) *usefulness* is, for the *individual* spider, a serendipity. By contrast, if a man manufactures a hunting net, *intending* to use it in the hunt, his net's future usefulness is not a serendipity, but a genuine reward for an H/N effort that had future pertinence.

In man, S/C training, which is by definition held to be future (and/or elsewhere) pertinent, tends to affect even the manner in which he learns (H/N) things that *do* exist H/N. Strange as it may seem, he learns them *as though* they did *not* exist H/N—but only partly because even *this* learning has largely future pertinence. A few examples will clarify this statement:

1. I am studying H/N a book on gravitation. Though gravitation keeps me firmly seated on my chair and prevents the book I am studying from floating off ceilingward, I am *not attending* H/N to these H/N manifestations of gravitation. I would attend to them H/N only if there occurred a *perturbation* of the laws of gravitation I am just now studying.

2. The situation would be exactly the same if I were just now reading a book about the functioning of the lungs. I would attend to the functioning of *my* lungs H/N only if "inexplicably" I suddenly had an attack of dyspnoea.

3. I am studying H/N a paper describing the process of learning through repetition. I would attend to *my* learning H/N about this process only if I realized that the *more* I reread that paper, the *less* I remembered its contents . . . which would be contrary to what the paper I am studying describes.

One of the conclusions one may draw from the data just cited is that, unlike animals, "learning man" is singularly estranged from the present: from "here-and-now." I note in particular the extreme rareness of situations in which true T/E learning (promptly rewarded by an H/N pertinent success) occurs. To the best of my recall, I found myself in such a situation only once in the course of the last year: my standing lamp ceased to function on a weekend (i.e., at a time when no electrician could be summoned) and just before nightfall (i.e., at an hour when a prompt repair of the lamp was imperative: the repair had H/N pertinence). I had to discover, by T/E, how to repair the lamp, *for* an H/N pertinent reward: *in order* not to spend *that* evening in the dark.

I deem it useful to analyze my performance on that occasion in some detail, for it permits me to highlight one special aspect of "intelligent" learning behavior, which I am provisionally inclined to connect with man's high degree of estrangement from the present, as exemplified by the future pertinence of many of his activities.

To repair the lamp, I had to *disassemble* it first, though lamps obviously operate only when properly assembled. In other words, I was, for all practical purposes, obliged to "move away" from my goal (a once more functioning lamp), the better to attain it. An apparent "moving away" from the goal pursued—the better to attain the goal—is highly characteristic of many day-to-day human activities. If my front door opens inward, I must first *back away* from the doorway, pulling the door inward, to be able to pass easily through the doorway. Similarly, one of the best ways of obtaining certain greatly desired things is, proverbially, "to play hard to get."

Such situations demand the construction of a "social-cultural space" in which what, in Euclidean geometry, *must* be *represented* as a "moving away" from the objective *can* be *represented* as a "moving toward."

As I indicated almost twenty years ago (Devereux 1956), physics provides us with a model for the construction of such a special "geometry." In Euclidean geometry, the shortest distance between two points, A and B, is the straight line. But in reality, if A and B are separated by a mountain, proceeding from A to B in a straight line (shortest line) obliges one to dig a tunnel through the mountain; this involves a great expenditure of energy. Much less time and energy would be expended if one proceeded from A to B by walking *around* the mountain, following the valleys, though this may, at times, *increase* one's distance from the goal B. In such an "economy of effort" geometry, the "shortest" path from A to B is the one that involves the least expenditure of effort.

It is, I think, only by representing the sociocultural "space" in a manner that so defines the "shortest" distance between A (situation to be coped with) and B (goal pursued by means of that "coping") that a provisional and "economical" (Euclidean) "moving away" from the objective pursued *during the T/E (coping) period* could be *represented* as a constant "decreasing" of the distance between A and B. In fact, sociocultural "space"/"time" can so be conceived that even past/future/elsewhere referable learning, *acquired H/N,* but having primarily a "future/elsewhere pertinence," could be *represented* on such a space/time map—or sociocultural manifold (multidimensional space)—so that H/N learning situation would be "situated" in the immediate "vicinity" of the (future/ elsewhere) point/event at which that learning will become pertinent (useful). In simpler terms, it is possible to construct a sociocultural time/space manifold in which my H/N "past referable" learning (e.g., that the eclipse of the moon, on 27 August 413 B.C., was fatal to an Athenian army) will, in terms of its time axis, be located in the immediate vicinity of the point at which that information will actually be *pertinent* (an examination in ancient history, or my citing this example in this paper).

Such "geometrically" contrived *temporal contiguities,* as regards learning (H/N) something that is *not* H/N relevant (past, future, elsewhere) and will "normally" be pertinent ("rewarding") only much later, are less artificial than they may seem. I am thinking here in particular of what is usually called the "timeless" aspect of dreams, but which could, more suitably, be called the "incessant H/N character" of all dream experiences, upon which a *sense* of "duration" or "sequentiality" is, in my opinion, *imposed* only during the secondary elaboration represented by the recalling of the dream. I view this matter as follows:

Consider an imaginary dream: X dreams that he is escaping from a bandits' lair and is heading for the safety of a friend's home. Let us now focus our attention on a *moment* of this dream, during which the dreamer dreams of racing *toward* his friend's home and *away* from the bandits' lair. So stated, my formulation *imputes* to the "running" dreamer an awareness both of "anteriority" ["I was (recent past) in a bandits' lair and escaped"] and of "posteriority" ["I am heading for the (future) safety of a friend's house"]. I hold that this formulation distorts the "running" dreamer's actual experience. The danger represented by the bandits' lair is, in dream, not "situated" in the past: it "exists" as an H/N *present* motivation (of the running). Likewise, at *that* moment in the dream the "prospect" of reaching the safe haven of a friend's house is psychologically not "situated" in the future: it is experienced in dream as a *present* (H/N) striving toward a goal. In fact, though the dreamer dreams of running, *just then,* from the bandits' lair to a friend's house, in his dream experience the lair does *not* "exist" elsewhere: it exists as a *(subsequently* past referred) *present* image ("push"). Similarly, the house of the friend which the runner seeks to reach is *not* situated "elsewhere"; in dream it exists II/N as a motivating preexperience (P/E "pull") *while* he dreams of running: it is only *subsequently* future referred.

In fact, since I might just as well be hung for a sheep as for a lamb, I admit that I am not certain that my two cautious clauses ("subsequently past referred" and "subsequently future referred") are more than somewhat timid attempts to temporize: to achieve some sort of compromise with the indubitable fact that, in the *remembering* of dreams, the events *seem* to be arranged in conformity with the traditional articulation of time into past, present, and future. Logically it is very probable that all dream content is originally experienced purely H/N—the "past" perhaps in the form of an "away from" (push) (present) motivation, and the "future" perhaps in the form of a "toward" (pull) (present) motivation.

I concede that this interpretation is very difficult to confirm directly. But it appears to shed some light upon the finding, known already to Aeschylus (*Agamemnon,* vv. 893f.), that long stories can be dreamed in a few minutes only. Also, there exists one phenomenon that may, perhaps, indirectly substantiate this view.

The crucial datum is the impossibility of causing an animal, particularly by means of a H/N experience, to *refer* that experience to the past: an animal can be taught neither history nor autobiography:

A puppy I once owned was in the habit of jumping on my lap and curling up on it. But by the age of about eighteen months, when he weighed 145 pounds, he discovered that he could no longer curl up on my lap. It would be crude anthropomorphization to assume: (1) either that my dog realized that he had grown from 20 pounds to 145 pounds; (2) or that he supposed that I had shrunk in the course of the first eighteen months of his life.

I concede, of course, that after covering the "outward bound" itinerary *a, b, c, d, e, f,* a cat can "reverse" this sequence and follow an "inward bound" itinerary *f, e, d, c, b, a.* I even concede that, on its return journey, the cat may take certain "shortcuts" (e.g., proceeding directly from *e* to *c,* without passing through *d* as it did on its "outward bound" journey). But, just as in dream, the bandits' lair and the friend's house do not seem to be *experienced* in the past or in the future, but have a strictly H/N "existence" even while the dreamer dreams of running *from* the bandits' lair *to* the friendly house, so the basket to which the cat seeks to return is (psychologically) *not* "referred" to the past; the effort made to reach it (soon, though still in the future) is, likewise, not "future pertinent" in the sense in which I define this term. Speaking in a consciously speculative manner, I imagine that the basket to which the cat seeks to return is, *before* it actually gets there, experienced in a *manner* that is the exact reverse of a "déjà vu." I realize that this hypothesis may, perhaps, be unprovable; I at least cannot think, for the time being, of an experiment which *could* prove it. But I hold, nonetheless, that the adoption of some such working hypothesis or "thought token" greatly simplifies the understanding of how mankind can, here and now (H/N), learn something that has a *sense* only if it is held to be relevant in terms of the past, of the future, or of the elsewhere, and has, admittedly, only future pertinence. I recall that I am *not* rewarded H/N for learning H/N the date 1776, the predictions of futurologists, or the fact that Mount Everest "is" elsewhere: in Asia.

And, though I have indicated that one can construct a sociocultural "space/time" frame of reference in which H/N learning (especially of a non-H/N relevant fact)—and the future pertinence thereof—can be "represented" as contiguous, it is nonetheless useful to be able to explain at least two commonplace phenomena (dreaming and the homing "instinct" animals) *without* imputing to the dreamer or to the cat an authentic awareness of the past and of the future, and even less the capacity to perceive that his (its) H/N learning activities are clearly future pertinent.

These considerations bring me to a final difficulty. As noted, though most S/C relevant teaching (communication) and learning occurs H/N, without real T/E, it is strictly future (and elsewhere) relevant *only*. Thus, one can teach the sixth commandment, forbidding adultery, to a six-year-old boy, though his learning of *that* commandment H/N is not likely to be useful (or, indeed, meaningful) to him until several years have gone by.

But even this is not the main problem. Nearly all S/C training concerns a hypothetical (if probable) future, rather than a *certain* one.

If I learn to swim H/N in sweet water, it is absolutely predictable that I will be able to swim even better if and when I have occasion to swim in salt water.

By contrast, in times of rapid change—especially if it is deliberately and masochistically of an anomic, driftlike type—nearly all S/C learning (acquired *in the belief* that it is future pertinent) ceases, when "the future" comes around at last, to have pertinence: the rules of the game will have changed or (in anomic situations) will have been abolished entirely. Hence, S/C type of knowledge learned (H/N) in the *expectation* that it will be rewarded twenty years hence, may, by that time, become a handicap or even be penalized. Persons trained to become (well-rewarded) model citizens of *one kind* of society may end up on the gallows of the *next* society. Even future pertinent inhibitions, learned H/N, may become severe handicaps. Percival was taught that proper gentlemen do not ask personal questions. But his failure to ask the ailing Fisher-King personal questions about his illness prevented him from finding the Holy Grail on his first attempt: he found it only after he had learned to discard his gentlemanly discretion.

Another, particularly striking, example may also be cited:

1. Twenty years ago even nonvirginal girls claimed to be virgins.
2. Nowadays some authentic virgins claim to be promiscuous.

Tempora mutantur et nos mutamur in illis.

Such observations oblige one to ask whether S/C training continues to be useful—or even possible—when it is likely to become "counterproductive" by the time the future, to which it *supposedly* pertained *when* it was learned, comes around; when the future, *for the sake of which* that S/C was acquired, proves to be unmanageable by the S/C tools one had acquired. Can one *really* persuade the young that saving one's money is worth one's while, at a time when inflation destroys the purchasing power of one's savings? Can S/C *responsibly* condition people to be truthful, loving, and considerate when what is manifestly more and more rewarded is lying, selfishness, and brutality? One even wonders whether one can teach the worthwhileness of the effort to think rationally when, in many places, even psychoanalysis itself—the one science that studies the irrational rationally—is lapsing into a near-delusional rhetoric.

These crucial problems must be reconsidered in the light of the radical distinction I first made nearly forty years ago (in a seminar report) between sanity and adjustment. Subsequently I specified that the main criterion of sanity is the capacity for a continuous *creative* readjustment (Devereux 1970), without a loss of one's sense of selfhood ("temporal Ego") (Devereux 1951, 1966).

According to Leibniz, time is the order of events. But it must be specified at once that, for Leibniz, an "event" was not a "happening," because, for him, the term "order" had a "meaning." And I hasten to add that *that* "meaning" is not impaired even by the most probabilitarian modern theories of causality.

Though I somewhat oversimplify matters, one can, in the first approximation, differentiate between two conceptions of Time: the conception of the chronicle writer, who lists—strings together— what he considers (in a way) as "happenings" and the conception of the historian, who elucidates objectively the *order* of "events." And I note that, at present, the dominant "historical" perspective is radically false, and much of the rest little more than chronicle writing. But that is by the way.

What matters is that responsible and rewarding S/C teaching/ learning is possible only within the framework of an authentic and valid *historical conception of time.* Where sociocultural change is viewed as a random sequence of "happenings," all S/C—which, as noted, *necessarily* passes from one mind to another—becomes inherently irrational. If a situation arises in which the knowledge and experience of the elders becomes—as Margaret Mead says (1970)— irrelevant to the young, society is headed for the anomie of the pseudonymous Iks tribe of Africa (Turnbull 1972), where, as among animals, nearly all learning seems to be of the T/E type and nearly all behavior appears improvised; irrelevant for the past, for the future, and for elsewhere and devoid of all true future pertinence. In that tribe—and in similar situations—all "coping" is related to H/N situations only: to random happenings in the chronicler's unilinear, overmeticulous, and *therefore* fractured time chaos. And one must firmly bear in mind that situations resembling that of the Iks tribe have existed throughout history—from the Athenian plague, as described by Thucydides (*The Peloponnesian War*, II, 47 ff.), to modern concentration camps, but nearly always only in the most marginal areas of society, or else during relatively brief and notoriously catastrophic periods of history.

The present generation of adults may not be able to transmit to the next one any particular *recipe* of the S/C type, learnable H/N, though rewarding only in the long run (future pertinent). But it *can* and *must* transmit to the next generation a *sense of*—or *feeling for*—the crucial sociocultural *and individual* importance of a non-T/E type H/N learning that has a *genuine* future pertinence, *whatever* that H/N learning and that future may be. Unless my generation accomplishes this, the very concepts "society" and "culture"—and even the concept of "person"—will lose any meaning whatever; —and the structures corresponding to them would cease to exist, as (for all practical purposes) they have ceased to exist in the Iks tribe, except for the sharing of a language and of a ghetto territory.

Thus, paradoxical as it may seem, it is *precisely* in times of excessively rapid and almost anomic sociocultural change, that the depositories of a *human* future are not the young, but the adults: they alone have had—for however short a time, and however tragically—the *actual* experience of an S/C learning (H/N), which had a *real* future pertinence. Deprived of this senior-mediated S/C *experience*, there is no alternative for the young but to cross the Iks desert and then to reconstitute slowly a generation capable of devising, experiencing, and mediating (H/N) a future pertinent S/C teaching/learning to the young. For the cornerstone of human existence is *Time*—history, if one prefers: an articulation of the H/N with the past, the future, and the elsewhere. That historians *are* beginning to grapple with the basic notion of Time is illustrated by a magnificent recent study of Alain Besançon (1971), who is my friend and also—*not by chance*, as he himself stresses—one of my former students.

In my experience, the present crisis does not have at its root a refusal of the young to learn—it is the refusal of some of their "disillusioned" seniors to teach. And, as one who has learned and still learns much from her writings, even if he often comes up with very different conclusions, I attest that Margaret Mead at least has never ceased teaching her juniors *in a future-pertinent manner.*

This is logically unquestionable: in terms of Bertrand Russell's theory of mathematical types (1903), a teaching concerning the irrelevance of *all* teaching is not applicable to itself. I can therefore say in good faith that without Margaret Mead's most recent teachings concerning the *irrelevance* of the teachings of the adults, this article—whose greater part goes back to drafts written in the early 1930s—would not have crystallized into a paper written in honor of one whose teachings are and remain future pertinent.

For it is the role of adults to *mold* all that is otherwise only a sociocultural *drift,* into history and then tradition. *This* role Margaret Mead has fulfilled: like the ancient Persians, she taught her contemporaries and her juniors alike "to shoot straight and to speak the truth."

REFERENCES

AESCHYLUS. *Agamemnon,* vv. 893 f.

BESANÇON, ALAIN. 1971. *Histoire et Expérience du Moi* (chap. IV). Flammarion.

DEVEREUX, GEORGE. 1951 (2d ed. 1969). *Reality and Dream.* New York University Press.

———. 1956. *Therapeutic Education.* Harper.

———. 1966. Transference, Screen Memory and the Temporal Ego, *Journal of Nervous and Mental Disease* 143:319–323.

———. 1970 (2d ed. 1973). *Essais d'Ethnopsychiatrie Générale.* Gallimard.

KÖHLER, WOLFGANG. 1927. *The Mentality of Apes.* Harcourt, Brace.

MEAD, MARGARET. 1970. *Culture and Commitment: A Study of the Generation Gap.* The Natural History Press.

RUSSELL, BERTRAND. 1903. *Principles of Mathematics.* Cambridge University Press.

THUCYDIDES. *The Peloponnesian War,* II, 47ff.

TURNBULL, COLIN. 1972. *The Mountain People.* Simon and Schuster.

Eidos and Change:

Continuity in Process, Discontinuity in Product

RHODA METRAUX

It is no longer open to question that a people may undergo even profound change and nevertheless retain their culture in its essential configuration and have a clear sense of their cultural and social identity. The difficult question is how this comes about: how cultural structures are carried by the total communication system so that, incorporating or overriding change, the processes by which members of older and younger generations organize their image of the world in which they live together are congruent.

In this paper I demonstrate that in a society in which a direct approach to this problem is not feasible, primarily because the premises that shape and inform cultural structures are not within articulate awareness, an indirect approach through the use of a nonverbal technique—in this case, performance on the Lowenfeld Mosaic Test—can give insight into cognitive processes that account for cultural continuity.

As background I characterize the kind of change that has taken place in the ongoing life of the Iatmul people of the autonomous village of Tambanum in the East Sepik District of Papua New

RHODA METRAUX is a research associate at the American Museum of Natural History, New York.

Guinea during the period between 1938, when Tambanum was intensively studied by Gregory Bateson and Margaret Mead, and 1967–1973, when I undertook a restudy of Iatmul culture in the course of three field trips to Tambanum.[1]

I then very briefly discuss the eidological structure of Iatmul culture as presented in Bateson's theoretical analysis in *Naven* (1936 and 1958),[2] based on field work in the early 1930s, and as it was manifested in thought and observed behavior during my own field work after a lapse of more than a generation.

Against this background I analyze two aspects—product and process—of adolescent and adult performance on the Lowenfeld Mosaic Test[3] and present a step-by-step outline of the design process in the making of two mosaics.

1.

Iatmul is a centripetal—an inward-turning—culture. The Iatmul regard themselves as unique and as the aristocrats of the Middle Sepik River. Peace, imposed by the government in the 1920s, did not break the pride of Iatmul men or alter their condescending

1. The 1938 field research by Gregory Bateson and Margaret Mead on the Iatmul of the Sepik River, carried out principally in Tambanum Village, was supported by grants from St. John's College, Cambridge University, and from the American Museum of Natural History, New York. My own field work on the Iatmul of Tambanum Village (1967–68, 1971, and 1972–73) was supported by grants from the National Science Foundation (Grant No. NSF GS-642, 1966–1970) and from the Jane Belo Tannenbaum Fund of the American Museum of Natural History, New York (1971——). Throughout my research I had full access to the unpublished field materials—notes and texts, still photographs and films—of the 1938 expedition. As a way of bridging the work of the two expeditions, Margaret Mead spent one month with me in Tambanum in 1967 and visited the village briefly in 1971. William E. Mitchell also worked with me in Tambanum for two months in 1967 and made valuable contributions to my understanding of the life of Tambanum men. In 1972, I visited all the up-river Iatmul villages where Bateson had worked in the early 1930s, research on which *Naven* (1936, 1958) was based. At this time it was still possible to work with some of Bateson's informants. My own thinking about Iatmul culture has been continually illuminated by correspondence from and to the field and by long conversations with both Margaret Mead and Gregory Bateson.

2. In this paper, with its diachronic emphasis, I draw heavily on Bateson's earlier research, particularly as it is formulated in the two editions of *Naven*.

3. For background, see Margaret Lowenfeld, *The Lowenfeld Mosaic Test*. In 1971, I discussed details of the Iatmul Mosaics with Margaret Lowenfeld and, more recently, with Theodora M. Abel. Both contributed valuable insights, but responsibility for the present interpretation is my own. Other aspects of the Tambanum Mosaics are discussed in a paper by Theodora M. Abel and Rhoda Metraux, "Universals and Cultural Regularities: Aspects of Performance in the Lowenfeld Mosaic Test" (1974).

attitudes toward the peoples around them, their former victims in headhunting raids. Work experience and, for the young generation, schooling, have broadened their horizon and whetted their appetite for new material goods. Forward-looking men believe that their educated children and the children of Europeans will "walk one road." Using the image appropriate to trading partners and reconciled enemies, they say that these children will "sit down together (and) eat together like brothers." At the same time most adults still prefer their autonomous life in the village.

In many respects change in the traditional way of life has been characterized by attenuation and internal shifts of emphasis, not by outright rejection of the old or acceptance of the new. Even the major change initiated by the big men of Tambanum in 1953, the decision to send the children to school, was intended to support Tambanum's preeminent position and further the good life—but in the village itself, not elsewhere.

The new freedom to move at will in the bush and on the far reaches of the river and its branches has enhanced the independence of women, who now go off in small clusters to fish and garden, work sago, gather weaving materials and wild foods in the bush or trade in the distant villages of former enemies. It has also heightened the emphasis on individual interpersonal relations as husband and wife or brother and widowed sister work as gardening partners, as young men pair up to play at hunting, to practice their guitar songs or to go visiting, or as men live with their close kin for weeks at a time in their houses in the garden suburbs.

Ceremonial life came to an abrupt halt with the Japanese occupation during World War II and has been only fragmentally reconstituted. The last initiations in Tambanum were carried out before the war. The cross-cutting initiation moieties described by Bateson (1958: 244–246) no longer function and no men under the age of about 40 can proudly display the traditional scarification.[4] The age-graded junior men's clubs have disappeared. Instead, young men and older boys wander quite freely, but in a subdued way, in and out of the clan and lineage clubhouses, where mature men come to gossip or carve or doze or hear the news or, somewhat infrequently, debate some issue of the day.

---

4. Sporadic initiations still take place in various up-river villages of the Central Iatmul.

Sorcery and the vicious, rivalrous battles of the sorcerers that kept Tambanum in a fever of excitement in the 1930s also died out after the war as the sorcerers died, it is said, without passing on their destructive powers. But belief in sorcery has not been rejected. It is well known that sorcery is practiced in the bush villages and up river. In 1972, after an epidemic had caused a great many deaths— too many, in Tambanum, for people to cope with—rumors began to circulate that perhaps sorcery had not completely died out in the village after all.

Supernatural sanctions, too, remain strong and effective. Sickness, accident, misfortune, and death (except of the very old) always require a ceremonial response. Marriage payments must be made. New houses must be built and ceremonially honored. The dead must be mourned and, after an interval, must be ceremonially sent on their way. Today, many small ceremonies focus on the dwelling house. On many days, late in the afternoon, one hears in some part of the village the beat of the hand drum (*kundu*) accompanying pairs of men who are chanting the sacred name songs (*tsagi*) for some ritual.

Many ceremonies are fragmented so that, often, some small part stands for the whole. I witnessed perhaps a dozen *naven* ceremonies —most often for the return of a child from his first visit to a town, once for the purchase of a shotgun by a young man, once for the purchase of an outboard motor by a mature man (actually a group of men) and twice during school theatrical performances when several mothers and father's sisters leaped out of the audience and danced in response to what they regarded as a first dancing performance by a group of small schoolboys. But only on one occasion was the ritual more than a slight gesture.

There is, however, always the possibility that the fragment may be expanded or that an appropriate innovation may be incorporated. At one small ceremony to end mourning (*teva*), inside a house a solitary elderly widow mourned in antiphonal response to the solemn chanting of *tsagi* by a group of older men, while down below, out of doors, the young danced to their own singing and the music of massed guitars from dusk to dawn. This, no less than much more elaborate and conventional *teva*, carried the significant, contrasting themes: the reluctance to let the dead go (the mourning woman), the proud assertion of the continuity of life in the face of death (the chanting men) and the vitality of the living (the young dancers and musicians). Modern dancing, an innovation in the *teva*, was introduced on this occasion to bring the young back into the ceremonial situation.

Tambanum men have become adept at handling new kinds of dualities. For example, they have enthusiastically applied the idea of "law" to old customs as well as to present-day government regulations. Armed with this two-edged weapon, big men can force the settlement of many kinds of disputes without resorting to the government court. And generally speaking, in matters of health they have no sense of contradiction between treatment in a hospital and ceremonial treatment of illness. Young men, questioned on such subjects, are reluctant to express an opinion and refer the questioner to the experts, the big men who know. Mature men, however, feel no need to reconcile alternative theories or explanations or to reduce concepts to those that fit within a single theme. One explanation does not cancel out the other. They have a lifelong experience in debating essentially irreconcilable differences without changing their views. Women talking amongst themselves often express views at variance with those of men and laugh scornfully at the things men do and say. And if young men have their own ideas, based on a different kind of knowledge, this only adds one more dimension to the complex whole.

There are, however, regularities that pattern interpersonal relations and the ways in which masses of detail are given order, fragments can be linked together and multiple beliefs can be related in different sets of circumstances. Bateson in his original full discussion of the Iatmul people (1936: 218–256) points out the essential *dualism* (the "tendency to see things, persons, or social groups related together in pairs," p. 238) in Iatmul social structure. He demonstrates that Iatmul dualism is expressed both as *complementarity* (which he then called "a sense of *direct* dualism: that everything has a sibling," p. 235) and as *symmetry* (which he then called "a sense of *diagonal* dualism—that everything has a symmetrical counterpart," p. 235, and the "idea that everything in the world has its equal and opposite counterpart," p. 239). The interplay of these premises, both strongly developed in Iatmul culture, as Bateson points out (p. 239), shapes and informs the cultural structure.

In "Epilogue 1938," he comments further that Iatmul individuals *"learn,* besides the symmetrical and complementary patterns, to expect and exhibit certain sequential relations between the symmetrical and the complementary" (1958:291).

A single example from my own field work on kinship relations is illustrative. Elder brother, younger brother, and sister (a triad incorporated in the masked figures of the *mwai,* who always appear together ceremonially) form one kinship set. Elder brother and younger brother stand in a complementary relationship to each other: younger brother calls elder brother *nyamun;* elder brother responds, *tsuambo.* Their names also may be paired in a complementary fashion. When they share one house, *nyamun* lives in and names the more prestigeful front half, while *tsuambo* lives in and names the back half.

Brother and sister also form a complementary pair. Brother calls sister *niangai* (actually "child of the house") and sister responds, *nyamun.* Brother and sister also may have paired names, differentiated only by a male and a female suffix.

But from the point of view of a sister, brothers form a symmetrical pair, as sisters address all brothers, elder and younger, as *nyamun.*

Sets of triads of this kind, combining symmetry and complementarity, pervade Iatmul culture and are highly elaborated in ceremonial and daily life and thought, and Iatmul children learn from their earliest experience "certain sequential relations between the symmetrical and the complementary."

But the question is whether—and if so, in what way—this eidological structuring of relationships is carried over into the organization of a world view in the younger generations of the Tambanum Iatmul, who know the traditional culture only in attenuated, fragmented, and continually changing form and whose life expectations differ radically from those of their grandparents and parents. I believe that Tambanum performance on the Lowenfeld Mosaic Test indicates both age-grade differences in the type of designs made and cross-generation continuity in the process by which the designs were achieved.

2.

The Lowenfeld Mosaic Test (LMT) is a free, nonverbal performance test. The subject is presented with a box of 256 small plastic tiles of five geometric shapes, each in six colors, and a tray (covered with white paper on which the design is later traced), which provides a bounded working surface. The tiles were demonstrated and, in Pidgin, I explained, "Nau mi laik yu yet wokim samting long laik bilong yu," that is, "I would like you yourself to make something as you choose to make it."

The work is timed, but no time limit is set. Each step in the process is recorded (with sketches to include changes in organization) and the tracing provides a permanent record of the final design. The LMT, which stimulates the subject's own spontaneous capacities, is also one of the few projective techniques in which the performer, as he works, can observe his own procedures and, at any stage, judge the product by his own standards.

The Tambanum mosaics were collected in 1971 in two consecutive series: (a) 50 adolescents (27 boys in Standard V and 23 girls in Standards IV and V, age range 11–16 years), who were individually tested in the village primary school setting, and (b) 32 adult volunteers (26 males and 6 females, age range early 20s to early 60s), who worked with me individually on the porch of my house where they were, by then, completely at home (see table 1). No subject, adult or child, had previously seen materials remotely like the tiles and no subject witnessed the performance or saw the finished design made by any other individual. The adults themselves decided that they wanted to participate in this "pilay" (game).

Taken as a whole, the Tambanum productions, adult and adolescent, are handsome, vivid, and spatially well organized. There were only two outright failures—one a schoolgirl who tried to build multicolor, multiform columns that collapsed and the other an older man who shook his head and gave up before he started. A very unusual feature was the request by eleven adults (2 women and 9 men) to make a second mosaic, either immediately or on a following day. Some treated their first effort as a trial; some wanted to work out a different idea. Others (adults and children) would have made a second—and a third—mosaic had there been an opportunity.

The designs fall into three general categories: *formal* (nonrepresentational), *naturalistic* (representational) and *emblematic* (those having reference to the ideational system of the supernatural in myths and rituals).

TABLE 1
DESIGN TYPES

Subjects by sex and age	Simple	Formal Complex	Experimental	Natural and experimental	Naturalistic Figure, house, etc.	Weaving	Emblematic	Failed
Females:								
Schoolgirls N = 23	4		7	3	8			1
Young Adults N = 7a			2		1	4		
Adults over 60 N = 1		1						
Males:								
Schoolboys N = 27	5		8	5	8	1		
Adults to age 32b N = 9c		1		3	4		1e	
Adults age 33–40 N = 9a	2		2	2		2	1f	
Adults age 41–49 N = 10d	1		2		1	1	5	
Adults over 50 N = 7a						2	4	1

Notes to table 1

a Two subjects made two mosaics included in this table.

b Adult ages were calculated in part by comparison with the 1938 household census; e.g., those not yet born in 1938 are 32 yrs. or younger, those under 8 yrs. in 1938 as under 40 yrs. in 1971, and so forth. Age was known for the youngest adult male, 22 yrs.

c One subject made two mosaics.

d Four subject made two mosaics.

e This young man is the senior male member of a large household; he is a talented and prolific carver of almost wholly traditional masks.

f This man also is raised out of his generation group as the senior male member (in direct descent) of his lineage and draws heavily on the past in support of his prestige.

In answer to the question, "What have you made?" those who had made formal designs might reply, "Em i piksa tasol," that is, "It's just a design." Or a schoolchild might refer to a geometric form (learned in school), such as a square or a diamond. Some subjects became fascinated with the different possibilities of color and form and experimented with a whole series of small designs which, however, usually filled the tray harmoniously.

Those who had made naturalistic representations were always specific. They had made a (Tambanum) house, a church, a heron, a bird trap with birds flocking in, a waterbird with a small red head, a flower or a poisonous shrub or a decorative leaf found in the bush, or a man smoking a pipe. Stars in many shapes were popular. Or they had demonstrated a weaving technique, either for basketry or wall panels (known as *belem*, a local dialect version of PE *blain*), which when new may be painted in bright colors. Finally, some of those who experimented with form and color made a series of small naturalistic designs.

Emblematic designs also were representational but they differed from naturalistic ones in that what was represented was, for example, a traditional named mask or a named supernatural crocodile, pig, fish, or other creature. Thus an elderly man said (but in PE), explaining his design, "It is Kamerangowiavwan. He is a *tumbuan* (mask or masked figure) belonging to the men's house of Mboi-Nanguisime."

A few subjects made quite simple formal (nonrepresentational) designs (see table 1). This is to be expected in any sample. But here the proportion is small; no such simple formal design was made by an older man and only three were made by adults—one by a man who later made a well-organized *belem* (wall weaving) design and one by a man who layered the tiles in a sophisticated way to obtain color contrast effects along the edges.

What is most immediately striking about the designs is that, with some overlapping, *there is age-grading in the type of design made.*

The adolescents, both boys and girls, and the youngest adults were both experimental and naturalistic in their approach, the younger men even more than the adolescents as their experiments in form and color were more likely to be interpreted by them as representational. The two men in the 33–40 age group who made formal, experimental designs were both literate (self-taught) in

Pidgin English and in this sense fitted into the next younger age group; one of them, who treated his experiments as practice, later made a very handsome *belem* design, like other transitional men. In the next age group (41–50) one man, an exuberant and highly gifted artist, treated his experiments as "play" and later made an elegant design based on an emblematic theme of his clan—the moon in clouds and a star.

Making a weaving design imitating *belem* was in some way characteristic of people in transitional positions. (The one weaving design by a schoolboy could equally well have been classified as a complex formal design.) The *belem* technique is familiar to Tambanum men and women but is not used in their traditional house construction. That is, it is something foreign. One man in the over-50 age group made two *belem* mosaics. He was an astute politician in clan and village affairs. As *luluai* (government-appointed official) 1953–1965, he led the first children to school. But he was also a man whose beliefs and practices were deeply imbedded in the traditional culture. In the 41–50 age group one man first made a weaving design and afterward a magnificent naturalistic waterbird. This man, too, faced both to the past and the future; when Tambanum entered the regional council system, he was elected councilman to represent the powerful clans at the top of the village. For such men making *belem*—using these new materials to imitate a local but "foreign" product—seemed to reflect their transitional position between the past and the half-known present into which younger men and women and their own children were moving.

The major break, however, occurs between the younger groups, who were largely naturalistic and/or experimental in their approach, and those men in their late 40s or older who consistently drew on traditional, ceremonial clan themes in their choice of subject matter. But their work (with two partial exceptions) also illustrates the extreme individualism of the Iatmul male. Faced with the problem of working with entirely unfamiliar materials, they did not attempt to reproduce the traditional style. Instead, each successfully created a wholly new, and individually conceived, image of, for example, a crocodile or a bandicoot. (See plates 7 and 8 for the versions of a crocodile made by two men.)

These older men also most clearly exemplify the approach to the task characteristic of adults and only to a lesser extent of the schoolboys. A man would begin working by placing one tile (for example, a red square) near the center of the tray. For some seconds or even a minute or two he would concentrate on this, as though he were focusing his attention. Then, with little hesitation and, usually, relatively few substitutions he would go about developing his design. The first "key" piece almost invariably was incorporated in the design. These carvers and musicians were men with long, disciplined experience in visualizing a mass of details as parts of an organized and integrated whole. They worked very much as Iatmul men do in carving, where one blunder with the adze or chisel may spoil a work in progress.

3.

In contrast to the *products*, the final designs, which differed in relation to age and individual orientation to past and present, the *process* by which individuals achieved their designs was common to the whole group, adolescents and adults of all ages, girls and women as well as boys and men. Two basic principles guided their constructions: symmetry and complementarity. The selection of each tile, as well as substitutions of one tile for another, in terms of form and/or color, in the course of the development of the design, were determined by the complex interplay of these two principles. The color plates illustrate the process. Plates 1–4 illustrate stages in the construction of one design; Plates 5–8 show the steps (by the numbering of the tiles) in the sequence in the completion of four designs.

The steps, outlined below, in the making of two simple formal mosaics demonstrate the process through which the principles of symmetry (Sm) and complementarity (Cm) come into interlocking play.

The first, reproduced as a diagram, is a Mosaic made by a mature woman to illustrate a basketry technique. It is the most minimal design made by an adult.

1. *Design A*: Subject places one white square, W-S-1, on tray at lower right.

2. Places W-S-2 to left of W-S-1: *Sm in color, form, position.*

3. Centers W-S-3 underneath: *Sm in color, form: Cm in position.*

4. Centers W-S-4 above: *Sm in color, form; in position, Sm to W-S-3, Cm to W-S-1 and W-S-2.* This completes Design A.

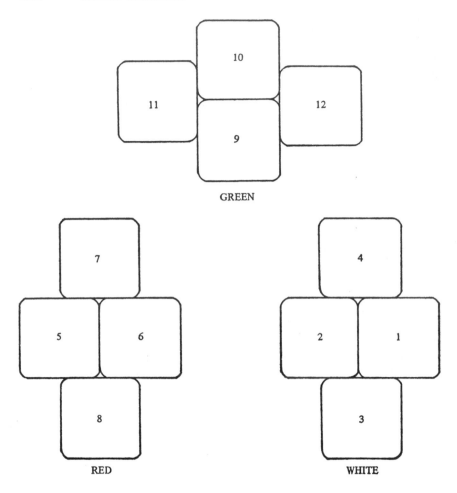

5. *Design B*: Parallel to Design A, but nearer center of tray, places red square, R-S-5: *Sm in form, Cm in color to tiles used in Design A.*

6, 7, and 8. In three steps, using in sequence R-S-6, R-S-7, and R-S-8, completes Design B, moving first from left to right (instead of from right to left, as in Design A) and then from top to bottom (instead of from bottom to top). *Design B is Sm in form and orientation, but Cm in color and process to Design A.*

9. *Design C*: Centers a green square, G-S-9, above Designs A and B: *Sm in form, Cm in color to tiles in Designs A and B; Cm also in position.*

10, 11, 12. In three steps, using in sequence G-S-10, G-S-11, and G-S-12, completes Design C, moving first from bottom to top and then from left to right, reversing the sets of sequences in Designs A and B. *Design C is Sm in form, but Cm in color, orientation (horizontal instead of vertical), and sets of sequences in both Design A and Design B.*

The final Mosaic design consists of a well-balanced triad in which the elements (Designs A, B, and C) are integrated through the symmetry of form and design (but with one change in orientation) and the complementarity of color.

The second illustration of the way symmetry and complementarity interlock in the process of construction is a formal (nonrepresentational) design made by a 14-year-old schoolboy, which he described (in English) as a "star in a diamond"—an idea that emerged as he worked. Stages in the construction are illustrated in plates 1–4.

Plate 1. Stages A-D: Exploration

This plate, which illustrates four successive stages, does not show where on the tray the subject actually placed the tiles, but only what the four initial sequences were.

1. Subject takes out of the mosaic box 6 tiles: a green square, a white equilateral triangle, a black scalene triangle, a red square and a yellow square. All are eventually used in the design.

2. *Stage A*: Sets green square, G-S-1, at center right. (His key piece.)

3. Sets aside equilateral and scalene triangles.

4. *Stage B*: Places yellow square, Y-S-2, at right of G-S-1, forms Cm pair.

5. Takes from box another green square, G-S-3; sets it as pendant to corner of G-S-1. Sets red square, R-S-4, symmetrically at corner of Y-S-2.

6. *Stage C*: Turns G-S-1 and Y-S-2 so that this small design, symmetrical in form and design, also forms one Sm pair and four Cm pairs.

7. *Stage D*: Reorganizes arrangement of the same tiles so that they form two diverging (Cm) columns that combine Cm and Sm pairs.

This gives him the beginning idea for his design. From this stage on, I shall in most cases only state the steps, not the progressive handling of Sm and Cm.

Plate 2. Stage E: Development of initial design, with one substitution.

8. *Stage E*: Opens up columns and sets two black squares, B-S-5 and B-S-6, moving from left to right, at the top of each column.

9. Sets white equilateral triangle, W-ET-7 (which was set aside earlier), at the apex.

10. Adds green squares, G-S-8 and G-S-9, moving from left to right, at the base of the columns.

11. Adds black squares, Bk-S-10 and Bk-S-11, moving from left to right, at the base of each column. Turns them so they slope inward, parallel to each other.

12. Closes base with two red squares, R-S-12 and R-S-13, moving from left to right.

13. Substitutes a yellow square, Y-S-14, for G-S-8, which he removes.

He has now achieved a closed design consisting of two diverging Cm columns with echoing colors, joined together at the base by matched Cm/Sm pairs and at the apex by a single tile, Cm to the whole in color and echoing the whole design Sm in form.

Plate 3. Stages F and G: Reorganization and elaboration of design. This plate shows simultaneously two successive stages in the development.

14. *Stage F*: Removes W-ET-7, and sets it aside.

15. Rearranges the pieces (without changing their order) so that they form four sets of three squares (one set as yet imperfect). The *interior space* now forms a diamond.

16. Inserts at the sides, now moving from right to left, white equilateral triangles, W-ET-7 (set aside earlier) and W-ET-15, emphasizing by these Sm triangles, which are Cm in color and form to the rest of the tiles, the Cm of the columns of squares.

17. *Stage G*: In the interior space fits together two opposing white scalenes, W-ST-16 and W-ST-17, now moving from left to right.

18. Sets two black scalenes, Bk-ST-18 (one of the tiles first taken out of the box) and Bk-ST-19, above and below white scalenes.

Plate 4. Stage H: The final design achieved, "Star in a Diamond."

19. *Stage H*: Replaces Bk-ST-18 with a white scalene, W-ST-20.

20. Opens up "star" and turns W-ST-20 so that the two pairs of scalenes (white and white, white and black) balance in their combined Sm and Cm.

The design made by this adolescent boy is a well-integrated

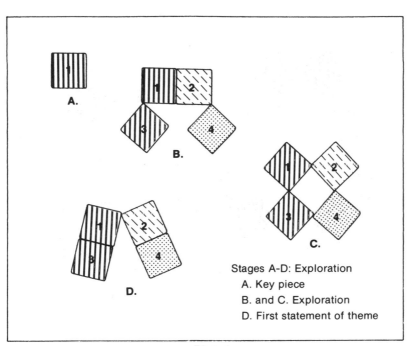

Stages A-D: Exploration
A. Key piece
B. and C. Exploration
D. First statement of theme

Plate I.

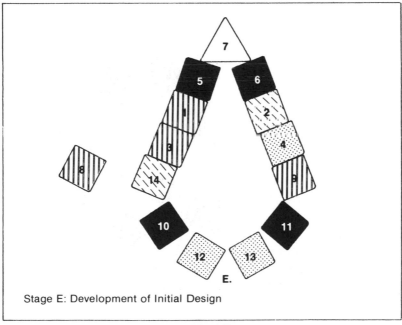

Stage E: Development of Initial Design

Plate II.

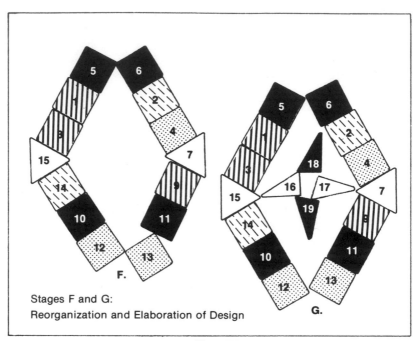

Stages F and G:
Reorganization and Elaboration of Design

F.

G.

Plate III.

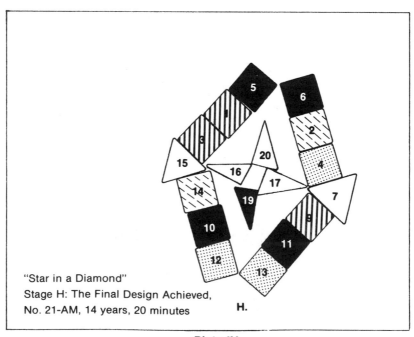

"Star in a Diamond"
Stage H: The Final Design Achieved,
No. 21-AM, 14 years, 20 minutes

H.

Plate IV.

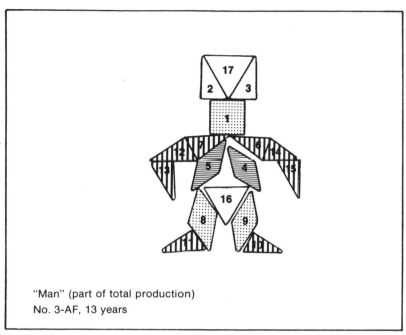

"Man" (part of total production)
No. 3-AF, 13 years

Plate V.

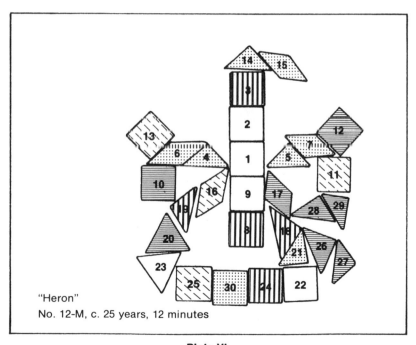

"Heron"
No. 12-M, c. 25 years, 12 minutes

Plate VI.

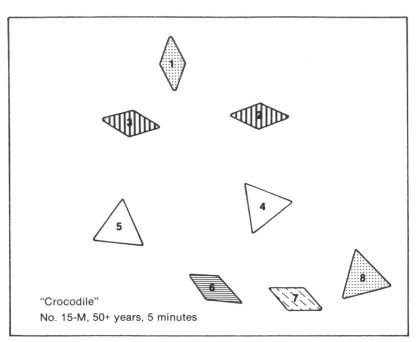

"Crocodile"
No. 15-M, 50+ years, 5 minutes

Plate VII.

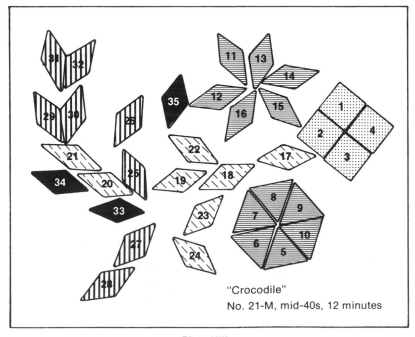

"Crocodile"
No. 21-M, mid-40s, 12 minutes

Plate VIII.

whole that displays a fine balance between symmetry and complementarity in the forms, colors, and placement of tiles. But without a step-by-step analysis of his procedure it would not be possible to understand how these basic principles guided the process of achieving this balance. It may be noted that the colors used are those of the traditional Iatmul palette.

4.

Analysis of two aspects of Tambanum Mosaic designs—product and process—indicates that the performance of adolescents and adults in this culture taps their life experience at two clearly differentiated levels.

Age-grading in the type of design made reflects the slowly changing mode of life. It also demonstrates the steadfastness of the older men in their preoccupation with the themes around which their rich ceremonial life was built and the shift of attention among the younger age groups, not to a different world but to the actual world around them of houses and people, birds and plants, women's basketry, and a technique used in house building elsewhere in the locality.

Younger people were more experimental in their fascination with the properties of the material—the actual mosaic tiles in their different forms and colors. Older men were experimental in quite another sense, that is, in their capacity to translate thematic material freely and with assurance from the traditional cultural style into something new and highly individualized. There is, however, a likeness between the best work of older and younger men in their disciplined artist's awareness of good design, well organized and harmoniously proportioned within the frame provided by the tray.

The analysis also disclosed that the process by which the designs, however different, were achieved by adolescents and adults, males and females, was based in and reflected the dualistic handling of symmetry and complementarity, the principles that integrate Iatmul interpersonal relations, ceremonial themes, artistic production and world view at a deep level of the cultural personality. It is at this level that one finds continuity in both sexes across the living generations. This is certainly one precondition for the survival of the cultural and social identity of the Iatmul, for whom their own culture is at the center of their consciousness and commitment.

REFERENCES

ABEL, THEODORA M., and RHODA METRAUX. 1974. Universals and Cultural Regularities: Aspects of Performance in the Lowenfeld Mosaic Test. Paper presented at the annual meeting of the American Anthropological Association.

BATESON, GREGORY. 1936. *Naven.* Cambridge University Press.

———. 1958. *Naven* (2d ed.). Stanford University Press.

LOWENFELD, MARGARET. 1954. *The Lowenfeld Mosaic Test.* Newman Neame.

Relations among Generations in Time-Limited Cultures

THEODORE SCHWARTZ

Although youth and age still follow one after the other, the circle of successive generations is not unbroken, for the paths of young and old extend through time and change. When adulthood is reached, youth may find itself (or think itself to be) in new terrain. In other words, discontinuities as well as continuities of culture exist through time. Such changes are not new, but the rate of change relative to the human life span—the longitudinal effect —has accelerated. The variability, distinctiveness, and relative isolation of cultures arrayed in geographic space has diminished greatly, given worldwide interdependence and the means for rapid and massive culture transfer. As a result, cultures may now be located more in time than in space. In the new experiences and identities of successive generations lies the replacement of the lost spatial variability.

The question "What is culture?" can no longer be answered in any way that does not consider what culture is becoming. Margaret Mead, with her sensitivity to crucial issues, has been preeminent among anthropologists in suggesting answers to this question. The span of time and change encompassed by her work in many cul-

THEODORE SCHWARTZ is professor of anthropology at the University of California, San Diego.

tures, particularly that of the Manus people of the Admiralty Islands of Melanesia, has contributed to her perceptiveness of the relations among cultural generations. It is now clear that the concept of generations is crucial to the understanding of the structures of cultures. Such relations range from the theoretical extremes of replication to complete discontinuity between cultural generations. In between lie the many compromises of relations among generations.

This paper discusses some aspects of the structure of generationally stratified cultures, which are seen as consisting of a set of coeval time-limited or generational cultures. The temporal structure of a culture varies with its cultural history, its historical situation, and its state or phase. All of these aspects determine the relations among coexisting generations—the bonds that unite and the gradients that differentiate their members in some degree of social and cultural integration.

A general statement on generationally stratified cultures is followed by an ethnographic example of narrower scope. The example is drawn from my research in Manus, which I began in 1953 as a participant in the longitudinal study conducted by Mead and others since 1928. The example deals with the relations between those who remain at home in their Manus village and the educated progeny of that village, now employed in all parts of Papua New Guinea. It discusses the derivation of bonds and intergenerational sanctions that continue to unite generations that otherwise appear to be markedly differentiated. The situation described is itself phase-relative, that is, subject to change in the process of culture change itself. It illustrates one of the as yet uncataloged possibilities of relations in generationally stratified cultures.

Anthropologists were not the first to focus on the importance of cultural generations. We were, perhaps, excessively concerned with the documentation or reconstruction of cultures "fixed" in time to become a part of the permanent record of human ways of being. The study of acculturation was concerned with relations between cultures from different places which had come into contact, rather than with the internal culture contact between generations. But internal acculturation may now be near in importance to enculturation in the overall cultural process. Temporal structures in the sense of age-grades or age-linked statuses and ritual transitions were, of course, well studied and are prerequisite to understanding a more dynamic structure.

Emergent generational cultures have long been important to historians and students of art and literature who were accustomed to examining such aggregates as the Spanish poets of the 1890s or the "lost generation." Generations have been explored by philosophers, particularly those concerned with the historical relativity or emergent character of human nature and ideas. The notion is central to the work of Ortega Y Gasset and richly analyzed by Julián Marías. Several sociologists, under the stimulus of Mannheim, have considered the question of generational change, character, duration, and identity. David Riesman, a sociologist and ethnographer of generations and institutions, began by identifying generations in American culture in terms of their social character. This was seen largely as their cultural orientations—as traditionalists attuned to the past, as status or cultural migrants guided by internalized motives, or as other-directed shoppers amidst the constant turnover of current peer styles. These were modes of conformity beyond which possibilities of autonomy were envisaged. Alvin Toffler evoked wide public response to his characterization of the effects of rapid culture change on the nature of culture itself. Margaret Mead's "postfigurative, cofigurative, and prefigurative" modes of cultural transmission parallel Riesman's types to some extent but reflect her cross-cultural perspective and the 1970s concern with commitment, perhaps the central problem of autonomy.

In this paper, the term "generation" is not being used in the traditional genealogical sense appropriate only to particular lineages. As obvious as it seems, we often have had to be reminded that, as P. T. Barnum put it (although he had something else in mind), "There's one born every minute." To which we must add that one dies every minute. The flow of cultural generations is a continuum to which each individual born contributes and from which each individual passing subtracts. But to classify and to segment is human, and to classify in particular ways depends on human motives and models. We must be reminded that cultural generations, usually conceived of as sequential, do not disappear as predecessors give rise to their successors, but that different generations are coeval and must relate, communicate, exchange, and otherwise interact to constitute a society.

If generations are segments perceived or imposed on a continuum, a "generation" may be defined as those individuals in the flow of population through time who see themselves or are seen by others as culturally distinguished from others who preceded or followed them. Bennett Berger has pointed out that we may all too avidly distinguish and name generations, and that the seeming acceleration of generational turnover may depend as much on this avidity as on real change. He correctly notes that even for the same age group, there exists a plurality of "generations" or cultural styles. We may term these "complementary generations"—that is, an age cohort may be divided among alternative generational cultures covering various time spans. At the same time, these complementary generations coexist with all predecessor and successor generations that still have living members. All such segments taken together—whether in the relations of complement, predecessor, or successor to each other—constitute the generation-stratified culture.

There are both objective and subjective boundary markers of cultural generations. Boundaries may be subject to various numerologies—decades and centuries being most obvious in the perceptions of Western historians. Such boundaries would seem totally arbitrary unless, perhaps, we have attuned our expectations for change to such units as the "sixties" or "twenties," as the current nostalgia fad might indicate. We have become a generation of generation watchers with the bumper-sticker motto, "Nostalgia isn't what it used to be." Less arbitrary is the delimitation of generations by natural and historic events marking discontinuities of experience for the members of sequent generations. Calamities—wars, droughts, depressions—make good generational watersheds, although paradoxically, perhaps, because they evoke nostalgia for the solidarity of adversity. (Italians say it another way: "We had it better when we had it worse.")

Boundaries may often seem vague and generations may intergrade or overlap, so that the span of a generation seems indeterminate or as arbitrary as it may be when reckoned in decades. Even so, most individuals will still have an anchor point. One's generation is not coterminous with one's life span. Halcyon days may serve as well as societal traumas as anchor points. In our culture, anchorage seems to occur in late adolescence and early adulthood.

In a school-centered culture, "class-years" occur at a suitable rate to serve as labels in the rapid turnover of academic "generations." For most, high school, physical and sexual maturity, dating or courting, and life in extrafamilial society among friends and peers are at their height. This period may be prolonged by extended education, perhaps even by war, or terminated by commitments to work or marriage. Adhering to each individual's generational anchor point is a cluster of emblematic traits much like those of space-bounded cultures (Schwartz 1975b)—food preferences, songs and musicians, language with its generational slang, clothing styles, causes, and culture heroes.

Of particular concern here is the question of the relations between coeval generations—of the bonds, gradients, sanctions, and conflicts among contemporaries who are members of differing generations. For this paper, Manus will be considered as a representative of those societies in which the repetitive cycle of generations has only recently and partially been broken, leaving certain transitional features in evidence.

Mead's first study of Manus was in 1928. Her books *Growing Up in New Guinea* and *Kinship in the Admiralty Islands* tell us more than we deserve, for that period of our science, of kinship behavior and of the relations of authority, nurturance, competition, obligation, and support that made up the circle of intergenerational relations. In a specialized culture of fishermen who lived on pile houses over the shallow lagoons within the reefs of the Admiralty Islands, we follow toddlers encouraged to independence, venturing into a mixed-age play group, exercising constantly their early competence in a hazardous marine environment. And in this play group, they stayed through childhood and youth until in marriage they reluctantly assumed the full burdens of adult responsibility. By at least eight years of age, girls served as child nurses. But even with their younger siblings on their hips or backs, they were not severed from the play group. Boys played at fishing, joined the expeditions of their elders, and contributed substantially as they got older. They played an important but passive cultural role, providing the occasions for the economy of ceremonial exchange that would revolve around the repeated validation of their future, their present, and their past marriages, the birth of their children, their deaths, and their later commemoration. The younger men began their adult responsibility deeply obligated to the kinsmen entrepreneurs who had financed their marriages. Their choice was either to contend for prestige at some level or to be regarded as rubbish, a man without a name, perhaps an unimportant supporter of a lesser "big man." From the freedom and comradeship of the play group and the youth group, the young man moved on to the prestige treadmill upon which his interests and values were to become focused. The woman was not exempt. She would be involved in exchange on behalf of her brothers, and her husbands; in recent times at least, she might herself be a party in exchange.

A further aspect of this discontinuity between youth and adulthood was the relatively late recruitment of the young to the full weight of the moral-religious system. In this system they had often provided the occasion (in their serious illnesses, for example) for their elders to invoke the ghosts of the lineage to diagnose the adult sins that had provoked the theft of their soul stuff. Not until early adulthood did their own behavior become a moral concern of the ghosts. In yet another pioneering paper, Mead (1932) discussed as an early counter-Piagetian argument (see Langness, Shweder, and LeVine in this volume) the relatively nonanimistic perceptions of causal relations by children in comparison with the explanations of adults. Again, this seems to indicate a delayed induction into the full adult culture.

If these observations had represented only a monographic fossil in the anthropological record, they would nevertheless have been of great interest as depicting one possibility in the process of enculturation. But in the context of another series of studies that Mead began in 1953, twenty-five years after her initial work in Manus, these discontinuities take on a greater importance in our understanding of the process of rapid culture change. Within the limits of their means, the Manus made a remarkably vigorous and in many ways successful adaptation to the challenge of seemingly overwhelming culture contact. Various aspects of Manus culture may have preadapted them to seek to acquire and master European culture, wealth, and knowledge. Contributing to the process was their adaptation to seafaring, fishing, trade, and ceremonial exchange in a prestige system that motivated so many to strive for renown. Mead states in *New Lives for Old* that delayed induction into the full adult traditional culture was one of the factors that enabled the immediately post-World War II generation of young men to chose entry into the European culture (or at least into a native version of it) rather than to take up the adult roles and ceremonial responsibilities that awaited them in their own culture.

In the initial phase of what was to become known as the Paliau Movement (named after its leader; see Mead 1956, and Schwartz 1962, 1975a), this Hamlinesque defection by an entire generation was at first resisted by the leaders of the parental generation. It seems likely that the sanction of ideological and physical withdrawal from the villages would have brought them around. While the question was still unresolved, all were swept into commitment to the movement by the tidal wave of a "cargo cult" that promised them immediate parity with the Europeans through the supernatural intervention of Jesus, who would lead their own modernized ancestors to a wealth-laden reunion with the living. The cult subsided, leaving the movement with an assimilative program and an increasingly routinized native separatist church in its place. The history of the next twenty-five years cannot be offered here. The movement accomplished much; a new way of life, in many ways disappointingly (to its followers) more native than European, was instituted. Intermittent plateau phases led to cult revivals, each more restricted in spread than those before it. The movement became acceptable to the Australian administration and then was increasingly absorbed into district and emerging national politics. While the Manus moved to the beaches and built more "European"-shaped thatch and scrap metal houses and reorganized their lives around new village routines, they still made their living by fishing from their outrigger canoes. Their incomes allowed only very limited access to the goods that would enable them to live in a more European manner.

The greatest discontinuity stemmed from the secular, government schools established in the mid-1950s which were part of a crash program to prepare for self-government in the near future. In each village within the area of the Paliau Movement, children left the free-form life of the play group at the age of six to spend long disciplined days reciting and being recited at in English; in the afternoons they returned to their home, language, and play. For at least fifteen years, most of these children went on to high school, vocational, technical, and agricultural schools, to the military or police service, or to jobs. Each of these destinations removed them from the village for most of the year, and their adolescence was filled with intensive training unrelated to their traditional cultures and the continuing activities of their parents. Recently other ethnic groups are catching up with the Manus. The job market has become more saturated and an increasing number of young people do not go beyond the village primary school or are returned to the village after a year or two of secondary school. The result, however, is that young men and women from Manus are disproportionately represented in the educated work force all over Papua New Guinea, which became self-governing in 1973. There are many Manus students at the University of Papua New Guinea and among its early graduates. Others hold government positions or are clerks, teachers, mechanics, or members of the police or armed forces.

During my four research visits of almost five years' duration over a twenty-year period, changes were seen in the lives of those who remained in the village. Many adults had grown up within the contact culture and the new way of the Paliau Movement but they had done so prior to the opportunity for modern education. The changes were far less than the adherents of the Paliau Movement had hoped for in 1946. During our visit in 1953, it seemed that so much of traditional practice was gone forever, having been deliberately discarded. This was initially disappointing to me, steeped as I was in the classic ethnographies. There were church services, village meetings, and court cases, but the drums, the dancing, the ceremonial seemed gone—looked upon with disdain as the "stinking ways of our ancestors."

On later visits, I learned to distinguish better between change in the "state" of the culture, responsive to changes in the perceived situation, and change in the culture itself. The past is not so easily extirpated. Expectations were gradually recalibrated as hope dwindled for the instantaneous or imminent achievement of a European way of life or, perhaps more precisely, a European (including American and Australian) standard of living. This hope was shifted back and forth from the cult to the movement, then to cooperatives, to local government councils, and to the schools and the careers they promised. But for adults, life went on increasingly as before, selectively reactivating core elements of the premovement past.

During this time, some exchanges were initiated on the occasion of marriages in the village. At first, there was embarrassment about these exchanges, which defied the attempts of Paliau, who had targeted them for extinction as dissipative of wealth and energy. But by 1963, they were being celebrated with "native" costumes and a revival of the older style dancing and drumming—without the traditional phallic exposure but with great hilarity over the gestures that once accompanied it. To my amazement (thinking back on earlier rigidities), Paliau staged such a dance in 1973 in which he, wearing the dog's teeth ornaments of a traditional "Big Man," was the featured dancer. The renascence of the exchanges was not a simple revival. There were new elements. Prestige was attached especially to the exchange of imported goods (such as clothing, bicycles, outboard motors, and watches) and imported foods (such as bags of sugar, flour, and rice) against large amounts of Australian currency, which had replaced the dog's teeth and shell money of old. The hope of wealth was displaced upon the exchange system that, as in the past, assembled large amounts of wealth momentarily in the name of the principals to the exchange, only to distribute it for reassemblage over other nodes in the network of exchange.

A revival of another updated form of the old ceremonial exchanges had begun in 1953. From that date through 1967, at least ninety instances of the "mother's teeth" exchange (explained later) had taken place in the Manus village, Peri. Each involved many participants and considerable amounts of wealth and consumables. These exchanges were continuing as a major focus of adult interest in 1973.

During a field period from 1963 to 1967, I conducted an ethnographic survey of all the peoples of the Admiralty Islands. It was then that I began to pick up instances of another "survival" among the Manus and others of the traditional belief in the power of the father's sister, her children and, more extensively, of the father's matrilineage to curse (or bless) the members of his patrilineage (Mead, 1934). In 1953, informants had discussed this as if it were a defunct custom. It was especially thought that they could strike the wives of men of the patrilineage with barrenness, or that the curse could cause a man or woman to lose interest in food and work, perhaps to the point of death. But usually long before this time, the cause of the disease would be diagnosed and separated from other

causes, such as ghostly wrath or an encounter with bush spirits, and
the father's sister would have been placated. By another incanta-
tion, she could remove the curse.

Why are the exchanges called "mother's teeth," and what has
this to do with the father's sister's curse? Manus and other Admiralty Island societies were organized around villages composed of
patrilineal lineages (grouped as clans). Depending on the ethnic
group, totemic food taboos, or simply the taboos themselves without the belief in descent from the taboo species, were inherited
matrilineally along with certain spiritual powers (of cursing or
blessing) over the related patrilineage. Each man's exchange network depends on his "sisters": the women of his patrilineal lineage
or clan who have married into other clans. These women are, in a
sense, compensated and armed with sanctions to protect their rights
in the patrimony of the clan they have enriched (in leaving) as well
as the residual rights of their progeny. From the point of view of
the patrilineal clan, its dispersed progeny through females are resources and potential recruits. These sanctions also would have
supported the Manus ideal marriage, in which cross-cousins arrange for the marriage of their children. Cross-cutting ties are carefully conserved on both sides, and spiritually, the demands of the
exogam and her progeny (one's cross-cousins through the father's
sister) are backed by the power of cursing and blessing.

Traditionally, then, the father's sister's curse has been an intersegmental sanction. We may picture it as interlacing the vertical
segments of the clan-lineage structure. With this, it is now possible
to see the mother's teeth exchange as the same relationship but acting, or at least initiated, in the opposite direction, accomplishing or
exploiting the same interlacing. In it, members of a clan (usually of
a specific lineage of the clan) will approach some of the progeny of
a woman (usually deceased) of the clan and will challenge them to
pay for the teeth of their mother. This woman had been "paid for"
many times over since her betrothal, but now her matrilineal descendants are reminded that she bore all of them or their parents
and that she "wore out her teeth" for them, premasticating the food
that she stuffed into their mouths as infants. It is interesting that it
is the mastication rather than her suckling that is used to evoke a
sense of obligation in her descendants. We could guess that the
sense of being stuffed with food and some anxiety (manifested in

other ways) about getting it down, through, and out may be the dominant memory of the oral stage (premasticated feeding starts within the first three months after birth). We could, less speculatively, link the demand for the mother's teeth with its traditional payment in dog's teeth—an obvious homonymy.

There are many complications, of course, but the above must suffice to indicate the essence of this traditional relationship. The intergenerational significance now becomes apparent when we turn to examine how these bonds and sanctions between the vertical segments of Manus society became converted, under recent circumstances, to bonds and sanctions between differentiated generations. These generations may be viewed as horizontal segments in a generationally stratified culture.

By 1963, the cash yield of village produce had changed little. And yet, more and more expensive goods and foods were turning up at marriage and mother's teeth exchanges. It is true that the appearance of wealth was magnified by the number of times the same cash or objects could be used in different exchanges. It is also true that in gambling with cards, amounts of money were won and lost in one night which few natives could earn in many months. Both winner and losers were participants in this symbolic magnitude, and the informal but strongly felt rule was that the winnings were not to be dissipated but rather kept in the gambling circuit. Nevertheless, it was apparent that there was by now a constant flux of new wealth from a major source—the salaries of the young people of the village who were working in all parts of Papua New Guinea. In some cases, money or articles requested were mailed or shipped back to the village, but it had also become a common practice for villagers to visit their kin in the towns and outstations where they were working. Visiting relatives often stayed for many months, had their fares paid, and were sent home by their kin loaded with gifts. In 1967, there had only been a few outboard motors in native hands at our base village. In 1973, there were thirty-nine—about half of them still in working condition. Between 20,000 and 30,000 dollars had been paid for them with money derived mainly from the salaried progeny of the village.

I had a discussion with one young Manus man, a university graduate who now held an important government position. We discussed his father, whom I had known for twenty years—an important figure in the Paliau Movement. The old man had spent about six months visiting with his son's family about a year before. In spite of the son's generosity—it took all his son could manage to provide for his father's trip and gifts—the old man had returned home dissatisfied with his treatment. Now the father kept writing for an outboard motor that would cost at least 800 dollars—a powerful motor commensurate with his prestige. The son complained bitterly to me that other relatives made demands on him as well, and that he never could save any money or, for that matter, stay out of debt. He felt that he should be able to use his money to live at a level commensurate with his needs and status as a highly educated government official living in the capital, but he saw no hope that he would be able to buy even a car. I asked him why he didn't resist the demands of his relatives: "*Oi kembule mamachi?*" (Is your forehead ashamed?) "No," he replied, "*Yo kwinyol.*" (My buttocks are afraid.) He told me that his father had cursed him (though he was not at the time aware of it) when the old man had returned dissatisfied to his village. As a result, the son had failed an examination and missed a job opportunity.

All the instances of the father's sister's curse I have heard of since 1963 have been similar to this one. They seem not to be based on grievances toward the young person's parents; instead, they are directed toward the young persons themselves as retaliation for some slight or for some unfulfilled request. The alleged effects of the curse were in every case a setback to the career of the young person. Failure of a school examination, being fired unjustly from a job, loss of interest or motivation in a job or school that leads the young person unaccountably to leave without explanation to return to the village, an impulse to steal from an employer that led to being fired or to a jail term—all of these were immediately recognized as the results of cursing. The slighted relative is found, the grievance is assuaged, and the situation is remedied if it is remediable. It also became apparent that the cursing power was no longer specific to the father's sister's line. The young people thought of it as something that older people of the parental generation will do when their wishes are denied. I encountered no instance in which a sibling or cousin considered of one's own generation used the curse. There were other sanctions as well applying generally between those who stayed at home—the noneducated and the nonemployed school leavers, and those who were away at work. One could not avoid making appropriate contributions to mother's teeth exchanges, affinal exchanges, or exchanges in the same social form occasioned by death and mourning. The absentee is not merely a donor. He is entitled to his part of the reciprocal distribution; but if he was not there, his kin were recipients on his behalf.

This situation, with perhaps widely differing kinship rationales, is a well-known phenomenon in developing countries that are making the transition from a kinship-based to a cash-based contractual society. In West Africa, it has often been discussed under the name of "parasitism." A gradient of wealth, knowledge, and power seemingly develops with the educated, salaried class at the high end of the gradient. And yet, in Manus at least, this gradient is nullified so far by the effective operation of what we may call "forward sanctions" operating from the older upon a younger generation and the ineffectiveness of "black sanctions" operating from the younger upon the older generation. The sanction of withdrawal, an effective back sanction under some circumstances (as in the early stage of the Paliau Movement), is nullified by the father's sister's curse, which can act over any distance, and by the practice that brings relatives to your door at your most distant posting.

In summary, what had been a sanction operating between lineages (cross-generational, or vertical segments) has been adapted as a generational sanction (operating between generations, or horizontal segments). There has been a corresponding shift in the set of kin who may use the sanction from the father's matrilineage to "the old people"—a generation. A branching of the younger generation is developing between stay-at-home and away-at-work complementary generations. The relation between the two is comparable to the relation between the endogamic and exogamic sexes—those who remain resident in the clan and those who marry out—in the traditional social structure. But the sanctioning power is reversed: it is the stay-at-home generation that has the compensatory sanctions to enforce their claims on the resources of the dispersed wage earners. Whether the younger stay-at-home generation will succeed to the use of the cursing sanction as they get older remains to be seen. They are able to make other claims based on less drastic kinship sanctions on the away-at-work generation.

It appears that the sanctions will remain effective as long as the generations remain a part of a single community of belief in spite of the educational gradient that separates them. They will continue to pay indefinitely for their mother's teeth and to ward off their father's sister's curse. All of those with whom I spoke shared these and comparable beliefs. In spite of their having been kidnapped by an alien culture, perhaps the early years, the afternoons, and the school holidays sufficed for their induction at the deeper levels of their culture.

REFERENCES

BERGER, BENNETT. 1971. *Looking For America*. Prentice-Hall.

FORTUNE, REO. 1935. *Manus Religion*. American Philosophical Society.

MANNHEIM, KARL. 1952. *Essays in the Sociology of Knowledge*. Routledge and Kegan Paul, Ltd.

MARÍAS, JULIÁN. 1967. *Generations: A Historical Method*. trans. by Harold C. Raley. The University of Alabama Press.

MEAD, MARGARET. 1930. *Growing Up in New Guinea*. Morrow.

————. 1932. An Investigation of the Thought of Primitive Children with Special Reference to Animism. *Journal of the Royal Anthropological Institute* 62:173–190.

————. 1934. *Kinship in the Admiralty Islands*. American Museum of Natural History Anthropological Papers 34, II.

————. 1956. *New Lives For Old: Cultural Transformation—Manus, 1928–1953*. Morrow.

————. 1970. *Culture and Commitment: A Study of the Generation Gap*. Natural History Press/Doubleday.

RIESMAN, DAVID, NATHAN GLAZER, and REUEL DENNEY. 1950. *The Lonely Crowd: A Study of the Changing American Character*. Doubleday.

SCHWARTZ, THEODORE. 1962. *The Paliau Movement in the Admiralty Islands, 1946–1954*. American Museum of Natural History Anthropological Papers 49, II.

————. 1963. Systems of Areal Integration. *Anthropological Forum* I, 1.

————. 1973. Cult and Context: The Paranoid Ethos in Melanesia. *Ethos* 1 (2):153–174.

————. 1975a. Cargo Cult: A Melanesian Type-Response to Culture Contact, *Responses to Change* (George De Vos, ed.). Van Nostrand. (In press.)

————. 1975b. Cutural Totemism, *Ethnic Identity: Cultural Continuities and Change*. (George De Vos and Lola Romanucci-Ross, eds.), pp. 106–132. Mayfield Publishing Co.

Becoming Modern:

Individual Change in Six Developing Countries

I. INTRODUCTION

Every era confronts its distinctive social and political dramas. In the mid-twentieth century, center stage has frequently been dominated by the struggle of the so-called "third world," first for liberation from the colonial powers and then for development and for entry into the modern world. The sixties were to be the "decade of development." Yet many of the emerging nations developed very little, if at all, and some slid backwards.

We must acknowledge that this sad outcome was contributed to by foreign intervention and colonial dependency, general political instability and specific tribal, religious, and ethnic conflicts. There was, however, more to the explanation. We have come, in time, to realize that nation building and institution building are only

ALEX INKELES is currently at the Institute for Advanced Study, on leave from Stanford University where he serves as Professor of Sociology and Margaret Jacks Professor of Education.

This paper summarizes the results of, and discusses some of the implications of the Harvard Project on Social and Cultural Aspects of Development, now located at Stanford University. Since the project was large and complex, the findings cannot be properly documented in this brief statement. For such documentation one must turn to the detailed report of the project by Alex Inkeles and David Smith (1974). Thanks are due to the Harvard University Press for permitting the use of material under their copyright incorporated in this book.

empty exercises unless the attitudes and capacities of the people keep pace with other forms of development. That such articulation will not result simply, or perhaps primarily, as a result of attaining political independence is clear from much of recent history.

Mounting evidence suggests that it is impossible for a state to move into the twentieth century if its people continue to live, in effect, in an earlier era. A modern *nation* needs participating citizens, men and women who take an active interest in public affairs and who exercise their rights and perform their duties as members of a community larger than that of the kinship network and the immediate geographical locality. In their turn, modern *institutions* need individuals who can keep to fixed schedules, observe abstract rules, make judgments on the basis of objective evidence, and follow authorities legitimated not by traditional or religious sanctions but by technical competence. The complex production tasks of the *industrial order,* which are the basis of modern social systems, also make their demands. Workers must be able to accept both an elaborate division of labor and the need to coordinate their activities with a large number of others in the work force. Rewards based on technical competence and objective standards of performance, on strict hierarchies of authority responsive to the imperatives of machine production, and on the separation of product and producer, all are part of this milieu, and require particular personal properties of those who are to master its requirements.

In addition, modern political and economic institutions alike make certain general demands on the people who work within them. They require a greater acceptance of personal mobility, occupational and geographic; a greater readiness to adapt to changes in mode of working and living, indeed a propensity to be an innovator; more tolerance of impersonality, of impartiality, and of differences that may characterize the diverse backgrounds of fellow employees in complex organizations. Neither the modern political nor the modern economic institution has much tolerance for fatalism or passivity. Rather both favor persistent effort and confident optimism.

These and related qualities will not be readily forthcoming from the people in developing nations so long as they continue in traditional village agriculture, are locked into near-feudal landholding patterns, are dominated by self-serving elites desperate to preserve their own power, are dependent on inadequate and antiquated public institutions, and are cut off from the benefits of modern science and technology as well as the stimulation of modern mass communication.

Naturally, every national population is large enough to include some individuals who have quite spontaneously developed the qualities that make for quick adaptation to the requirements of the modern world. Some ethnic and religious groups also seem more likely to generate individuals of this type. Swiss Protestants, East European Jews, the Parsis in India, and the Ibo in Nigeria have been nominated by various scholars as groups representing this tendency. Most men and women throughout the world, however, must acquire their modernity on a more individual basis.

The Project on the Social and Cultural Aspects of Economic Development, initiated at Harvard University and now located at Stanford, set itself the task of explaining that process whereby people move from being traditional to becoming modern personalities, hence our title, *Becoming Modern*. Our main objective was merely to attain greater understanding of a vitally important social process. But we entertained as well some hope that from this scientific understanding might come some increase in our ability to select wise and effective policies to guide national development.

II. THE DESIGN OF THE RESEARCH

We started with the assumption that no one is born modern, but rather that people become so through their own particular life experience. More specifically, our theory emphasized the contribution of man's work experience to making him modern. We believed that employment in complex, rationalized, technocratic, and even bureaucratic organizations has particular capabilities so to change men that they move from the more traditional to the more modern pole in their attitudes, values, and behavior. Among such institutions, we gave prime emphasis to the factory as a school in modernity. We also thought that urban living and contact with the mass media should have comparable effects. While emphasizing such modes of experience as more characteristic of the modern world, we did not neglect to study education, which earlier research had shown to be a powerful predictor of individual modernity, as well as other personal attributes such as age, religion, ethnic membership, and rural origin.

These and several dozen other variables that our theory, or other theories, identified as plausible explanations for individual modernity were taken into account in the design of our research. Interviewers trained by our project staff questioned almost 6,000 men from six developing countries: Argentina, Chile, India, Israel, Nigeria, and East Pakistan, now Bangladesh. The interview was extensive, up to four hours long.[1] Our samples were highly purposive, each including subgroups of cultivators, migrants from the countryside newly arrived in the city, urban workers earning their living outside large-scale productive enterprises, and workers in industry. The industrial workers were the largest group in each country, some 600 to 700, whereas the other subgroups were to be 100 each. The selection of cases was on the basis of the respondent meeting certain common characteristics as to sex (all male), age (18–32), education (usually 0–8 years), religion, ethnicity, rural or urban origin, residence, and, of course, the occupational characteristics already mentioned.

Since we are not making generalizations to the national populations, we gave greater emphasis to keeping the subsamples like each other in all respects except occupation, rather than selecting them to be representative of any "parent" population. Our strategy, then, was to treat the research in each country as essentially a replication of our basic design, on the assumption that any relationship that held true in six such different countries would be a powerful connection indeed.

III. DEFINING AND MEASURING INDIVIDUAL MODERNITY

The ultimate meaningfulness of our sample design rested on our ability to construct a reliable, cross-national measure of individual modernity. We do not claim to have invented the idea of the modern man. The concept was already there when we began our work, even though its content was vague. Inventing "types" of men has, after all, always been a fundamental preoccupation of sociologists. Yet it has been the rare instance, indeed, in which any systematic attempt has been made to measure whether there are real people in the world who, in their own persons, actually incorporate the qual-

---

1. The initial interviews were conducted during 1963 and 1964. Subsamples of 100 each were reinterviewed during 1968 and 1969 in India, Israel, and Bangladesh.

ities identified by these ideal types. We were determined to break with this tradition, and firmly committed ourselves to testing how far the set of qualities by which we defined the modern man actually cohered as a psychosocial syndrome in real men.

The characteristic mark of the modern man has two parts: one internal, the other external; one dealing with his environment, the other with his attitudes, values, and feelings. The change in the external condition of modern man is well known and widely documented, and it need not detain us long. It may be summarized by reference to a series of key terms: urbanization, education, mass communication, industrialization, politicization. The particular focus of our interest, however, was in the psychological characteristics that might distinguish the more modern from the traditional man.

Among the traits we saw as important were: openness to new experience, a strong sense of personal efficacy; a high degree of autonomy in dealing with the family, clan, and religious authority; valuing education and technical competence; and taking an interest in public affairs. In addition, research by various scholars argued the probable relevance of qualities such as being positive towards family limitation and the adoption of birth control; being an active participant citizen; and granting women some equality of rights in basic social, legal, and economic matters.

To convert our conception of the modern man into a tool useful for research, we created a long and fairly complex interview schedule yielding answers each of which could be scored to indicate whether a respondent was more inclined to the modern or the traditional pole. On numerous issues, using a separate subset of questions to reflect each topic, we explored all of the themes we had built into our own conception of the modern man as well as themes that other theorists had identified as relevant to judging individual modernity. One of the major challenges facing us was to discover whether these discrete elements held together in a more or less coherent syndrome that one could sensibly speak of as designating a "modern man," or whether they would prove to be a mere congeries of discrete and unrelated traits, each of which characterized some modern men and not others.

In fact, it proved possible to develop a composite scale to measure individual modernity in general. This scale has considerable face validity, meets quite rigorous standards of test reliability, and can be effectively applied cross-culturally. We called it the OM scale to reflect its status as our overall measure of modernity. In one group of people after another differentiated by occupation, religion, ethnicity, educational level, and country of origin, the same set of qualities went together. We therefore felt quite confident in affirming the empirical reality of the psychosocial syndrome our theory had originally identified.[2]

The modern man's character, as it emerges from our study, may be summed up under four major headings. (1) He is an informed participant citizen; (2) he has a marked sense of personal efficacy; (3) he is highly independent and autonomous in his relations to traditional sources of influence, especially when he is making basic decisions about how to conduct his personal affairs; and (4) he is ready for new experience and ideas, that is, he is relatively open-minded and cognitively flexible.

As an informed participant citizen the modern man identifies with the newer, larger entities of region and state, takes an interest in public affairs, national and international as well as local, joins organizations, keeps himself informed about major events in the news, and votes or otherwise takes some part in the political process. The modern man's sense of efficacy is reflected not only in his belief that either alone, or in concert with others, he may take actions that can affect the course of his life and that of his community, but also in his active efforts to improve his own condition and that of his family, and in his rejection of passivity, resignation, and fatalism towards the course of life's events. His independence from traditional sources of authority is manifested in public issues by his following the advice of public officials or trade union leaders rather than priests and village elders, and in personal matters by his choosing the job and the bride *he* prefers even if his parents prefer some other position or some other person. The modern man's openness to new experience is reflected in his interest in technical innova-

2. Different specialists in scale construction prescribe different standards for judging whether or not a set of questions or subscales "cohere" well enough to be acknowledged as constituting a general syndrome. Our standard scale OM-500 achieved a comfortable median reliability of .80 or above in all six countries in our study, as judged by the Kuder-Richardson formula. The coherence of the scale cross-nationally was also confirmed by a factor analysis of the version based on 19 subscales.

tion, his support of scientific exploration of hitherto sacred or taboo subjects, his readiness to meet strangers, and his willingness to allow women to take advantage of opportunities outside the confines of the household.

Although these are the principal components, they by no means exhaust the list of qualities that cohere as part of the modernity syndrome. The modern man is also different in his approach to time, to personal and social planning, to the rights of persons dependent on or subordinate to him, and to the use of formal rules as a basis for running things. In other words, psychological modernity emerges as a quite complex, multifaceted, and multidimensional syndrome.

Our results then provide definitive evidence that living individuals do indeed conform to our model of the modern man, that they do so in substantial numbers, and that essentially the same basic qualities that define a man as modern in one country and culture also delineate the modern man in other places. The modern man is not just a construct in the mind of sociological theorists. He exists and can be identified with fair reliability within any population where our test can be applied. Moreover, since the modernity scale enabled us to distribute men validly and reliably along a dimension of individual modernity, we were in postion to ask the next basic question: Why did particular individuals fall at one or the other end of the continuum, in other words, what makes men modern?

IV. EXPLAINING HOW MEN BECAME MODERN

Just as we had adopted a rather catholic position in considering a wide range of potential elements that might delineate the modern man, so we considered a large number of forces as possible determinants of individual modernity. Many of these were, however, only alternate ways of measuring the same thing, and we were able to reduce the explanatory variables to a basic set of some eight to ten major dimensions. These dimensions included: education, work experience, contact with the mass media, consumer goods possessed, father's education, urbanism of residence, skill level, length of urban residence, the modernity of one's factory, and the modernity of one's home and school background.

By using a composite measure summarizing each individual's

total exposure to such presumably modernizing experiences and institutions, it proved possible to sort out our samples with great precision. Of the men with minimum contact with modernizing institutions, only about 2 percent achieved scores on our attitude and value test which qualified them as modern men. Each step up the ladder of exposure to modern institutions brought a regular increase, so that by the time we reached those with the most extensive contact 76 percent scored as modern. The results are summarized in table 1.

TABLE 1
PERCENT MODERN ON THE OM SCALE WITH INCREASING EXPOSURE TO MODERN
INSTITUTIONS: BY EXPOSURE DECILE AND COUNTRY

Exposure Decile[1]	Argentina	Chile	East Pakistan	India	Israel	Nigeria
1	0.0	2.2	8.3	0.9	11.0	1.3
2	4.9	6.1	15.6	5.2	21.1	4.8
3	18.7	4.9	26.3	8.6	26.4	12.7
4	28.6	20.9	28.2	17.0	28.4	9.7
5	31.8	23.4	29.0	24.8	27.7	34.2
6	38.0	36.4	38.5	40.7	43.1	47.8
7	32.7	49.1	36.3	52.1	30.6	40.0
8	51.0	43.8	44.5	52.6	38.0	50.6
9	65.9	62.9	53.1	66.7	46.7	66.7
10	73.8	78.6	71.4	80.3	56.4	80.6

[1] Those in decile 1 were rural resident farmers with the least education, least contact with the mass media, and least urban experience. The more contact with the factory, the city, the media, and the school, the higher the decile position of the respondent.

Taken together this limited set of independent variables produced multiple correlations with the individual modernity scores of .56 to .79, depending on the country. This meant that we were explaining between 32 and 62 percent of the variance in modernity scores, with the median for the six countries at 47 percent.[3] This performance compares quite favorably with results obtained in the more developed countries in studies using comparable measures of complex personal attributes. Indeed, we can more fully account for what makes a man modern in Chile or India than our political scientists can account for what makes him liberal or conservative in the United States.[4]

3. The detailed results by country are shown in table 19–5 of Inkeles and Smith (1974).
4. For the justification of this assertion, see the evidence presented on pages 422–423 of Inkeles and Smith (1974).

SOCIALIZATION OF MODERNITY: EARLY OR LATE?

Our battery of measures taken together explained enough of the variation in OM scores to make meaningful an attempt to sort out the *relative* contribution of different kinds of influence. For us, the critical competition was that between those that exerted their effect early in life and those that came into play mainly in adulthood. We see individual modernity, measured by the OM scale, as being a quite basic personality characteristic. Yet, in the theories of personality most dominant in our time, it is generally assumed that the basic attributes of personality are laid down in the early period of development. If this assumption were correct, there would be little hope of changing people from traditional into modern men, psychologically speaking, once they had reached adulthood. Instead, efforts to increase the proportion of modern men would have to be focused mainly on the family and early schooling.

We assumed, however, that men could be changed in quite fundamental ways *after* they reached adulthood, and that no man need therefore remain traditional in outlook and personality merely because he had been raised in a traditional setting. Putting these ideas to an empirical test, we measured how much variance in OM scores was accounted for by the set of *early socialization variables*—notably father's education, own education, ethnicity and urban or rural origin—as compared to the explanatory power of a set of *later socialization influences,* including occupation, standard of living, urban experience, and mass media exposure. In three of our six countries the late socialization experiences played an even more important role in determining a man's modernity score than did the earlier formative influences. Indeed, when each set was used standing alone, the early socialization variables typically accounted for about 31 percent of the variance while the late socialization variables accounted for about 37 percent.

These results indicate that under the right circumstances any man may become modern after he has passed his adolescence. And, since the forces that can make men modern after the formative years seem to be embedded in the institutions that developing countries are most eager to adopt, the prospect is substantial that over time more and more of the men in those countries will develop the attitudes, values, and behavior patterns we have identified as defining the modern man.

In addition to observing the effect of the explanatory variables grouped as early and late socialization influences, we naturally wanted to know how the separate variables performed independently, in their own right. The answers could be obtained in a global way by considering the zero order correlations of OM scores with the standard explanatory variables, as in table 2.

TABLE 2
CORRELATIONS OF TEN INDEPENDENT VARIABLES
WITH INDIVIDUAL MODERNITY SCORES (OM-500), BY COUNTRY

		Argentina	Chile	East Pakistan	India	Israel	Nigeria
1.	Formal education	.60c	.51c	.41c	.71c	.44c	.52c
2.	Months factory experience	.24c	.36c	.26c	.11b	.26c	.29c
3.	Objective skill	.34c	.25c	.24c	.33c	.23c	.23c
4.	Mass media	.43c	.46c	.36c	.55c	.42c	.43c
5.	Factory benefits	.09a	.13c	.10b	.25c	.17c	.28c
6.	Years urban since age 15	.35c	.37c	.20c	−.02	n.a.	.22b
7.	Urbanism of residence	.45c	n.a.	.11b	.25c	−.01	.36c
8.	Home-school modernity	.11b	.22c	.01	.26c	.01	.02
9.	Father's education	.33c	.33c	.21c	.42c	.02	.17c
10.	Consumer goods	.44c	.35c	.35c	.38c	.17c	.42c
N's for rows 1, 4, 7, 8, 9, 10		817	929	943	1198	739	721
N's for rows 2, 3, 5		663	715	654	700	544	520
N's for row 6		239	305	654	700	0	184

Significance levels are as follows:
a = at .05 level; b = at .01 level; c = at .001 level or better.

In all six countries, education emerged as unmistakably the most powerful force. Indeed, judged by the number of points on the OM scale a man gained for each additional year of schooling, education was generally two or even three times as powerful as any other single input. In this, our conclusions are not new but rather confirm findings in several other studies of modernity.

The distinctive emphasis of our project, however, lay in its concern for the potential impact of occupational experience, and particularly of work in modern large-scale productive enterprises such as the factory. Although each year in a factory yielded only one-third to one-half the increase in points on the modernity scale which an additional year in school could bring, the variable of factory experience was generally second in importance after education. Moreover, the association between work in a factory and individual modernity did not result from factories having selected only modern men to be their workers. Retesting the same individuals after a lapse of four years, we found that every year they had continued working in a factory had contributed to making them more modern. No such change was found in men who, over the same span of time, had continued working in agriculture.

Exposure to the mass media generally showed itself to be more or less equal to occupational experience as a force making men modern. By contrast, some of the institutions most commonly associated with the process of modernization failed to substantiate their claim to standing as important schools for modernity. Most notable of these was the city, whose failure to qualify was not corrected by taking into account either the size or the relative cosmopolitanism of different urban centers. Ethnic origin and religion also proved to be relatively unimportant variables, at least once the educational and occupational differences usually characterizing such groups were brought under control. We were struck, and rather surprised, to find that the relative modernity of the school a man attended and of the factory he worked in, at least so far as we were able to measure that quality, also played a very small role in determining a man's modernity when compared to the sheer *duration* of his exposure to those institutions.

These conclusions are of necessity stated here in very general terms, and do not reflect the many variations we observed when the forces at work were studied in greater depth. These more complex patterns were manifested in many ways, one of which is reflected in the contrasting direct and indirect effects of the explanatory variables as described in table 3.

We discovered that factory experience had a much greater impact on men of rural background and of little education than it did on men of urban origin who had had more education. Indeed, in explaining the modernity scores of the less educated men of rural origin, we found that their occupational experience could be of equal, or even greater, importance than was the amount of schooling they had received.[5] This was partly because such men entered

5. This was most notably so for Argentina and Chile, as judged by the Beta weights of a regression including education, mass media, and years of factory work as predictors. For details see chapter 19 of Inkeles and Smith (1974).

TABLE 3

TOTAL DIRECT AND INDIRECT EFFECTS OF MAIN INDEPENDENT
VARIABLES ON OM-500: MEDIAN FOR SIX COUNTRIES

| Independent variables | Six Country Median Effects For: | | | | | |
| | All subjects | | | Factory workers only | | |
	Total[1]	Direct[2]	Indirect[3]	Total[1]	Direct[2]	Indirect[3]
Rural-urban origin[4]	—	—	—	.28	.10	.18
Ethnicity-religion	.19	.09	.10	.23	.09	.14
Father's education	.27	.05	.22	.22	.03	.19
Education-literacy	.52	.37	.15	.55	.37	.18
Occupational experience[5]	.41	.16	.25	.30	.12	.18
Mass media exposure	.45	.18	.27	.40	.16	.24
Living standard	.39	.10	.29	.33	.08	.25
Urbanism	.19	.04	.15	.02	.04	−.02
Life cycle stage	.03	.04	−.01	.06	.01	.05
Nature of present factory	—	—	—	.10	.06	.04

1 Total effects are the zero-order Pearsonian correlation coefficients.
2 Direct effects are the Beta weights (path coefficients).
3 Indirect effect equals total effect minus direct effect.
4 Rural-urban origin was measured only in Argentina, Chile, and Nigeria.
5 In total sample this variable measures occupational type; in the worker sample it is a complex measure of factory experience.

the factory with lower scores to begin with, so that they were not yet near the "ceiling," and hence had more room to develop as modern men under the tutelage of the factory. We also assume the factory effect was greater for men of rural origin because for them the factory was their first extensive contact with modern organizational principles and the large-scale inanimate use of power. In other words, with those men the factory could and did produce a more powerful "demonstration effect."

While we were persuaded by our data that the factory was certainly a school in modernity, other results indicated that the factory is probably not the only form of occupational experience with that potential. Thus, some types of urban nonindustrial employment also seemed to be at least a modest stimulant to modernity, a fact that we attributed to the contact with a diversified public and to relative autonomy in arranging one's own work. In addition, men pursuing traditional occupations, such as those of porter, but doing so in the context of large-scale bureaucratic organizations, also become somewhat more modern, presumably because the organizational context exerted some influence, even if the job itself did not.

We were most struck, however, by the dramatic changes in the level of individual modernity which were manifested by the peasant farmers who came under the special influence of the Comilla cooperative movement in what was formerly East Pakistan. Holding other factors constant, every year in a factory in East Pakistan was worth only about 1 point on the OM scale; every year in school produced a gain of about 1.5 points; whereas each year of exposure to the co-op movement as a nonmember netted approximately 1.7 points, and every year spent in the co-op as a member yielded a gain of 4 points or more per year. Since the cooperatives did not rely very heavily on new machinery to raise the productivity of the farmers, the exceptional impact of agricultural cooperation in Comilla must be accounted for by reference to other influences. We assume the success of the Comilla co-ops came, in part, from the models of alternative ways of doing things which the cooperative instructors provided, and in part from the new principles of social organization and interpersonal relations which the cooperatives introduced.

In summary then, we may say that at the point at which he left school, half the story of a man's eventual modernity score had been told. But this was true only "on the average." Actually, for many men the story really ended at that point. The score they had attained at the time they left school was basically the same one they were going to record when our project staff eventually came by to test them. Others would add a few points over the years. Still others, however, were to have later life experiences that would raise by many points the OM scores they had had at the time they left school. This increase was frequently as much as 50 percent, and in some cases was almost 100 percent, of the score these men had had on leaving the village. This outcome depended largely on the interaction between the stage at which the men left school, and the nature and extent of their later contact with modernizing institutions. Of these later experiences, the two that were critical were the occupations they entered and the extent of their contact with the media of mass communication.

Rural men who stayed in the countryside to farm as their fathers had were most likely to be frozen at the level of modernity that had characterized them when they left school. Few things in the nature of their work stimulated them to new ways of looking at things, to a heightened sense of personal efficacy, or to any of the other changes that would have made them more modern.

The greatest change in individual modernity was experienced by the men who left the countryside and associated agricultural pursuits to take up work in industry. As a result of this set of experiences, men of rural origin with modest education, say with three years of schooling or less, often moved almost completely to the opposite end of the continuum of individual modernity from that occupied by their former neighbors who continued agricultural pursuits in their natal villages. Indeed, such migrants often benefited enough from the combined stimulus of factory work and mass media contact to attain a modernity score the equal of that of men who had had twice as much education as the migrants, but had remained in their traditional villages to work as farmers.

V. SOME REMAINING ISSUES

There remain a few issues related to measuring the process of individual modernization which may be put in the form of simple questions, to which I will essay brief answers.

1. Is the process of modernization continuous and lifelong, or is there a definite plateau that people reach, after which they no longer continue becoming ever more modern?

Our experience with the OM scale suggests that the process of individual modernization can continue, if not indefinitely at least for a very long time, without any obvious limit being reached. This was most clear for education where, at least up to the twelfth year of school, each year of contact produced pretty much the same increment in OM scores as the year before. The growth curve for modernity rose on the chart in virtually a straight line in every country, without any visible dip in the latter years.

Examination of the "curve of growth" in modernity for men at different stages of industrial seniority indicates that there, too, the process of modernization is relatively continuous over time. During a span of at least twelve years in the factory, which was generally the maximum seniority of men in our samples, workers continued to become more modern, year by year, the longer they continued in industrial employment. I cannot be sure that becoming modern is a "lifelong" process, because our samples cut off at age thirty-five. Up to that age, however, a man in the right institutional setting can experience a continuous process of movement up the modernity scale.

2. Granted that change toward modernity is continuous so long as men remain under the influence of modernizing institutions, what happens to those who lose that contact? Is modernity irreversible, or will such men return to the more traditional mold?

That is unfortunately a question we cannot answer on the basis of any substantial empirical evidence. I can only say, therefore, that I believe that becoming modern represents a fairly basic change in personality, and such changes generally tend to be relatively enduring. How long they endure will, of course, depend on various circumstances, including how persistent the given individual is in preserving his character, how deeply rooted were the modern attitudes and values he had adopted, how much his subsequent experience reinforces his newly acquired traits, and how strong are the countervailing environmental forces working to move him in different directions.

For example, I assume men who leave industry to start their own small shops will probably be among the most modern and, furthermore, that their subsequent experience in entrepreneurial activity will itself further conduce to increasing individual modernization. By contrast, a man who leaves the urban industrial setting to resume both peasant agriculture and the whole set of his traditional role obligations, would likely become less modern under the influence of such life conditions.

3. Considering that the modernization process seems to work so consistently in so many different cultural settings, is there then no choice? Must everyone become modern, and to the same degree?

My image of man's nature is not that of a sponge soaking up everything with which it comes in contact. In my view individual change toward modernization is a process of *interaction* between the individual and his social setting. Quite contrary to the conception of men as putty passively taking on whatever shape their environment imposes on them, I see the process of individual modernization as one requiring a basic personal engagement between the individual and his milieu. In this engagement the individual must first selectively perceive the lessons the environment has to teach, and then must willingly undertake to learn them, before any personal change can come about.

If the qualities of industrial organization are truly alien to a man, he will not incorporate them. And even if the environment is benign and the individual ready to learn, the process will not work if the environment itself is confusing and the messages it conveys are unclear or even contradictory. All in all, then, I see little reason to fear that the modernization process threatens to impose on us a deadly, passive, totalitarian uniformity, especially if one keeps in mind that among the most outstanding characteristics of the modern man are his openness to new experience and his readiness for change. Indeed, our data indicate that, at least in the kind of developing countries we studied, the more modern men were also the more radical, in the sense that they much more frequently asserted the need for immediate and total transformation of the existing socioeconomic system.[6]

4. Since a whole set of institutions including the school, the factory, and the mass media, all operated to make our men modern, the question arises: must a nation be able to bring all these forces to bear, and do so simultaneously, to stimulate the development of individual modernity?

The issue is a sore one, since the key problem of many underdeveloped countries lies precisely in their lack of schools, factories, and media of mass communication. My experience suggests that it is not necessary that all, or even most, of the more effective agencies be available and working simultaneously to bring about individual modernity. On the contrary, any one modernizing institution seems to be able to operate independently. Moreover, contact with any one modernizing institution evidently can be more or less readily substituted for contact with any other, making allowance for the fact that some institutions are more effective than others. Indeed, the evidence from the Comilla cooperative experiment indicates that even in quite isolated villages, new forms of social organiza-

6. The "radicalism" index was based on a special question CI-52: "In your opinion what is it that Chile (Argentina) most needs: (1) a total and immediate change; (2) a total but gradual change; (3) a partial but immediate change; (4) a partial, slow change." The correlation of position on this scale and overall modernity was for Argentina .39 and Chile .34, both significant at better than the .001 level. See Inkeles (1969) for an analysis of the complex pattern of relations between measures of modernity and indexes of political orientation.

tion can be highly effective in making men modern without the aid of machinery or electronic communication. The means for bringing about greater individual modernization are, therefore, potentially within the reach of even the least advantaged nations and communities.

5. Does the concept of individual modernity and the measurement of it through the OM scale apply only to men, or are the concept and the measure relevant to understanding the characteristics and the situation of women as well?

Our project studied only men solely because of practical considerations arising from the limits on our budget and the concentration of men in the industrial jobs in which we were especially interested. I am firmly convinced that the overwhelming majority of the psychosocial indicators we used to identify the modern man would also discriminate effectively among women. And I am quite certain that the same forces that make men modern—such as education, work in complex organization, and mass media exposure—also serve to make women more modern. Of course, some adjustments in the content and scoring of the OM scale might be necessary to make it maximally effective in distinguishing modern from more traditional women, and some influences might play a different role in shaping the modernity of women rather than men. Nevertheless, I believe the pattern that will eventually emerge for women will be broadly similar to what we observed for men. I am given confidence in this assumption by some preliminary evidence already available.[7]

6. Are the individual modernization processes we studied in several developing countries likely to take place also in more advanced industrial and postindustrial societies?

---

7. A special version of the OM scale was administered by Donald Holsinger (1972) of Stanford University to boys and girls in the third to fifth grades of schools in Brazilia. At each grade level, the modernity scores of the girls were equal to those of the boys, and the girls gained as many points on the OM scale as did the boys during each additional year of schooling. In a study of Black women in Boston, Richard Suzman (1973a) administered a modified version of the OM scale. Basically the same items that had been used with our men in underdeveloped countries combined to yield a reliable OM scale for the Boston women. Moreover, the OM scores for women, using the Boston scale, could, in turn, be explained by much the same influences that explained the modernity of men in our samples from underdeveloped countries. It should also be noted that the Kahl (1968) modernity scale, originally developed for use with men in Brazil and Chile, evidently worked quite well when used to study the responses of women in the United States.

My answer is "yes." Societal modernization is always a matter of degree. Even the most highly developed nations have more and less modern portions of their populations, according to differences in exposure to modernizing experiences. In the United States, I would expect the forces that make men modern to have their most dramatic impact on immigrants from less developed countries, on rural subsistence farmers who leave their farms and on "dropouts" who leave their schools to enter industry, and on members of disadvantaged minority groups. In general, however, I believe that the same qualities that are summed up in the OM scale would distinguish the more from the less modern individuals in the industrialized countries, and that the same forces that made individuals modern in our samples would emerge as important causes of modernity in the economically advanced countries.

7. Is all this purely an academic exercise? In particular, does it have any practical contribution to make to national development? Are not attitude and value changes rather ephemeral and peripheral? Can we offer any evidence that all this has much to do with the real problem of underdevelopment?

In response, I affirm that our research has produced ample evidence that the attitude and value changes defining individual modernity are accompanied by changes in behavior precisely of the sort that I believe give meaning to, and support, those changes in political and economic institutions that lead to the modernization of nations. As table 4 indicates, men more modern in attitude and value

TABLE 4

PERCENT OF MEN HIGH ON BEHAVIORAL MODERNITY[1] IN EACH COUNTRY, WHO ARE LOW, MEDIUM, OR HIGH ON ATTITUDINAL MODERNITY

Standing on attitudinal modernity[2]	Argentina	Chile	East Pakistan	India	Israel	Nigeria
	%	%	%	%	%	%
	..	..	%	%	%	%
Low	13	14	15	5	16	18
Medium	35	32	34	27	35	29
High	52	54	51	68	49	54
Total N high on behavioral modernity	100% (271)	100% (308)	100% (373)	100% (448)	100% (261)	101%[3] (286)

1 Behavioral modernity is measured by a score on the summary (objective plus self-reported) behavior scale. Men in the upper third of the frequency distribution on this scale were considered "high" on behavioral modernity.

2 Attitudinal modernity is measured by scores on OM-1, trichotomized as to the frequency distribution in each country.

3 Percentages do not total 100 because of rounding.

were much more likely to act or behave in more modern ways in their various social roles.

We were able to document most extensively those behavioral changes accompanying attitudinal modernization in the realm of political and civic action. The modern man more often than the traditional man took an interest in political affairs, he kept informed and could identify important political events and personalities, he often contacted governmental and political agencies, more often joined organizations, more often voted—and all these by large margins. He was in every way a more active participant citizen of his society.

Beyond politics, the modern man showed himself to perform differently from the more traditional man in many realms of action having practical bearing on the process of societal modernization. The modern man is quicker to adopt technical innovation, and more ready to implement birth control measures; he urges his son to go as far as he can in school, and, if it pays better, encourages him to accept industrial work rather than to follow the more traditional penchant for office jobs; he informs himself about the goods produced in the more modern section of the economy, and makes an effort to acquire them; and he permits his wife and daughter to leave the home for more active participation in economic life. In these and a host of other ways, the man who is more modern in attitude and value acts to support modern institutions and to facilitate the general modernization of society.

In saying this I am not espousing some form of naive psychological determinism. I am not unaware that a modern psychology cannot alone make a nation modern. I fully understand that to be modern a nation must have modern institutions, effective government, efficient production, and adequate social services. And I recognize full well that there may be structural obstacles to such development stemming not only from nature, but from social, political, and economic causes as well. Narrow class interests, colonial oppression, rapacious great power, international cartels, domestic monopolies, archaic and corrupt governments, tribal antagonisms, and religious and ethnic prejudices, to name but a few, are among the many "objective" forces that we know act to impede modernization.

Nevertheless, I believe a change in attitudes and values to be one of the most essential *preconditions* for substantial and effective functioning of those modern institutions that most of the "more practical" programs of development seek to establish. Our experience leads us to agree with many of the intellectual leaders of the third world who argue that, in part, underdevelopment is a state of mind.[8] It is admittedly difficult with presently available techniques and information to establish the case scientifically, but I am convinced that mental barriers and psychic factors are key obstacles to effective economic and social development in many countries.

REFERENCES

HOLSINGER, DONALD. 1972. The Elementary School as an Early Socializer of Modern Values. Ph.D. dissertation, Stanford University (partially published in Holsinger 1973).

————. 1973. The Elementary School as a Modernizer: a Brazilian Study. *International Journal of Comparative Sociology* 14:180–202.

INKELES, ALEX. 1969. Participant Citizenship in Six Developing Countries. *American Political Science Review* 63:1120–1140.

INKELES, ALEX, and DAVID H. SMITH. 1974. *Becoming Modern: Individual Change in Six Developing Countries.* Harvard University Press.

KAHL, JOSEPH. 1968. *The Measurement of Modernism.* University of Texas Press.

SUZMAN, RICHARD. 1973a. The Modernization of Personality. Ph.D. dissertation, Harvard University (partially published in Suzman 1973b).

————. 1973b. Psychological Modernity. *International Journal of Comparative Sociology* 14:273–287.

8. In his unpublished contribution to the conference on Alternatives in Development sponsored by the Vienna Institute for Development in June, 1971, Dr. Salazar Bondy, a leading intellectual of Peru, wrote as follows: "Underdevelopment is not just a collection of statistical indices which enable a socioeconomic picture to be drawn. It is also a state of mind, a way of expression, a form of outlook and a collective personality marked by chronic infirmities and forms a maladjustment."

ERRATA

page 68, line 32: ictures *should read* pictures

page 76, line 21: *Insert following "cognitive dissonance"*: (But see Schwartz, 1976.)

page 77, line 20: automatic *should read* autonomic

page 83, line 33: *Insert at end of paragraph*: (See Schwartz, 1975, p. 126.)

page 90, line 18: 1975a *Should read* 1976
line 21: 1975b *should read* 1975

page 134, lines 1–4: *Should read* With regard to dream events, it seems to us the choice among rival forms of understanding is subject to diverse constraints. All knowledge available to the organism, whether preadapted in the evolutionary history of the species or the cultural history of the group, or postadapted in the life history of the individual, begins with external perception . . .

page 161, footnote: classification *should read* clarification

page 182, line 24: obstructure *should read* obstructive

page 191, line 7: N/N *should read* H/N

page 192, line 6: "appy" *should read* "happy"

pages 198 to 199, passim: Iks *should read* Ik